George Mifflin Dallas

This volume was published with the cooperation and support of the Pennsylvania Historical and Museum Commission in its continuing attempt to preserve the history of the people of the Commonwealth.

George Mifflin Dallas

Jacksonian Patrician

John M. Belohlavek

The Pennsylvania State University Press
University Park and London

Library of Congress Cataloging in Publication Data

Belohlavek, John M
  George Mifflin Dallas.

  Includes bibliography and index.
  1. Dallas, George Mifflin, 1792–1864. 2. Vice-
Presidents—United States—Biography. 3. United States—
Politics and government—1815–1861.
E340.D14B44   973.6'1'0924 [B]   77-1415
ISBN 0-271-00510-6

For those who believed:
My mother, father, and sister

Contents

Once there were two brothers. One ran away to sea; the other was elected Vice President. And nothing was ever heard of either of them again.

Thomas Riley Marshall

Acknowledgments

Several years ago, as a graduate student at the University of Nebraska, explorations into the Jacksonian period resulted in my discovery of George Mifflin Dallas. Dallas did not appear as a savior, an inspiration, or as one of the most misunderstood men of antebellum America. He revealed himself much more subtly in my readings; first as Senator, then Vice-President, and, finally, as diplomat. While apparently a secondary figure in American political and diplomatic history, Dallas aroused my curiosity and fascination by the longevity and prominence of his career. Further investigation revealed no biography of the Philadelphian had been written.

A debt of gratitude is owed Professor James A. Rawley for his encouragement in filling this gap in historical literature. He provided guidance, structure, a keen eye for style and documentation and a modest amount of sympathy. Professors Jack M. Sosin and Lloyd Ambrosius were equally vigilant and energetic in both praise and criticism of the manuscript. More recently, Professor George H. Mayer of the University of South Florida gave unselfishly of his time and talent. His ability to turn a phrase, enliven a passage, or point out a stylistic flaw has undoubtedly contributed to the readability of the book.

Professor Philip S. Klein of Pennsylvania State University reviewed the manuscript and suggested important changes which now make Dallas a private, as well as a public, figure. John M. Pickering and Carole Schwager of The Pennsylvania State University Press showed their concern and perseverance through a maze of delays. The staffs of the Library of Congress manuscript division, the Temple University Library, and particularly the Historical Society of Pennsylvania provided the needed materials, advice, and support.

There are several special people. Marcia Lee Mann shared the joy and pain of the difficult years and demonstrated her patience and affection by encouraging an aspiring young historian. David H. Hoober, who makes the best martinis west of Council Bluffs, understood and cared, both as friend and colleague. Susan C. Turner provided warm smiles, positive words and shared my faith in George M. Dallas.

Thanks must also be expressed to my friends, colleagues, and students at South Florida who cared about this project. They share in the credit, but assume none of the liabilities that may accrue from any error in judgment or mechanics that follows in this work.

Introduction

George Mifflin Dallas died over a century ago, but neither his contemporaries nor subsequent generations of historians endeavored to reconstruct the details of his life or career. The few historians who did, like Philip S. Klein and Charles M. Snyder, dealt with Dallas only insofar as his political activities illuminated the behavior of more famous public servants. Focusing on the domestic scene, these accounts virtually ignored his stewardship as a diplomat. This persistent lack of curiosity about Dallas invites the judgment that he was an obscure, secondary figure: an ineffective although energetic political dilettante. Far from undermining that verdict, the fact that he served one term as vice-president of the United States has usually been cited to reinforce it. This dubious honor guaranteed that posterity would never forget him—indeed high school and college students often feel obliged to memorize his name—but it also branded him a lightweight. Irrespective of what the Founding Fathers had intended, the vice-presidency was universally regarded as a retirement home for mediocre politicians by the time Dallas held the post.

There is no point in challenging the conventional view of Dallas, or in making him a subject of research in the hope that a minor figure can somehow be converted into a major one. The justification for a detailed study of his career must arise from an opposite perspective: his views, ideals, and fears were so average and typical that he mirrored the American mind with perhaps greater fidelity than a Daniel Webster or a Henry Clay, and the other giants of mid-nineteenth-century America. An assessment of Dallas from this perspective is all the more promising because, like many if not all of his contemporaries, he suffered the anxieties of a political moderate obliged to grapple with two great crises—nullification and Civil War. Growing up with the outlook of a Philadelphia patrician, Dallas was forced as a young man to attempt some accommodation with Jacksonian Democracy as the price of political survival. Likewise, in his old age, he faced the painful problem of all Democrats who had to choose between union and the Constitution or state rights and secession. Dallas grappled with sacrificing state prerogatives for emerging nationhood. Unwilling to give up politics in an era of turmoil, he assumed the role of acrobat. But, more visible than most citizens who were confronted with the same dilemmas and who made the same decision, his acrobatics can be charted. The ensuing effort to do so is undertaken in the hope that the maneuvers and rationalizations of Dallas will deepen our insight into the responses of the American rank and file.

Since Dallas adhered to a prevailing canon of oratory so platitudinous that pronouncements could mean anything, the paucity of his private papers for his early years in politics is a handicap. Yet enough exist to allow fairly firm conclusions to be drawn about his motives for action.

His political operations and his personal antecedents, both relevant to an understanding of his career, warrant some attention at the outset. A lifelong resident of Philadelphia, Dallas could pursue his large but ill-defined political aspirations only as a spokesman for the entire state of Pennsylvania. This circumstance was both an advantage and a disadvantage. On the one hand, he enjoyed the political leverage associated with citizenship in a large and uncommitted state, the wishes of which could not be ignored by national party leaders. On the other hand, Dallas labored under the endemic handicap of trying to ascertain those wishes in a state as paralyzed by particularisms as ancient Greece. Pennsylvania on the eve of the Jacksonian era was a commonwealth containing some 1.3 million people of diverse social, economic, and religious backgrounds. Geography was a complicating factor, cutting across cultural divisions and making loyalties all the more unpredictable. Mountains and river valleys separated Pennsylvanians physically from each other into five distinct regional groups: the southeast, with its gently rolling hills, oriented toward Philadelphia; the Susquehanna Valley, which drew the interest of its residents southward and into a web of economic relations with Maryland; the northern tier of counties, originally inhabited by New Yorkers and New Englanders who clung to their traditional affiliations; the central counties, walled off by the Appalachian Mountains from the rest of the state like a modern Sparta; and the still more isolated enclaves of population along the Ohio border, with topography dictating closer ties to people further west than to fellow Pennsylvanians.

Although most Keystone residents were farmers of one kind or another, three cities and their hinterlands acted as a barrier against the emergence of a monolithic agrarianism. Pittsburgh, the burgeoning "Gateway to the West," claimed 20,000 inhabitants and had already earned the reputation as the "Smokey City" for its numerous mills, factories, and foundries. In the southeast, Lancaster, with a population of 7,000, was the focal point for marketing the goods of the fertile lands tilled by the Pennsylvania Dutch. Finally, there was Philadelphia, the nation's second largest city (behind New York) with almost 200,000 people. A hub of domestic and foreign trade and industry, it combined culture, banking, educational institutions, and an articulate press to provide leadership for, if not dominance over, the remainder of the state. By 1800 the city had lost its status as the nation's capital to Washington, D.C., and by 1830 its position as the leading commercial center had been lost to New York. But the wide thoroughfares, the red-brick, green-shuttered houses, and the grandeur of the public buildings provided sufficient warmth and elegance to awe the most skeptical visitor. The residents could also be proud of the host of doctors, artists, scientists, and philosophers who lived there. Music and theater, the University of Pennsylvania, and the American Philosophical Society enhanced leisure opportunities and provided an intellectual climate for members of the upper class.

Moreover, Philadelphia had a heart. Numerous societies were at work distributing funds for the relief of foreigners and the impoverished; launching free schools for the blacks and the poor; and promoting everything from abolition to vaccinations. Philadelphia pioneered a municipal water system in the Jeffersonian era and coordinated it with the activities of the fire department. By the 1850s the city was creating a central police system and subscribing to a new quarter-million-dollar opera house. This was Dallas's Philadelphia, but innovative as it was, the city remained politically conservative and a stronghold of Federalism until the advent of Andrew Jackson.

While there were other towns and villages throughout the state (Harrisburg, the capital, was but a village of 4,500), the scattered nature of the populace made a statewide political organization in the modern sense almost impossible. What evolved then was the rise of a group who resembled "Chinese war lords": powerful men—like Dallas, James Buchanan, William Wilkins, and Samuel McKean. Dominant in their own "provinces," none could achieve statewide success except through alliances with one or more of his rivals. These politicians could readily find support for Pennsylvania's favorite project in this era—internal improvements. Anxious to connect the east and west (as rival New York has already done through the Erie Canal), both farmers and manufacturers supported a costly system of turn-pikes, canals, and ultimately railroads to bring all parts of the state together. Although there were chronic disputes about such projects, the debate was not over whether they would be constructed, but where.

The aspiring politicians, interested in building a state machine, also were confronted with the problem of ethnic diversity. The major po-litical force in state politics was the Scotch-Irish. Involved in state government and demanding much from it, they occupied a broad belt of counties from the center of the state to the Ohio Valley and reach-ing the northern tier. Like their pure Irish kinsmen of a later genera-tion in Boston, they had an appetite for politics and frequently pro-vided statewide leaders. The Germans, more concentrated than the Scotch-Irish, were important politically in the southeastern and south-western sections, where most of them resided. Isolated, uneducated, and often apathetic, they nonetheless tended to vote for candidates of Germanic extraction. Thus the fact that three of the four governors of Pennsylvania in the 1830s and 1840s were of German origin (the other was Scotch-Irish) could hardly be regarded as accidental. The English represented the bulk of the southeastern population, especially in the greater Philadelphia area. Many of the families could trace their lin-eage back five or six generations. They constituted the political back-bone of the state and exercised a conservative influence in commerce and industry as well. The northern counties blended the Scotch-Irish with New Yorkers and New Englanders to produce a frequently unique response to political and reform issues. Although the tidal waves of German and Irish immigration did not strike the Common-wealth's shores until the 1840s, alert politicians, like Dallas, became aware of their political potential very quickly and accepted them as a force to be reckoned with.

If George M. Dallas had been born thirty years earlier he would have been first a Federalist and later a Whig, rather than a Jefferso-nian who became a Jacksonian. Dallas had neither the background, temperament, nor traits of the mythical frontier Democrat who fol-lowed "Old Hickory." A distinguished upper-class family, which educated Dallas to perpetuate its traditions, did its work well. He took his lofty social and intellectual status in the community as a matter of course, but he had also been trained for it. In addition to the conventional accomplishments of a Philadelphia aristocrat, he wrote poetry and spoke excellent French. Tall and distinguished, perhaps even handsome, Dallas possessed a compelling voice which served him well on the hustings. His aquiline nose, soft hazel eyes, and long sandy-brown hair (turning prematurely white), which fell gently on his neck, invariably captivated women, at least in the drawing room. He, in turn, was ever conscious of his personal appearance, and he distinguished himself from the crowd by wearing expensive clothes and cultivating the manner of the aristocrat.

A fortunate marriage widened his social contacts and gave him access to the old Federalist families, who were arbiters of culture as well as politics in Philadelphia. Prestige came without money, a circumstance that was doubly unfortunate because he had developed extravagant tastes as a youth. For this reason he continually lived beyond his means and was constantly in debt, a situation that caused him on more than one occasion to reject otherwise acceptable political posts.

Aside from money, his most serious handicap as a politician was a lack of will to implement his ambitions. He demonstrated time and again in the courtroom that he possessed the intelligence and forensic skill of his more successful rivals. Yet he was an erratic and lethargic office-seeker. He recoiled from the sustained and uninspiring work of party management. This antipathy was reinforced by his disdainful attitude toward the adventurers who staffed the lower rungs of the political organizations, to say nothing of the voters themselves. He could tolerate both when they were deployed in orderly rows beneath him at party rallies, but he had no stomach for intimate personal contact with them. Thus it was no accident that, although Dallas held many political offices, the vice-presidency was the only one that he owed to the voters. If he possessed some charismatic qualities, he concealed them lest they encourage the familiarity distasteful to him. The urge for political recognition was strong enough to draw Dallas into the Jacksonian movement in Pennsylvania, but he never felt at home in it and remained to the end an antique—a silk-stocking Jeffersonian in an age of egalitarianism. For these reasons, he had to reconcile himself to the role of a semiclandestine manipulator and factional leader. Yet Dallas was never happy over his decision. He wanted to be a king, but instead became a kingmaker, and a rather ineffective one at that. His shrewdness was wasted because of his self-imposed aloofness from the arena of practical politics. In the end it deserted him altogether, and during the late 1840s he nursed the delusion that he was a serious presidential candidate.

Dallas viewed politics almost with a feeling of *noblesse oblige*, expecting public office to seek him. Only occasionally did he campaign or engage in speaking tours to facilitate personal advancement. Like many before and since, he enjoyed the game of politics more than the rewards of the game. Although he held many posts, he grew bored and restless with the daily drudgery after his initial excitement subsided. He would then return to practice law, which he found more financially rewarding. He was unable, however, to give up the game altogether, and he returned sooner or later for an encore performance.

There is no doubt that Dallas's wife and mother exerted a strong influence over him. He was a loving and devoted—if not doting—husband, son, and father of seven children. Every foray into politics and diplomacy was made with the welfare of his family in mind. He did not hesitate to sacrifice himself or his career to preserve its unity and happiness. After all the factors are taken into account, the impression survives that Dallas was a complex individual. He was a capable and articulate barrister, a family man, and a fixture in the upper strata of Quaker City society. He loved the law and had a deep respect for the Union and the Constitution. Anything that threatened or violated these pillars of the Republic, he firmly opposed. To his way of thinking, the Founding Fathers had spoken the last word on nullification, secession, and slavery, and he would tolerate no deviation from their handiwork except through constitutional amendment. Throughout his career the Philadelphian echoed loudly and insistently what he took to be their views.

Dallas began his political career in what has been euphemistically labeled the "Era of Good Feelings." This misnomer could not be applied to Pennsylvania in the years between 1817 and 1825. The Commonwealth was in a politically turbulent situation, which terminated in the emergence of two major factions—the "Family Party" of Dallas and the "Amalgamators" of James Buchanan. Dallas had built a powerful state and local machine, with centers at Philadelphia and Pittsburgh, which controlled Pennsylvania politics intermittently for over a decade. The Family Party had first backed John C. Calhoun and later Andrew Jackson for the presidency. In both cases, it acted from expediency rather than principles. If it stood for anything substantive, it was what George Dangerfield aptly termed the "awakening of American nationalism."

When Dallas emerged on the political stage after the War of 1812, he reflected this nationalistic fervor and fierce pride in his support of Calhoun, who was then a champion of the "American System." The loyalty Dallas gave to Jackson before 1828 was merely lip service, since the general was a popular favorite. The Philadelphian became a thoroughgoing Jacksonian when the Tennessean staunchly defended the Union against the doctrine of nullification, while Calhoun was simultaneously moving in the direction of sectionalism.

Dallas does not fit the stereotyped mold of the frontier Jacksonian. He deserted Calhoun for Jackson because the latter stood for the Union, but also because his followers had supported the high protective tariff of 1828, which benefited the economic interests of Pennsylvania. The idea of Old Hickory as president of the common folk was important to Dallas only because Jackson seemed to be a nationalist presiding over a nationalist movement. Jacksonian principles—if such things existed—were not part of Dallas's intellectual baggage, unless they could be used advantageously. Dallas was pragmatic and realistic on basic issues; some may label him a "trimmer." As a senator, he voted on the bank and tariff as his state desired, not with the bulk of southern and western Jacksonians. His stand on the need for a national bank alienated him from the president. Dallas accepted this act of political suicide calmly and after his retirement from the Senate came out against the bank. In 1832 Jackson was in the process of reconstructing a national Democracy, and Dallas felt he must maintain a dual loyalty between the state and national parties.

Between 1834 and 1844 the leadership of the Commonwealth Democracy shifted from Dallas to Buchanan. Nevertheless, Dallas showed his political durability by preserving his strength in the Quaker City and winning the vice-presidential nomination in 1844. Dallas's dreams and ambitions for himself and the nation reached their zenith during his tenure. While he was not particularly influential with the austere president, he viewed the post as a springboard to the presidential campaign of 1848. The Buchanan-Dallas rivalry came to a climax in this period. Dallas hoped to capitalize on his casting vote, which helped to save the Walker Tariff of 1846. He tried to make himself still more eligible for the White House by associating himself with the most extreme nationalist doctrines. Buchanan, who controlled the state machinery, was a trimmer and more in touch with public sentiment than Dallas. He out-distanced the Philadelphian in the struggle for state convention delegates, and thereby killed Dallas's presidential prospects.

After 1848, for all practical purposes, Dallas was ineffective as a national politician. Although he was mentioned in each of the three succeeding conventions, he was never seriously considered. He lacked a state alliance and a large personal following and had only limited sectional support. Dallas's major political contribution in the 1850s was the well-publicized stand he assumed on the Compromise of 1850. Steadfastly opposing all such arrangements as unconstitutional, he believed the only way sectional difficulties could be settled was by constitutional amendment. Dallas personally felt Negroes were inferior and accepted the institution of slavery as written into the Constitution, but he was not conscious of any racism. He viewed the problem of slavery both as a potentially destructive force to the Union and as a social and economic problem that would not be solved by the ineffectual Fugitive Slave Law. Instead, he favored amendments guaranteeing the rights of both northerners and southerners, but providing an advantage to neither.

He continued to advocate such a remedy for national ills until the firing on Fort Sumter in April 1861. By that time the Philadelphian was old and tired and out of touch with the realities of American political life. While he had always been a states rights Democrat and a supporter of southern institutions, he was primarily a Unionist. He was bitter and disillusioned as well over the secessionist movement, which challenged everything he had cherished throughout his life. Unfortunately, Dallas died before the Union had been restored.

During two of the interludes in his political career, Dallas served as a diplomat with distinction. Although his first mission—St. Petersburg in 1837—was the result of political intrigue rather than political reward, Dallas served his country well. He attempted to settle the northwest boundary to the benefit of the United States, but he received little support for the 54°40′ claim for the administration. This failure, combined with the lack of social and intellectual stimulation at the Court of Czar Nicholas I, led to Dallas's request for recall in 1839. The most important result of the Russian mission was that in Dallas's absence Buchanan was able to solidify his political position in Pennsylvania.

Dallas's subsequent five-year ministry at the Court of St. James's was the climax of his public career. His genteel and patrician manner served him well in dealing with the British aristocracy and it, in turn, accepted him. This social compatibility enhanced his effectiveness. At first, he worked for President Franklin Pierce, arriving in London in 1856 to settle the outstanding differences between Great Britain and the United States. Shortly thereafter he negotiated the ill-fated Dallas-Clarendon Convention. This agreement would have accelerated the American drive for political and economic hegemony in Central America by providing for peaceful British withdrawal. It was killed by skeptical senators who hoped for greater gain and fewer sacrifices under the incoming Buchanan administration. Once James Buchanan assumed power, Dallas was excluded from policy discussions. Although he was kept in London for political reasons, all correspondence of importance was deliberately routed around him. Despite this affront, Dallas attempted to play an active diplomatic role and eagerly accepted any duties the State Department assigned him. The minister involved himself as much as possible in the solution of the "visit and search" controversy with Great Britain, as well as the San Juan Island dispute. Yet he ended his mission in December 1860 on a note of frustration and returned to the United States, where the still greater frustration of the Civil War awaited him.

1

The Young Politician
(1792–1824)

Pennsylvania politics in the nineteenth century has been referred to by historian Philip Klein as "a game without rules." For a quarter of a century prior to the Era of Good Feelings the "game" had been dominated by two master Jeffersonian Republicans, Albert Gallatin and Alexander James Dallas. Operating in the western and eastern halves of the state, respectively, these two men insured Democratic-Republican control. Dallas's rise, while hardly meteoric, was nonetheless impressive, and it deserves passing attention because his son George Mifflin Dallas might never have entered politics without a successful father to serve as an example and mentor.

Alexander Dallas was born in 1759 at Dallas Castle, Jamaica, the third son of Dr. and Mrs. Robert Dallas. Mrs. Dallas died soon after and the doctor remarried, taking his new wife and family to England in 1769. Young Alexander began his studies there, but his father's death forced him to leave school. In 1774 he took a job in a bank. When the business failed two years later, he moved to Devonshire, where he resumed his studies and lived with his stepmother, who had remarried. There he met Arabella Smith, the teenage daughter of British army major George Smith. Despite their youth the couple planned to wed. The flowering of their romance happened to coincide with the absence of Arabella's father, who was in Jamaica. So they sought the consent of Arabella's aunts, on the theory that temporary guardians are more easily stampeded than permanent ones. Thwarted in this tactic, the young lovers crossed the Caribbean and made a personal appeal to the major. This, too, was fruitless. The aunts saw no reason to reconsider, so the determined youngsters simply eloped. Alexander was twenty-one and his bride just sixteen. After a brief stay in London they moved to Jamaica, where Dallas began to practice law. Unfortunately, the climate of the island seriously affected Arabella's health. Just as the Dallases were about to return to England, the major died, leaving Arabella with enough money for them to get out of Jamaica. On the recommendation of a friend, they changed their destination and emigrated to the newly independent United States in 1783.

Only a decade later Alexander Dallas had become a successful Philadelphia lawyer-politician and a patron of culture, with a mansion on Fourth Street and a country house, "Devon," on the banks of the Schuylkill River. In 1791 Governor Thomas McKean appointed Dallas secretary of the Commonwealth, a position in which he served with distinction throughout the stormy Federalist era. As partisan loyalties hardened, Alexander Dallas emerged as one of the driving forces within the Democratic movement. Stockily built, meticulously dressed (usually in an olive-brown suit), the ambitious barrister was particularly eye-catching because of his abundant, carefully powdered hair. An excellent conversationalist with a vivacious manner, he excelled in the parlor as well as the courtroom by persuasion rather than power. His conspicuous role in the election of Thomas Jefferson resulted in his promotion to the post of United States attorney for the Eastern District of Pennsylvania in 1801. He survived the controversies of the Jefferson administrations unscathed. Managing to make himself useful to James Madison as well, he was appointed secretary of the treasury in 1814. After Dallas grappled for a year with financial crisis triggered by the War of 1812, Madison also made him acting secretary of war. Dallas's major achievements in the Treasury Department were to facilitate the rechartering of the new Bank of the United States and the institution of a protective tariff. He resigned in October 1816 and returned to private practice to recoup the financial losses he had sustained through years of public service. In January 1817, while arguing a case in neighboring New Jersey, he was stricken with "gout in the stomach"—a chronic ailment since youth, when he had almost drowned in a Hyde Park pool. If artificial respiration had saved his life, it had also damaged several organs. In any case Dallas had been afflicted with pain and dizziness throughout his life. This particularly severe attack, however, proved fatal and he died just hours after arriving home. His sudden illness and death left his family with social and political pretensions—unfulfilled in part because of his Jeffersonian politics in a Federalist city—but insufficient wealth to sustain them as effortlessly as others of the second generation who belonged to the Philadelphia gentry.[1]

George Mifflin Dallas, the second of six children and second of three surviving sons, inherited his father's relish for politics and poetry. He soon became experienced in law and diplomacy, and by 1824 George was the leading Democratic politician in Pennsylvania. Born on 10 July 1792, in a North Front Street residence, he had been named after a family friend, Governor Thomas Mifflin. Ties between the first families and within the Dallas family remained close. Indeed, George recalled many years later that some of his happiest moments were spent with his father, whom he regarded as his "most delightful companion, instructor, and pride." Dallas particularly remembered a household institution known as the "cold cut." This fragmentary supper was held between ten and eleven o'clock, after his father had worked through the evening and allowed Alexander and the children to rally "for a lively chat and a gay good night." Undoubtedly the desire to emulate the elder Dallas drew George into a legal career.[2] After receiving elementary education in Germantown with Mr. Dorfeuille and at a Friends' School in the city with Provost Robert Andrews, Dallas transferred to Princeton in 1807 and was graduated three years later at the age of seventeen with highest honors. His valedictory address was a preview of the later ideas he held on the Constitution and the Union. Inheriting the patriotic sentiments of his father, who would refer to the War of 1812 as a "holy war," George glorified the brief history of the fledgling Republic and rhapsodized about its future. "Who," he asked, "can follow the aerial track of the American eagle without kindling into enthusiasm?"[3] Full of visions, the bright and aspiring future lawyer nonetheless spent the next three years in the pedestrian task of preparing for the bar examination in his father's office. George chafed under the drudgery and relentless application of the legal routine. Early in 1813 he volunteered for the militia to escape this regimen. His strong-willed father already had one son, Alexander, in the navy and his plans for George did not include lengthy military service. When requested to return to his studies, the obedient son reluctantly obeyed. He wrote his brother on board the frigate *President:*

> You know how heartily I despise the profession I have undertaken . . . I am becoming far too useful in the office for my comfort, and I sometimes feel a strong inclination to rebel against a continued round of copying, but I am fated to be, a lawyer, a word which conveys in itself every idea of labour and drudgery and misery, that a man can possibly suggest.[4]

But good fortune intervened suddenly and lifted Dallas from his obligation to pursue a legal career.

The author of this good fortune was Albert Gallatin, temporarily in Philadelphia in the spring of 1813, before his departure for Russia to explore the czar's offer to end the War of 1812 through mediation. As a trusted family friend, Gallatin offered to take young Dallas as his private secretary—if his father would cover his expenses. Alexander quickly agreed. George's military duties at home were terminated, but he was allowed to depart for Russia with the rank of major.

The members of the mission left the United States on 9 May. Gallatin and Federalist Senator James Bayard of Delaware, the other envoy, accompanied by Dallas, arrived in St. Petersburg on 21 July. There they were disturbed to find their hosts pursuing a bloody war with Napoleon and disappointed to learn that the English had turned down Russian mediation proposals. It was not until October, however, that the diplomats adopted a new course of action. In the meantime Dallas traveled extensively, exploring Russian life and society. This interlude ended when Gallatin responded to the prodding of Alexander Baring, a British financier, and dispatched Dallas to London to open a direct channel of communication with Lord Castlereagh, the foreign secretary. Gallatin instructed his secretary not to seek information, provide opinions, or report rumors, but merely to relay communications from Baring, Count Lieven, the Russian ambassador in London, the British government, and other reliable sources.

Dallas arrived in London in early December on the pretext that he had come to visit relatives. His appearance, however, caused a furor both in the press and in Parliament. A confrontation between Baring and Castlereagh followed, in which the former was obliged to acknowledge that the young American had come in an unofficial diplomatic capacity. Meanwhile, Castlereagh had made an offer on 4 November to Secretary of State James Monroe to negotiate directly with the United States. This fact was relayed to Dallas on 15 December by Count Lieven. Although Dallas was instructed to be the "eyes and ears" of the Americans, he had no power to negotiate with the British. For this reason he declined an offer of introduction to the foreign secretary, stating that he was not authorized to take any formal steps. Castlereagh had indicated to Lieven previously that he would receive Dallas and listen to any proposals he had to make. But the frustrated Philadelphian could only wait silently week after week for instructions from Washington or St. Petersburg.

Dallas's ill-defined status was terminated when he learned on 25 January 1814 that the American mission had lost faith in the czar and had left Russia for Amsterdam. Dallas joined Gallatin there in mid-

March, and during the subsequent negotiations at Ghent, he served as attaché. The talks dragged on from early July until late August, at which point Dallas carried the preliminary draft of the peace treaty to President Madison. Arriving home in October, he was more than ready to abandon his role as a glorified messenger boy. If the experience did not sour Dallas on public life, it did simplify his immediate career objectives. He turned from diplomacy to the "great game" of politics, a wise choice in view of the fact that his father was available to run interference for him. The first post to materialize was remitter of the treasury in 1814. The duties left Dallas plenty of time for speechmaking and exposed him to numerous invitations. His most notable effort was on the Fourth of July 1815, when he lashed out at critics of the recent war with England. The Federalists in general and the Hartford Convention in particular provoked his unsparing condemnation.

Oratory was only one manifestation of his cultural pretensions. As early as 1810 he had produced an essay "Upon the Moral Effects of Memory" for the prestigious literary digest *Portfolio*. It was predictable that abstract philosophy would give way to poetry sooner or later, because George, like his father, had a way with the ladies. Inundating them with verse was one technique of courtship that George employed fearlessly. He struck the contemporary theme of romantic melancholy and managed to sound like a cross between Goethe's *Werther* and Byron's *Don Juan,* as the following tribute to an unidentified charmer indicates:

> I am formed of hardened steel
> Such charms and arts I can't withstand
> My heart though long it ceased to feel
> Will throb again at your command
> That eye of love and word of fire
> Have ever proved resistance vain
> I dare not hope I don't desire
> To break my fetters e're again
> Thus sacred victims smile to see
> The altar redden with their gore
> They die to please their deity
> And bless the flame and still adore[5]

Whether poetry was a decisive factor in breaching the defenses of Sophia Chew Nicklin is unclear, but George had begun to pursue her in earnest by the end of 1815, and he proposed to her the following spring. Sophy was highly eligible, both because she was spirited and because she was the eldest daughter of a prominent Philadelphia businessman, Philip Nicklin. At the beginning of the courtship it was evident that the infatuation was mutual. This led to much teasing by Sophy, particularly when George was away in Washington plodding through his dreary office routine. A typical sample of mock desolation appeared in his mail:

> you play your part admirably in Washington . . . the ac-
> knowledged beau of one lady who is married [his mother], the
> declared admirer of another who is on the verge of becoming a
> bride—gallantries—and compliments to every lady of any note
> who will be pleased to listen to you. You do not require again to
> be told to take all possible advantage of your privileges.[6]

The touch of asperity was barely visible in the humor, but as the years passed the former would grow at the expense of the latter. At the time, however, it was the sort of appeal to bring George back to Philadelphia, the more so because he was a victim of loneliness and low pay.

Law seemed more promising than bureaucracy, and with the encouragement of Sophy he made preparations to pursue a legal career, in partnership with a family friend, Charles J. Ingersoll. Nonetheless, like most youngsters, he experienced misgivings almost as soon as he had made up his mind, confessing to a friend: "I tremble as the time approaches . . . and feel as if I were about to begin the world again."[7] Apparently Dallas overcame his doubts quickly. In any case Ingersoll reported satisfaction over the way his apprentice had won initial cases against two mutineers "without my interference." Even in this early stage of active practice, Dallas had begun to display the characteristics that ultimately won him a reputation for honesty and erudition. Whether by chance or design, his habit of talking slowly and emphasizing each word created the feeling that he was reasoning his way to a conclusion on the spot. Since he also prepared cases carefully in advance, his apparent groping for the right word—and finding it— reinforced the initial impression that a great mind was at work. Dallas did not relish the fast exchange in the courtroom, but he was seldom tongue-tied or caught off balance by rival lawyers. Although he could not be called a great legal scholar, he respected the law and was knowledgeable enough to tangle fearlessly with the better jurists of his generation.[8]

Over the next decade Dallas held two time-consuming legal positions—solicitor of the Second Bank of the United States (1816) and deputy attorney general for Philadelphia (1817–20). Yet he also was developing a healthy private practice. Working extensively in the local Court of Common Pleas, Dallas handled numerous civil and criminal cases, including property claims, divorce, and burglary. He defended men and women of varying socioeconomic backgrounds and seemed willing to take any case that offered him adequate remuneration.

As soon as he was established in law, he married Sophy. The wedding, which took place on 23 May, united two families as well as two individuals. Young George quickly fell into the routine of family man and provider for a wife and, finally, eight children—Alexander James, Julia, Elizabeth, Sophia, Philip, Catherine, Susan, and Charlotte.[9] Initially, George and Sophy lived with his mother on Fourth Street, where in 1817 their first son was born. The boy was a victim of hydrocephalus and died at the age of nine, but the parents apparently adjusted to this situation very well. Dallas was a devoted husband and father. He employed the conventional terms of endearment when addressing his wife, and he appeared to mean them as well because he was continually buying clothes for her and ornaments for the house, which he could ill-afford. Dallas's affection was not tempered with time, and on their twenty-eighth anniversary he gave her a portrait of himself and a bit of verse:

> By truthful Sully sketched, how plain appears
> The change produced by eight and twenty years
> Sophia, mark that dimming eye,
> That rigid brow of care
> The fallen cheeks, congenial dye,
> Those folds of whitened hair
> How well in unison they chime
> The triumph of remorseless time.
>
> The outward casket these, whose depths disclose,
> A gem, which never flaw nor fading knows;
> What if old age invites decay,
>   And form and feature wane
> That gem, though all its case gave way,
> Will sparkling still remain,
> Within enshrined, from changing free,
> Undying glows the love of thee.[10]

Such strong feelings existed equally for his children. He delighted in their company and in family activity. One of their favorite games was a variation of "follow the leader" called "so does the Mufti," in which George and the children usually ended up on the floor exhausted from laughter. The next morning the aching barrister would make the familiar walk along Walnut Street carrying his green bag filled with legal briefs. The future was his; as he confided to his brother, "I flatter myself with the hope that I shall always be content to live as I do now, without ostentation and without ambition." But politics, not law, would become George's forte, and at the age of twenty-four he seemed to be headed for political advancement as rapidly as his father had been at the same age.

Fortunately, George was also moving into a vacuum, for by 1817 most of the old guard of the Pennsylvania Democratic-Republican Party had been removed through death, retirement, or political defeat. A new generation of leaders had already begun to occupy the stage and would soon command the limelight by identifying themselves with the redoubtable Andrew Jackson. They crept along the low road of faction, but imagined they were taking the high road of statesmanship, even though tranquillity abroad blocked the principal avenue through which it had hitherto been pursued. Fooled by their own rationalizations, such prominent Pennsylvanians as George M. Dallas, James Buchanan, Samuel D. Ingham, Isaac D. Barnard, Joseph Ritner, and Henry Baldwin competed vigorously for power throughout the next decade.

The two chief factions in the party in 1817 were the "Old School" followers of William Duane, editor of the Philadelphia *Aurora,* and the "New School," led by John Binns of the *Democratic Press.* The former was composed of conservative, old-line Jeffersonians located in the rural east and dependent upon the German vote. The latter was an economically progressive element combining Hamiltonian means with Jeffersonian ends, led by Philadelphians but centered in the west, where it was sustained by the Scotch-Irish vote. Normally, factional animosities were heightened by squabbles over patronage. Yet Pennsylvanians managed to quarrel just as furiously, although the lion's share was routinely siphoned off to New York and Virginia during the Era of Good Feelings.[11]

In the election for governor that year the regular party headed by the New School nominated William Findlay, the state treasurer, in caucus at Harrisburg. The Federalists, calling themselves "Independent Republicans" and possessing real strength in Philadelphia and Pittsburgh, joined with the dissident Jeffersonians of the Old School to nominate Joseph Hiester, a Berks County congressman. Findlay's selection was the result of his own hard work and the indulgent attitude of aspiring eastern politicians who hoped to use him to build a new party. This cadre consisted of Dallas, Thomas Sergeant, Richard Bache, Samuel Ingham, William Wilkins, and a few others who, because of their marital connections, were quickly dubbed the "Family Party." Ingham was the front, Bache the propagandist, and Dallas the brains of the organization. Findlay won the October election with 66,000 votes to Hiester's 59,000, in a contest of personalities rather than issues. Philadelphia was the sole disappointment. Still solidly Federalist, it voted against Findlay and Dallas, who had run as the candidate of the Family Party for the Assembly.[12]

For the next three years Dallas widened his contacts, solidified the "Family" organization, discharged his official duties competently, and still found time to speak out on national issues. In 1818 he commended President Monroe for supporting the controversial General Andrew Jackson's pursuit of hostile Indians into Florida, which was still a Spanish colony. Dallas ran little risk by being forthright because neither the Spanish nor the Seminoles could evoke much sympathy from American voters. He courted unnecessary trouble, however, by plunging into the controversy over the Missouri Compromise. Then and later his innate caution deserted him because he was incapable of resisting a debate on the Constitution or of changing his position. Fortunately for Dallas, he mobilized forthrightness and erudition behind a view that minimized his political liabilities until the penultimate stage of the agitation over slavery. Strictly speaking, his outlook was shaped less by legal philosophy than by a deep-seated antipathy to all forms of agitation that threatened the stability of the Union. For this reason, he regarded the Constitution as a barrier to all legislative improvisations calculated to intensify sectional animosities over slavery. His standard posture was to denounce them as unconstitutional in the secret hope of shutting off debate. He parried accusations of rigidity by contending that constitutional amendments were a proper remedy, but his lifelong record suggests that he would have opposed them as well if they polarized opinion. In 1819 amendments were a remote possibility, so Dallas did nothing more to give them an abstract endorsement and deny that Congress possessed the power to regulate the status of slavery in the territories.[13]

The political honeymoon for Findlay, Dallas, and his other supporters ended suddenly in late 1819, when the opposition moved to impeach the governor. To this end, John Binns, angered over his declining influence in Harrisburg, struck up an alliance with William Duane. The opening shot was fired on 8 December 1819, when Josiah Randall, one of Binns's henchmen in the legislature, initiated an inquiry into the conduct of the governor. Binns and Charles S. Coxe represented the petitioners, charging the administration with corrupt and illegal behavior. Dallas and Samuel Douglass rallied to the cause of the governor in a battle where neither side was interested in ascertaining the truth. In his capacity as deputy attorney general Dallas countered by placing the petitioners on trial. Binns in turn tried to discredit Dallas, alleging that the latter was secretly trying to undermine the governor. The "trial" lasted until 3 February 1820 and featured a parade of witnesses with amazingly poor memories. It ended when the House committee found Findlay innocent of all charges. Enough voters were unimpressed by the verdict to reject Findlay's bid for reelection in 1820, and he lost by 1,500 votes out of the 134,000 cast. Identified with the governor, Dallas resigned as deputy attorney general before he was fired. Ostensibly, he returned to the practice of law, but he continued to be active behind the scenes, trying to arrange a comeback through an alliance with promising presidential hopeful John C. Calhoun.[14]

This project engrossed Dallas between 1820 and 1824, although he supported his family by acting as legal counsel for the Bank of the United States in Pennsylvania. His interest in Calhoun was part of a larger strategy to forge an entente between local Democratic-Republicans and the state organizations in Ohio and South Carolina, which would break the ascendancy of New York and Virginia in Washington. As secretary of war and a leading nationalist who favored the bank, the protective tariff, and internal improvements, Calhoun was especially attractive to Pennsylvanians. Dynamic and eloquent as well, he became the darling of the coalition that Dallas was trying to construct. Calhoun welcomed the interest and after mending his political fences in the South, visited Pennsylvania in August 1821. His "tour of observation" lasted one month and he left the Keystone State confident that he had impressed the leaders of the Family Party. His surmise was correct and bore fruit in December, when Family congressmen, led by Thomas J. Rogers of Easton, called on Calhoun and formally invited him to stand for the presidency.

Calhoun wasted no time feigning reluctance, so the Family quickly went into action, spreading pro-Calhoun editorials and literature over the state, as well as stepping up attacks on his principal rival, John Quincy Adams. Plans to secure a legislative endorsement of Calhoun in 1822 backfired. Dallas alluded to obstacles in July, wryly observing that a slight difference existed among state party members on the presidential question, but optimistically predicting that the dissidents would switch to Calhoun.[15]

Meanwhile, the Family Party shaped its strategy for the 1823 state elections with Calhoun in mind. What it wanted was a staunch Calhoun supporter to run for governor. Unfortunately, the leading aspirant, George Bryan of Lancaster, was uncommitted. Moreover, he was strongest in the rural areas and loathe to identify himself with the Family for fear of alienating farmers who suspected urban-oriented party factions on general principles. Since Bryan as a former state auditor had a wide following, the Family wanted to undermine his candidacy without arousing suspicions. The formula of the Dallas men was to assure Bryan that they would throw him the support of the Family after voting for their own candidate, Samuel Ingham, during the initial balloting. Bryan viewed this tactic warily, but he was in no position to complain because he had resisted the concessions that would have assured him the firm adherence of the Family. His misgivings would have deepened if he had realized that Dallas and Ingham were consulting Calhoun in Washington during February to work out a carefully timed doublecross.[16]

The plan called for the transfer of Family delegates from Ingham to John A. Shulze, a rheumatic, retired Lutheran minister from Dauphin County, instead of Bryan. The switch occurred on the fourth ballot and enabled Shulze to carry the nomination by a vote of 95 to 35. Eliminating Bryan was not as helpful to Calhoun as the Dallas forces had anticipated. Whether the relatively obscure Shulze, despite lengthy service in the state legislature, broke his part of the bargain, or whether the delegates were resentful of the scheming by the Family is unclear. In any case, the temper of the convention militated against an attempt to endorse Calhoun and none was made.

Embarrassed by his failure, Dallas nonetheless pretended that bad news was good news in dealing with Calhoun. He took the ingenious line that no endorsement was better than the tepid one available at the time, intimating that the silence of the convention would actually improve Calhoun's prospects. This kind of logic meant little to the latter, who had expected support from two-thirds of the delegates, and he was bitterly disappointed. Calhoun did not know whom to blame, but he felt betrayed in a state where his avowed retainers ostensibly controlled the government while pleading their inability to control the party machinery.[17]

If Calhoun was temporarily unwilling to breakfast on the illusions served by the Family, he soon developed a voracious appetite for them. Indeed, by 25 January 1824 he had written J. G. Swift that his candidacy was flourishing in the North and singled out Pennsylvania as being "firm as a rock."[18] Events soon demonstrated that the secretary of war was wrong on both counts. For one thing, Shulze—who was indebted to the Family for both his nomination and election as governor—persistently evaded a commitment to Calhoun. Moreover, a rump caucus of Pennsylvania congressmen met in late January and nominated William Crawford. Finally, an unmistakable tide of sentiment for Andrew Jackson began to sweep over the state, demolishing the organizational structures that local politicians had erected so painstakingly in the previous three years.

Spotting the swells from a distance on 27 January, Dallas dismissed Jackson's "excessive popularity" as "an effervescence that can accomplish nothing" and predicted afresh that Calhoun would be nominated. Three weeks later, when the wave from the west was lapping at the foundations of the Family organization in Philadelphia, Dallas decided that a salvage operation was in order, so he hastily dropped Calhoun for Jackson. Since some explanation of his acrobatics was mandatory, Dallas castigated the rump caucus that had endorsed Crawford as a "miserable infatuated minority" and hailed Jackson as the only statesman capable of uniting the party and the country. To Calhoun, he offered a wilted rose: the vice-presidential nomination. The Family caucus dutifully ratified the proposal and instructed its delegates to vote for Jackson at the Harrisburg convention.[19] The only casualty was the good faith of Dallas, and it seemed like a small price to pay for the privilege of clamoring onto a captious bandwagon. What such belated enthusiasm meant to Jackson was a matter of conjecture. But as a self-appointed kingmaker Dallas was an immediate success, because the Harrisburg convention endorsed Jackson over Crawford by a vote of 124 to 1. Consciences great and small took comfort by securing the vice-presidential nomination for Calhoun. Dallas made a virtue of duplicity by assuring Calhoun on 11 February that his cause was lost and that the Family had testified to its fidelity by conferring the vice-presidency on the bewildered South Carolinian. Calhoun was far from reassured by this protestation of good will. On the contrary, he countered with the assertion that he would have secured the presidency if Pennsylvania had done its duty.[20] Calhoun's supporters were more outspoken and complained bitterly about being deserted. Whether treachery was a tribute to the prescience of Pennsylvania is debatable. The sequel vindicated treachery, however, because within eight years Calhoun had transformed himself from a nationalist into an apostle of sectionalism. Moreover, the switch rewarded Dallas, who emerged from the controversy with a stronger grip on Family policy than ever before. His descent into the snakepit of Pennsylvania politics hardly entitled him to feelings of pride, but it paved the way for his emergence as the top figure in the political hierarchy of the state.

In retrospect, it is apparent that Dallas had expected more than he got during his flirtation with Calhoun. What he had wanted was the recently available Mexican mission, but old enemies combined with the new ones he made in the sparring over the presidential nomination in Pennsylvania. John Binns, for one, was determined to block Dallas's appointment and found a ready accomplice in Secretary of State John Quincy Adams. As the principal rival of Jackson in 1824, Adams recognized that he was a target of Dallas, and he operated behind the scenes to successfully thwart the Philadelphian.

2

The Rise and Fall of
The Family Party
(1824–1831)

The succession of rebuffs administered to Dallas on the eve of the 1824 election would ordinarily have discouraged a man who experienced misgivings about politics even when things were going well. On this occasion, however, adversity goaded him into a fighting mood and he made preparations to take over the Jacksonian movement in Pennsylvania. It was a decision made in the face of depressing odds. For one thing, no amount of effort could convert Dallas into an authentic Jacksonian. As a silk-stocking patrician and spokesman for the economic interests of eastern Pennsylvania, he had nothing in common with the mechanics, small farmers, and pioneers in coonskin caps who called themselves supporters of "Old Hickory." If ideology had loomed large in the calculations of Dallas, he would have emerged from the impending political realignment in the upper ranks of the Whig organization and thereby would have escaped the lifelong necessity of pursuing his socioeconomic preferences in a party for the most part unresponsive to them. From the outset, however, personal ties meant more to Dallas than principles, and these ties were the decisive factor in drawing him into the faction that would soon be known as the Democratic Party. The prospect of identifying himself with a winner and settling old scores turned him into a Jacksonian.

For better or worse, Dallas became imprisoned by the rhetoric of self-apology. Each successive deviation from orthodoxy made him vulnerable to attacks that necessitated frequent and largely unconvincing explanations of his position. As the discrepancies accumulated, the hapless Dallas became afflicted with chronic political disability. Occasionally, he was assertive and launched offensive action, but for the most part he spent his time countering the denunciations made against his integrity and motives.

Handicapped by his outlook and behavior, Dallas labored under the additional disability of being a late convert to the Jacksonian cause. Before he tried to scramble onto the bandwagon, there were two groups already occupying it. Each group distrusted the other, but both felt a greater antipathy toward sharing the ride with any newcomers because of the elementary perception that patronage would have to be shared with them as well if Jackson won and recognized their contribution.

The first group that claimed to be "original Jacksonians" was a diffuse combination of small-town editors and rural politicians. Operating more or less spontaneously throughout Pennsylvania, they generated the grassroots movement for the general. Their strong suit was enthusiasm rather than organization, a consideration that made it easy for the professional politicians to minimize their contribution. The second group—old Federalists and Democratic-Republicans—also tried to seize Jackson's banner. They mistook the advent of the general for the second coming of George Washington and aspired to the role of the elect on judgment day, which they thought was imminent. Called Independent Republicans or Amalgamators, they lined up behind Henry Baldwin, Isaac Barnard, and other holdovers from the 1790s. They had a long record of hostility to Dallas and the Family faction, but it could be attributed to the competition for power rather than to ideological differences. Although both paid lip service to egalitarianism, neither took it very seriously. Since the Amalgamators were the first in the field for Jackson, they dubbed the Family faction the "Eleventh-Hour Men," insinuating that the latter would drop the general after one term and switch to Calhoun in 1828. Jackson probably had misgivings as to the sincerity of his more belated supporters in Pennsylvania, but he professed to love them all. They responded, in turn, by giving him an easy victory over Adams and Crawford in November 1824.[1]

The Family Party and the Amalgamators, to say nothing of Jackson's rural followers, watched with great interest the maneuvering in the House of Representatives that followed the deadlock election. Dallas tried to influence the vote by firing off letters in all directions, alluding to the need for electoral reform and declaring that the selection of either Adams or Crawford would be a "contemptuous mockery." Inspired by his newly found faith in democracy, Dallas announced that the cause of General Jackson had become "the cause of popular government." The House took a more relaxed view of the issue and chose Adams for president, a decision that Dallas denounced as the product of a "corrupt bargain." For once his morality and interest converged. This happy coincidence freed him to attack the new president and to bid for control of the Jackson organization under the impression that he was launching a crusade.[2]

Dallas's first target in Pennsylvania was Henry Simpson, a Philadelphia Amalgamator and Jacksonian whom he dubbed "a fool and a madman" for his method of handling large political meetings. Confiding his irritation to Samuel Ingham, Dallas went on to say, "If Jackson has not the understanding enough to perceive the inevitable effects of this man's [Simpson] interference, we ought not to support him. Let him take his choice—or rather let his friends take their choice."[3]

The rhetoric was misleading because neither Dallas nor his collaborators had any intention of waiting for a blessing from the Hermitage. Jackson was a valuable symbol and they intended to exploit him for their own purposes in Pennsylvania irrespective of what he had to say. Fortunately, they already knew he would say as little as possible. So the Family men forged ahead. They organized Hickory Clubs, issued circulars setting forth their new champion's merits, and purchased newspapers to carry their message. Through these efforts they spearheaded the anti-Adams movement in Pennsylvania, and thereby stole the thunder of the other Jacksonian newspapers. For all their outspokenness, they were thinking in dynastic terms: four years for Jackson and eight for Calhoun. Indeed, Dallas spoke airily of a political revolution like the one that brought Jefferson to power and kept his organization intact for twenty-four years.

The Amalgamators, however, would not concede control of the party to the Jackson-Calhoun men so easily. Between 1825 and 1828 the contest for dominance in Pennsylvania became increasingly heated, but it went on mostly beneath the surface, because each faction had to fight the other without appearing to damage the prospects of Old Hickory. So the rival organizations displayed harmony in public and knifed each other quietly in private.

Despite the determination of the Family, the Amalgamators fought them on nearly even terms, strengthened in 1826 by the addition of James Buchanan to their ranks. Obscure at the time, Buchanan would ultimately dominate the counsels of the Amalgamators. His subsequent rise paralleled that of Dallas in the Family, and the two rivals were destined to confront each other in every Pennsylvania election for more than a quarter of a century, even though Dallas shunned

nominations for elective office. Buchanan was as much the patrician
or gentleman in politics as Dallas, but the Lancastrian matched or
surpassed his foe in political savvy and organizational ability. Elected
to Congress in 1820, the tall, blond, blue-eyed ex-Federalist was just
the man the Amalgamators needed; and they were just the faction for
a man without a party. He excelled particularly in the drawing room,
where he invariably made a good first impression. Capitalizing on an
eye defect, which caused him to develop an odd posture of tilting his
head sideways in an appearance of deference or interest, Buchanan
added a folksy charm to his mellifluous speaking voice to disarm
friend and foe alike.

Buchanan's strategy was to forge a coalition of erstwhile Federalist
German farmers and Scotch-Irish Democrats in the west; like the
Family, he planned to support Jackson for one term, perfect a new
party organization in the process, and then consolidate its supremacy
in Pennsylvania by backing Henry Clay. This strategy was shaped by
the belief that the rural vote could be mobilized against the predomi-
nantly urban organization of the Family. The Eleventh-Hour Men
countered with obstructionist tactics designed to thwart the polarization of Pennsylvania along urban-rural lines. The principal one was
applied to increase the warfare against Adams. The immediate hope
was to discredit Governor Shulze, who had won reelection in 1826,
and who tended to aid the Buchanan faction while cultivating a posture of independence.[4]

The clandestine factional struggle became public on the eve of the
1828 election. The immediate cause of the eruption was the ouster of
a Family man, Richard Bache, as postmaster of Philadelphia, ostensibly for using government funds to fight Adams's administration.
Bache was disposed of without an investigation, and Postmaster General John McLean, a Calhoun man, replaced him with Thomas Sergeant. Dallas was alarmed because the Jacksonians had lost Philadelphia in 1827 and he feared the odor of corruption surrounding the
Bache affair raised doubts about the ability of the Family to deliver
the votes for Jackson in its own stronghold in 1828. If Dallas felt any
distress over his association with people of questionable political morals, he managed to conceal it. The guilt or innocence of Bache was a
side issue. It concerned Dallas only insofar as it might minimize Jackson's political utility of the Family and thereby invalidate its claims
for patronage in the event that the general won the presidency.[5] Ele-
vating the welfare of the organization above all else, Dallas testified to
the preoccupation with spoils, which would become general and ob-
sessive during the next decade.

The subsequent presidential election confirmed the obvious: that Jackson was more essential to the quarreling factions in Pennsylvania than they were to him. Nobody needed scientific polls of public opinion to spot the trend. For those versed in the classics or capable of absorbing them secondhand, Jackson was venerated as a reincarnation of the simple, upright Roman republican. He came into focus as the Cincinnatus of Tennessee: indifferent to power, and reluctant to leave his farm, but so imbued with patriotism that he would heed the call of his countrymen. The rest of his numerous supporters simply viewed him as the perfect embodiment of the pioneer spirit because he bristled at insults from foreigners and echoed the aspirations of a restless, dynamic society bent on overcoming all the obstacles to expansion westward. The adoration depended less on what he said than on what he had done. His triumph over the British at New Orleans and his repeated chastisement of Indians, Spaniards, and sundry others who obstructed the quest of American settlers for land had assured him a near immunity from criticism. Jackson's popularity was further enhanced by the belief that the popular will had been thwarted in 1824. Voters otherwise immune to his appeal took it for granted that the vindication of Jackson was inseparable from the vindication of democracy.

Under the circumstances, issues meant little in Pennsylvania or elsewhere, except possibly New England. The indifference to them suited Jackson, who cheerfully allowed his political managers to identify him with whatever local voters found appealing. In Pennsylvania, this meant the Tariff of 1828, which offered protection to a variety of nascent industries. Jackson said nothing about the tariff, but both the Amalgamators and the Family assured the freeholders that he was a zealous friend of the iron manufacturers, the turnpike builders, and the merchants. It was a tribute to the mindless Jacksonian frenzy that the electorate discounted the incontestable exhortations of Adams for a protective tariff and gave the credit to the silent, inactive occupant of the Hermitage.

The upshot was that Jackson swept the country in November and piled up a plurality of 50,000 votes in Pennsylvania, disrupting old political alignments in the process. The role of the Family and the Amalgamators in the upheaval that convulsed the state was at best a modest one. Whether by chance or design, the Family recovered from its setback of 1826 in Philadelphia, receiving the good news a month in advance because Pennsylvania held its state elections in October. The Dallas faction managed to secure a majority of 6,000 in the city and county of Philadelphia, and to send three Jacksonians to Congress. Of more importance for the health of the Family, it flooded the common and select councils of the city with enough of its retainers to insure the election of Dallas as mayor of Philadelphia. The latter feat was all the more remarkable because hitherto the Federalists had dominated the councils that selected the mayor. If the Family had demonstrated that it was alive and well, the Amalgamators had compiled a more ambiguous record. They had plainly failed in their major endeavor to unify the old Federalists and the Adams supporters behind their banner. But in the evident confusion over who had done what for Jackson, they were able to make a plausible claim that they were the real architects of his victory. The one political reality that they could not deny was the revival of the Family and the derivative realization that Jackson dared not ignore its contribution, except at considerable personal peril.

An impartial observer surveying the political devastation in the wake of the Jackson landslide was bound to pity the new president, who faced the thankless task of choosing between the manifold and conflicting claims of his professed supporters. As already noted, the original Jackson men were the only ones the president could safely ignore, because they lacked any organization worthy of the name. The Amalgamators had to be considered, but many were erstwhile Federalists who had committed the grave error of supporting Henry Clay in 1824. The Family was tainted by its long identification with Calhoun and by the fact that its persistent championship of business interests was intolerable to the small farmers of western Pennsylvania, who had supported Jackson in large numbers.

The president-elect entered the no-man's-land of Keystone politics as warily as if he were tracking Seminoles in the swamps of Florida. His initial gesture elated the Family and took the form of an invitation to Samuel Ingham to enter the cabinet as secretary of the treasury. The offer was all the more remarkable because Ingham had lost a Senate seat to the Amalgamators the previous year. Ingham lost no time in accepting, which drove the Amalgamator candidate for the post, Henry Baldwin, into retirement. His precipitous withdrawal from politics was accompanied by jeers from the Family press, and it weakened the Amalgamators in western Pennsylvania, where Baldwin had long been an influential figure, reviling the Family's Judge William Wilkins. Far from being a casual decision of an inexperienced president, the elevation of Ingham to the Treasury foreshadowed a trend. Whether Jackson liked the Family or merely disliked Buchanan is not altogether clear, but the bulk of federal patronage was conferred on Buchanan's enemies. Although each successive setback diminished Buchanan's enthusiasm for Jackson, the unhappy Amalgamator and his retainers haunted the executive offices until June 1829, when all of the jobs earmarked for Pennsylvanians had been filled. Thwarted in Washington, Buchanan retreated to Harrisburg and lavished his considerable energies as a manipulator on the creation of a state organization.[6]

The momentum generated by presidential favors was too much for Buchanan to arrest initially, and he watched with dismay throughout 1829 as the Family tightened its grip on Pennsylvania. Their most notable triumph was in the gubernatorial election. Dominating the state convention and shelving the recalcitrant Shulze, they nominated George Wolf, a popular Mason from Northampton County who had served three terms in Congress. The joint support of the Masons and the Family made Wolf invincible, and he swamped Joseph Ritner, a former speaker of the lower house and avowed foe of the Masons. With both federal and state patronage at its disposal, the Family methodically completed the rout of the Amalgamators and the remnants of the Adams organization.[7]

During the turmoil, which he had done so much to promote, Dallas was ostensibly engrossed in the affairs of Philadelphia. He officiated at the sessions of the Mayor's Court and, together with the council, busied himself in the cause of civic improvements. He launched plans to pave streets and to widen footways, removed the market carts from Chestnut to Dock streets, and resolutely blocked the extension of the lottery system. His philanthropic impulses also found an outlet in the effort to establish a House of Refuge for Orphans. The mayor also found time to load the city payroll with loyal followers of the Family.

Like Napoleon on Elba, Dallas became bored as he ran out of projects to launch. His zeal for municipal administration was spent by April 1829. He did not dream of anything as dramatic as the reconquest of France, but he imitated the restless Corsican by exploring more inconspicuous avenues of escape. Ennui reduced him to the uncharacteristic role of suppliant, and he wrote to Ingham asking for the appointment as district attorney for the eastern district of Pennsylvania. Although his eagerness for the post verged on desperation, he was neither a vote-getter nor an asset to the Jacksonians outside Philadelphia. Fortunately, Vice-President Calhoun was still influential with the president and intervened decisively in behalf of Dallas. Receiving the post in mid-April, he resigned as mayor with only perfunctory expressions of regret and resumed his intrigues on the larger and more congenial stage of state politics.[8]

His new duties took some time to master, but Dallas soon began to concentrate his energy on strengthening the relations of the Family with Governor Wolf and studying the political role of the Second Bank of the United States. What emerged was an informal division of labor, with Dallas supervising the operations of the Family in Pennsylvania and Ingham performing the same function in Washington.

As befitted the managers of a temporarily thriving organization, both men allowed themselves the luxury of speculating about the political future and the selection of an heir to Jackson, even though they agreed that the moment of decision was nearly eight years away. Torn between the desire to put the ultimate winner under obligation by discovering him early and the fear of backing a loser, they were reduced to exchanging confidences. At first, only their old patron Calhoun appeared in their crystal ball, but by the summer of 1829 Martin Van Buren had also materialized as a possible competitor. Mindful that Jackson would play a decisive role in naming a successor, Dallas prudently urged silence on their collaboration, noting that "the best laid plans will be made and remade a dozen times."[9]

Obsessed as Dallas was with factional politics and the presidential succession, he was not impervious to issues. Normally cautious in such matters, he gradually became involved during 1829 and 1830 in what would be the most explosive issue of the decade: the Second Bank of the United States. His preoccupation developed naturally because, since the founding of the institution in 1816, Dallas had been a lawyer of the bank as well as one of its stockholders. He fancied himself an authority on its charter, which had been written by the elder Dallas, and was prone to scrutinize its operations critically inasmuch as its president, Nicholas Biddle, allied himself with foes of the Family. How far political animus shaped Dallas's approach to interpretation of the charter is a matter of conjecture, but his initial objections sounded like the antibank manifestos of the more militant Jacksonians a few years later. As he put the matter to Ingham in 1829:

> It was never intended by those who made it, that the Bank should be independent of the government, if it were why has the Executive the appointment of four directors . . . ? It was avowed on the floor of the House of Representatives by the framers and friends of the Bank and also in the Senate that these features were introduced into the Bill, for the very purpose of giving the government a certain influence and control over the administration of its affairs.

Specifically, Dallas objected to what he considered the excessive power of the private directors and stockholders, who took their cues from Nicholas Biddle. The political considerations lurking behind the legal position of Dallas became clearer when he worked up a paper in the fall of 1829 to confer on Washington (i.e., Secretary of the Treasury Ingham and the Family) greater control over the bank's policies. Presented to Biddle and the bank board, it was accepted with "sulky submission." Dallas received the report of Biddle's reaction with jubilation and expressed regret that he had not been present to watch the "successive contortions" as they registered on the "pretty face" of the president. He was especially elated to learn that Biddle had been too upset to attend the opera that evening. He took a kindred pleasure in the rumor that the bank might move to New York and thereby rid the Family of the financial Trojan horse in its midst.[10]

Through the influence of Ingham, Dallas was offered a government-appointed bank directorship, but initially he preferred to snipe at the bank from the outside. Personnel rather than principles were at issue, a point Dallas made clear by contending that the bank should be continued but that its president should be dropped. The reappointment of Biddle, he asserted, would indicate a "most preposterous weakness" in the government. The transparent campaign for the ouster of Biddle failed, but Dallas drew comfort from Jackson's annual message, delivered in December 1829, expressing doubt about the constitutionality of the bank and the uncertainty as to whether its charter should be renewed. Apparently the admiration was mutual because Jackson renewed the offer of the bank directorship and Dallas accepted it in January 1830. Attracted by the salary, he found it expedient to slip from the role of critic to that of booster. Indeed, he assured Ingham in disarming fashion that he favored neither the destruction nor the reform of the bank.[11]

It was predictable that Dallas would continue to grumble about the bank as long as it was managed by Nicholas Biddle. He soon developed the suspicion that Biddle was gaining access to the palace through Peggy Eaton, the wife of Secretary of War John Eaton, and a favorite of the president. Dallas relayed his apprehensions to Ingham in a coded letter, reporting that bank representatives had entertained Mrs. Eaton and presented her with gifts. He also mistrusted Van Buren for espousing the cause of the notorious Peggy and snorted that "petticoats should not interfere with politics."[12] He went on to deplore the divisive intrigues in Washington, by which he meant factional activity detrimental to the welfare of the Family.

The cumulative effect of the maneuvering by Dallas and Ingham was to undermine the alliance between Jackson and the Family. The deterioration of relations between the president and Calhoun, paralleled by the rise of Van Buren, accelerated the process. The upshot was that Jackson began to withhold patronage from the Philadelphia organization. Taking his cue from Washington, Governor Wolf did the same. Internal quarrels and disappointed office-seekers hastened the collapse of Family ascendancy in Pennsylvania. The greed and ambition of the leaders eroded the discipline of the rank and file. As the mutual animosities burgeoned within the organization, outsiders exploited their opportunity. Anti-Masonic elements and agrarian Jacksonians absorbed some of the malcontents. The Buchanan faction revived and echoed the traditional objection of western Pennsylvanians to domination by an eastern urban machine. Dallas watched helplessly as the situation worsened and complained about the aloofness of summertime friends. What vexed him most was "the utter indifference and inactivity" of Calhoun. Why Dallas imagined that the intervention of the South Carolinian would have made any difference is unclear. Common sense suggests that his aid would have been counterproductive because by 1831 Calhoun was on a collision course with the president. Perhaps the lamentations of Dallas were merely intended to justify his impending desertion of the vice-president. In any case, Calhoun soon provided an ideal excuse for the Family to sever relations with him by launching his doctrine of nullification.[13]

While writing off Calhoun, Dallas was grumbling about the "deplorable state of politics." He informed Ingham in November 1830 that "the party here is distracted to an extent I never before witnessed." Recounting the divisions, he blamed them on the personal ambitions of the members. Nevertheless, he contended that the trend could be reversed by the election of a Family man to the Senate in December. Dallas probably had himself in mind because his supporters in Harrisburg had floated a trial balloon. If so, he found the response discouraging and withdrew his name—as he always did on such occasions—by professing inability to make the financial sacrifice. He then threw his strength behind his brother-in-law, Judge William Wilkins of Pittsburgh. Residing in the west, Wilkins was able to pick up some wavering Democrats who would not have voted for Dallas. Even so, it took twenty-one ballots before the feuding Democrats in the legislature coalesced behind Wilkins and selected him over his Anti-Masonic opponent. It was a Pyrrhic victory for the Family rather than a revival of its fortunes.[14]

Meanwhile, an assortment of old-line politicians with varied antecedents had begun to toy with the idea of recruiting Dallas as a vice-presidential candidate on a ticket with Judge John McLean of Ohio. Since McLean had been postmaster general during the Adams administration and a Calhoun supporter, the use of his name was intended to unite the foes of Jackson. This motivation was denied by Philadelphia politicos Charles and Joseph Ingersoll, who approached Dallas as agents for McLean on 26 October 1830. Denying hostility to the general, they merely professed interest in promoting a suitable candidate if Jackson chose retirement. Dallas was not deceived, but he couched his refusal in gracious terms. Pleading "youth and inexperience," he also expressed apprehension that the movement was "premature and unadvised." Undeterred, the schemers repeated the offer in January 1831, and Dallas again rejected it with appropriate expressions of regret.[15]

The flirtation between McLean and Dallas continued through intermediaries, however, until March. At that point, Dallas urged McLean not to run, lest he collide with the president and disrupt the fragile Democracy by throwing the election into the House. The two men finally met in April, and McLean must have acquiesced in the strategy of Dallas, who later reported the views of the judge to be "just and proper." Dallas then made a magnanimous assessment of McLean. Predicting that the judge would be an important man in the future, he added: "His danger is in the present. . . . I do not think any circumstances will induce him to take the field against General Jackson."[16]

The same spring a fatal instability overtook the political conglomerate that had formed around Jackson in 1828. The embroilment of the entire cabinet in the affairs of Peggy Eaton was the incident that launched the process, but it was not its cause. Sectional rivalries had intensified the cleavage within the administration and had achieved a partial focus in the Calhoun–Van Buren feud. Forced to choose between them, Jackson espoused the wily "Little Magician" and drove Calhoun into the arms of his opponents. The Family suffered severe repercussions because it had lingered in the camp of the South Carolinian too long and could not evacuate rapidly enough to avoid his fate.

The axe fell quickly and almost without warning upon Ingham. Offered the Russian mission as a sop, he refused indignantly and soon withdrew from politics altogether. Dallas waxed eloquent about Ingham's record in the Treasury Department, but the former secretary was inconsolable. He became bitter as well when Jackson began his all-out assault on the bank. The removal of Ingham in Washington started a chain reaction that eventually leveled the already anemic Family organization in Pennsylvania. By May Dallas had stopped trying to cheer Ingham and had begun to brood about his own future.

I have long taken it for granted that I should be regarded as an early and incurable Calhoun man, and therefore entitled to be treated cavalierly whenever the proper periodical occasion came around. I know myself utterly inaccessible, except to the office of District Attorney, and were that to be called for tomorrow I don't think that except as an indication of ill will it would ruffle my temper for half an hour. As to my political action, it cannot be altered, on any consideration of this sort.[17]

For the moment Dallas was so depressed that he contemplated yet another retirement from politics. Extravagant at all times and by his own admission incapable of saving money, he nonetheless nursed the delusion that he would wipe out his debts and increase his annual income of $6,000 a year fourfold through the practice of law. While still cultivating these fantasies, Dallas was catapulted back into politics by the decision of the ailing Isaac D. Barnard to resign from the United States Senate. Only mild persuasion was required to extract a pledge from Dallas that he would be the Family candidate for the vacant seat. He faced competition from the political veterans: Richard Rush, who carried the Anti-Masonic banner, and Judge Joseph Hemphill, who inherited the remnants of the Adams machine. Both men were Philadelphians and old friends of Dallas. The same could not be said of the fourth candidate, Henry A. Muhlenberg, who was a strong antagonist but from the still rising Amalgamator faction. The final contestant was Jesse R. Burden, a veteran Democrat and member of the state senate from Philadelphia County.

The balloting of the 132-member legislature began on 13 December 1831. The first tabulation showed Dallas leading (34 votes), followed by Richard Rush (33), Joseph Hemphill (27), Jesse R. Burden (18), and Henry A. Muhlenberg (17). Dallas received his initial support only from areas where the Family was normally strong. Indeed, thirty out of his thirty-four votes on the first ballot came from the eastern tier of urban counties, the Cumberland-Perry district, and Washington County. The distribution of votes remained virtually the same for the next six ballots. On the eighth a shift to Dallas was discernible in the ranks of Burden and Muhlenberg and both men withdrew before the ninth ballot. In Muhlenberg's case, he and Buchanan warily watched the steady strength of Rush and Hemphill and rather than risk the complete destruction of the Jacksonian Party, they threw their support to Dallas. The rapid increase in his total vote enabled him to reach the needed sixty-seven votes on the eleventh ballot. He garnered many of Burden's old backers, especially from Philadelphia, and most of Muhlenberg's from Berks and York counties. These combined with a scattering of votes from rural northern counties to give Dallas the victory. If Dallas had depended solely on his own political strength, he would still have fallen short of the necessary total. It was the desperate efforts of the men who preferred Dallas, the avowed Jacksonian, to Rush, the Anti-Mason, that provided the key to success.[18]

If the votes of the state senators for Dallas in 1831 can be considered representative of popular will, a passing comparison can be made to Jackson's sources of support in 1828. Both men drew strength from a statewide base, urban and rural. The only solid Dallas counties to go against Jackson in 1828 were Adams and Bucks, and only by slight margins. Both lost Erie and Delaware counties and were strong, but not victorious, in Beaver County. The major difference in the balloting was that Dallas never won the trust of the Jacksonians in the rural areas. Perhaps he did not garner more of the president's dormant strength because of the all-pervasive influence of the state's Anti-Masonry, which would sway some Jackson men from voting for Dallas, who was a Mason. Dallas's strength came from the heavily populated areas of eastern Pennsylvania, while the general's was spread more evenly throughout the Commonwealth. Nevertheless, Dallas won because he was now recognized as an authentic Jacksonian by the bulk of the state politicos who dared not desert him for fear of damaging the nascent Democratic Party in the process.[19]

The result of the senatorial election provoked bitter attacks in opposition newspapers. Dallas was abused equally by the anti-Jackson and Anti-Masonic press. His "Eleventh Hour" arrival in the president's camp, his Masonry, and his Family Party ties were revived. Dallas was reviled as "shallow," "heartless," "unprincipled," and "a pretender," who would disgrace Jackson, the state, and the party. Since his brother-in-law was also a senator, Dallas faced the charge that he had launched a new blood-kinship party to replace the old Family organization. The critics were half right. The old Family faction, which had controlled Pennsylvania for almost a decade, was dying. When Dallas departed for Washington in December 1831, he was a leader without a visible following. For better or worse, he could not foresee the issues of the next year and a half, or how his responses would draw him into the tangled web of national politics.[20]

3

The Bank War and Beyond (1832–1833)

By 1832 the Pennsylvania Democracy was trapped in the whirligig of national politics. The new Family Party, the heir to the recently dominant faction in the Democratic Party, was caught in the crossfire among the warring forces of President Andrew Jackson and the White House aspirants Vice-President John C. Calhoun and National Republican Henry Clay, and would be destroyed by the events of 1832–33. Like the prodigal son, James Buchanan would return from his exile as American minister to Russia in 1834 to give the Democrats new direction and stimulate a career that would carry him to the presidency a quarter of a century later.

The Democracy of the Keystone State was warily defensive as the election of 1832 approached. Its two senators, George M. Dallas of Philadelphia and William Wilkins of Pittsburgh, and its governor, George Wolf, were avowed Jacksonians, but the party was tainted by its former ties with the Federalists or Calhoun supporters in the Era of Good Feelings. Old Hickory looked skeptically at the Pennsylvanians, especially after he dismissed his Calhounite, Philadelphia-bred Secretary of the Treasury Samuel D. Ingham in the cabinet shake-up of 1831. At the same time the president, responding to Van Buren's advice, had dispatched Congressman James Buchanan to Russia in January 1832, which eliminated another potent force from Pennsylvania Democratic—although not the nascent Family Party—circles. This left only freshman Senators Wilkins and Dallas in Washington to combat the rising influence of New York's "Red Fox," now the president's heir-apparent. Van Buren hoped to build a coalition of his own using a divided Pennsylvania Democracy, and it was the task of Dallas and Wilkins to frustrate this effort through development of a strong political and social bond with Jackson. Unfortunately for the Pennsylvanians the "Bank War" of January–July 1832 would totally smash their state's national influence and damage their own careers for over a decade.

Dallas journeyed to the capital almost immediately after his election. He arrived in time to eat Christmas dinner with his "quondam favorite," John C. Calhoun. Dallas informed his wife, Sophy, that the outer show of civility that passed between the two men would have amused her. They talked of everything but politics or the past. Dallas still held the vice-president in high regard, writing to Sophy that "he is a noble fellow, and deserves a better fate than the one which his headstrong friends and lofty faults have prepared for him." For the next few weeks the new senator visited the appropriate people in Washington, making fresh contacts and renewing old ones. He barely had time to complete these formalities before the heavy burden of the Bank Memorial for a recharter was placed in his inexperienced hands.[1]

There was no question about how the people of Pennsylvania viewed the Second Bank of the United States. The Philadelphia-based institution was Pennsylvanian by interest, location, and legislative initiative. Although it was charted by the Democratic-Republicans, men of all factions came in time to respect it. The chief issue in 1832 was whether the National Republicans or the Jacksonians were the stauncher friends of the bank. The president's followers responded vociferously when the opposition accused Jackson of hostility to a recharter movement. In late December 1831 the state legislature passed a resolution in support of the bank's renewal by an overwhelming majority. Such an endorsement by his state should have made Dallas's posture on the question easy to foresee. However, rumors were common that the president viewed the bank and the recharter as a personal and political challenge in an election year. These rumors placed the young senator on the horns of a dilemma.[2]

The plan for rechartering the bank had been carefully conceived by leading bank officials and politicians in December and early January. The only problem was when it would be put into operation. Bank President Nicholas Biddle considered conflicting procedural advice; while Jackson's cabinet members, on one side, urged waiting until the next session of Congress, congressmen and lobbyists, on the other, advised immediate action. Dallas agreed with the former group. Representative George McDuffie, a Democrat from South Carolina and an old Calhounite, was chosen to present the petition in the House, but determination of a Senate leader was a more difficult decision. Although General Samuel Smith, a Maryland Democrat and chairman of the Finance Committee, was the first choice, he objected to raising the issue at this session. It would be made a "Jackson/anti-Jackson vote," and few men would convince the president that they favored the bank and were not hostile to him. Smith urged the recharter leaders to wait until the following winter. He felt the bank would lose at least ten friendly votes, including those of Dallas and Wilkins, if its sponsors pursued their present course.

On 20 December Thomas Cadwalader, the bank's lobbyist in Washington, called on the two Pennsylvania senators to ascertain their sentiments. Cadwalader formed the impression that Dallas would aid him in any possible way, although the senator, like Smith, opposed renewal for that session and anticipated a presidential veto unless a two-thirds majority could be gained in support of the institution. Dallas said that Wilkins was as yet undecided and could not be counted upon to support the bank. In an interview one week later the agent learned that both men were still torn by contending calculations and, knowing they would urge postponement, Cadwalader did not ask for their advice. At that time Wilkins indicated a warmer feeling for the renewal than Dallas, apparently because he was "more linked in the great points of state interest—to which as he admits the extinction of the Bank would carry a death blow." Dallas, however, because of financial interests, family background, and personal ambition emerged as the second choice of the bank men. On 6 January he received a note from Biddle advising him of his selection as the institution's champion.[3]

Dallas was fully aware of his awkward predicament. He knew that the president and all his friends opposed the recharter and would consider it a political attack. Consequently, the senator feared introducing the memorial, an action which on any other occasion he would have been delighted to initiate. Yet when it was presented to him, as a representative from Pennsylvania—and Philadelphia—he could hardly refuse the application. Despite his legislature's endorsement, Dallas ran the constant risk of political harassment from acquaintances he was hoping to cultivate. The fear of being misrepresented and misunderstood throughout the entire country haunted him. Dallas had said many times, and would say again, that he opposed renewal activities before the election of 1832: "To bring it forward is certainly contrary to my judgment—but if they will advance, can I refuse to be their organ?—chosen because of my residence, my paternity to the bank, and because of my avowed politics."[4]

Dallas reiterated this theme when he presented the Bank Memorial to the Senate on 9 January 1832. He spoke of his reluctance to admit the petition in this session, for he felt "deep solicitude and apprehension, lest, in the progress of inquiry and in the development of views, under present circumstances, it might be drawn into real or imagined conflict with some higher, some more favorite, some more immediate wish or purpose of the American people."[5] The same day a Select Committee was established to study the memorial. It was composed of Dallas, Daniel Webster (Massachusetts National Republican), Thomas Ewing (Ohio National Republican), Josiah Johnston (Louisiana Democrat), and Robert Hayne (South Carolina Democrat). All except Hayne were avowed friends of the bank. The reaction of the administration to the petition was predictable. The *Washington Globe,* Jackson's organ, made no mention of Dallas, but immediately identified the movement with Henry Clay and his political interests. In an editorial on 10 January it stated that "the design is to forestall the election of the President, and to extort, from the circumstance of its pendancy [*sic*], submission on the part of the President and his friends, to the demands of the Stockholders of the Bank." Dallas, recognizing that his presence was unpalatable to many Jacksonians, refrained from attending the festivities held in honor of the president in mid-January.

Dallas never doubted that the bank's strategy was dangerous and imprudent. He quickly advised Biddle that someone with veteran ability was needed to manage the institution's campaign, since he was "legislatively inexperienced and in entire ignorance of the strategy so often successful." Dallas was becoming too old and crafty to continue this time-worn ploy and Biddle rejected it without acknowledgment, responding that he could not personally come to the capital, but that Horace Binney would be sent as his liaison man. Binney arrived within a few days and promptly met with McDuffie, rather than Dallas, about an officially planned strategy for the bank war. The senator, meanwhile, discounted rumors that his committee would return a report urging postponement of the memorial. His colleagues were eager to have it forwarded, and he conjectured that they would concede "any reasonable and not injurious modifications" to accomplish this.[6]

The battle over these modifications was fought not only in the committee but on the floor of the Senate as well. Dallas spoke on three occasions on behalf of the bank, usually in response to attacks by Senator Thomas Hart Benton, the spokesman for the administration. The Pennsylvanian first defended the institution on 20 January:

> To me the bank of the United States is nothing but a bank—a mere bank—enacted under the influence of the purest motives, for admirable purposes. If it shall have prostituted its faculties by embarking in the contests of political party, it will find me . . . an implacable opponent. But if, as I unhesitatingly avow my expectations it shall appear uprightly and impartially and efficiently to have achieved its great public duties, and to promise still further usefulness to the country, I must and will, wish it to have justice, stability, and success.

Although this typified Dallas's speeches on the subject, there is little reason to believe that he was naive enough to assume the bank question could or would be isolated from politics. Dallas knew the political importance of the issue and thus felt the Senate would vote to postpone it. This would mean defeat as far as the bank was concerned, and its representatives were becoming increasingly disgruntled with Dallas's attitude and actions. He moved too slowly and spoke too infrequently to suit their tastes. In an effort to stimulate his campaign the bank officials unwisely began to pressure the senator.[7]

By the first week of February Biddle had resolved in his own mind that the situation had reached a crisis for the bank and the administration. He developed a plan to be implemented by Dallas that would work for the benefit of the government, the institution, and the senator. Biddle realized that Dallas had strong ambitions to contest the vice-presidency with Van Buren in the state convention in March 1832. Agents of the bank were instructed to advise Dallas that his chances for the nomination would improve immeasurably if he would stand up for the interests of Pennsylvania, especially those to which the Little Magician was hostile. On 3 February the legislature of the state passed a new set of resolutions in support of the bank. Biddle's plan called for Dallas to approach the president with these resolutions and, after warning about irritating a state so loyal to him, offer to act as an intermediary between the bank and the government. With Dallas as the liaison modifications suitable to both parties could be agreed upon. The bank would be rechartered as an administration measure, increasing the president's support in Pennsylvania, and the senator would win national consideration for this distinguished contribution. Biddle instructed Horace Binney to relay this scheme to Dallas and added, "if in half an hour afterwards he is not on his way to the President, why then the stars have conjoined for him in vain."[8] But the cautious Pennsylvanian was becoming more agitated each day over the bank question. He exploded to his Philadelphia colleague Henry Gilpin:

What in the name of all that is reasonable do the Bank sages want? Are they disposed to see me degenerate into a heated partisan? If so, they mistake me, and are blind to their own policy and interest. I can do the institution no service, the instant I become as headstrong and headlong as themselves. Do they really imagine that I can or ought to forget that I am a Senator, in order to become an advocate?[9]

A strong advocate was almost exactly what the bank wanted and desperately needed. For the next month, until the bill was reported out of committee on 13 March, the bank's agents exerted a steady, daily pressure on Dallas to promote their institution more actively. The more pressure they applied, the more they alienated the senator. They tried to "rouse him to a proper sense of his situation," which they deemed "no easy matter," by pointing out his father's example and memory and the votes of the state legislature. Charles Ingersoll, a former congressman and old family friend, attempted to inspire Dallas. On 6 February Ingersoll advised Biddle that they must be "patient and constant" with Dallas, adding that "the affair cannot be hastened." But the bank men were beginning to panic. In the House the recharter petition was languishing in the hands of McDuffie, a Calhoun supporter. It was vital that Dallas, who was recognized as a loyal Jacksonian, assume the initiative. After spending a frustrating week attempting to move the senator off dead center, Ingersoll on 15 February told Biddle in despair, "the fact that Mr. Dallas is always selfish and never cordial, and will require all your superintendence . . . request Mr. Binney to be in constant urgency of him." Ingersoll reported that he tried to approach Dallas, "but he is so cold, selfish, wary and solicitous of office . . . that I must be very circumspect." As an additional weapon, Wilkins was recruited to talk over the matter with his relative. Biddle understood what his men were experiencing in Washington and urged them to keep reminding Dallas that he was serving his father's memory, the state, and himself. The senator had been insensible to these appeals in the past, however, and Biddle expected that any future progress would be made through influencing the president rather than Dallas.[10]

The bank agents did not quickly surrender their struggle with Dallas, but their renewed efforts brought no results. Biddle remarked to Ingersoll that "it requires a strong blower to ignite this block of granite." To which Ingersoll replied that to inspire Dallas was "impossible." By the end of February the close contact the lobbyists had with Wilkins was beginning to show results of an unexpected kind.

While the western senator was unable to move his brother-in-law, he revealed to the agents that he was warm to the bank and had ambitions of his own. He, too, had visions of the vice-presidency and was willing, unlike Dallas, to identify solidly with the bank. On 7 March Ingersoll approached Wilkins with almost exactly the same speech he had presented to Dallas a month earlier. A golden opportunity was waiting, Ingersoll prophesied, if only he would seize the prospect his colleague had declined. Wilkins, on the eve of receiving Pennsylvania's favorite-son nomination for the second slot, eagerly assented and promised he would talk with the president at once.[11] On 11 March Ingersoll and Wilkins discussed the latter's "road to the stars." While Wilkins agreed to pursue the proposed plan, it was "not so heartily as before." It can be assumed that Wilkins, who had been selected on 10 March as his state's vice-presidential choice, suddenly realized the predicament in which he had placed himself. Not only was he opposing Van Buren, but he was acting as a mediator for the bank as well. The only indication of Wilkins's obvious failure to convert Jackson to the bank is found in a letter of 22 March from Dallas to his wife. He pointed out that in a recent brief absence from Washington he had "escaped one question . . . the only one on which I should differ with Wilkins. I did not wish to be a participant. It was a matter of secret business." By openly confronting the president, his ignominious reward would be to head the Russian mission in 1834.[12]

Between 13 March, when the recharter bill was reported out of committee, and 11 June, when it was voted on, Dallas and the representatives of the bank became more estranged. Nervous over rumors he had heard from friends reporting the bank was bribing certain New York editors with loans to gain their support, he confided to Sophy, "I expect the Bank to make me sick. The reports are distressing and dirty beyond measure." Dallas felt the bank directors now realized their folly in pursuing the early renewal. If Biddle was guilty of bribery or regretted the bank's course, he did not indicate it to the senator. In fact, when Biddle visited the capital in April for a strategy session, he did not even see Dallas. Wilkins felt this oversight was an unpardonable affront to senatorial dignity, but Dallas was "rather pleased than otherwise."[13]

As the month of May passed, Dallas seemed increasingly eager to settle the issue. On the twenty-third he made another major speech in behalf of the bank, describing the fine work it had done. He also praised the committee's bill, although he felt that many of the modifications were either injurious or unnecessary, but that they had been made in the spirit of compromise and conciliation. Dallas favored the present long charter of fifteen to twenty years, so that Congress could not interfere with its activities or re-create the warm excitement of a bank fight every few years. He emphasized that the proposed charter contained every restriction necessary for preventing any mischief by the bank. Dallas still did not consider himself an advocate of the institution, but rather a man discharging a public duty. By the end of May there was no question in his mind that the bill would pass the Senate. The ordeal ended on 11 June when both Pennsylvanians voted with the 28 to 20 majority to approve the re-charter.[14]

On 3 July the bank bill passed the House of Representatives by a 107 to 86 margin. The Pennsylvania delegation voted 24 to 1 (with Henry Muhlenberg abstaining) in favor of the measure. Most of these men were strong Jacksonians who were unwilling to speak out for the bank, but who held firm in their ballots. Without regard for the comfortable majorities the bill had received in both houses and the overwhelming support of the Keystone State, Jackson sent his veto message back to Congress on 10 July. Dallas felt that the president viewed the bank as unconstitutional and no longer expedient. He regretted the "dreadful and unmerciful handling" of the veto and feared its impact on his state. But Dallas did not change his vote, joining the losing side on 14 July in an unsuccessful 22 to 19 attempt to override the president's veto.[15] The senator was not shattered by Jackson's action. He was far more concerned with the political rather than the economic aspects of the move. He did not like Biddle personally and opposed his strategy in the bank war. As for the institution, he advised Gilpin to "let that go—we ought to have it, but we can do without it." That same July Dallas told a Philadelphia gathering (which later adopted resolutions approving the veto) that the president was more important than the bank. In 1834, when Jackson removed the government deposits, Dallas commented to Governor Wolf: "I mourn over its [the bank's] downfall as over the offspring of my father—but I think I can perceive that its directors have insured its destruction by perverting its principles, and by shamelessly as well as unwisely throwing away the very grappling irons which my father had given them to hold on to popular favor and good will."[16]

The reaction of the Pennsylvania Democratic press was similar to Dallas's. The bank was a popular institution in the state, especially in the Pittsburgh and Philadelphia areas, and many people supported its renewal. Yet if the president said it was unconstitutional they would accept his argument and support him in 1832—"Bank or no Bank." The veto message might even have been well received, some editors guessed, by the faithful yeomanry outside the two cities. Unfortunately for the Keystone Democracy, the people were not as understanding as the press had hoped. The president also would not forget the votes of the Pennsylvania delegation, especially those of its two freshman senators. Jackson's veto and his ensuing attitude toward the state party, combined with his views—or lack thereof—on internal improvements and the tariff, would have a serious impact upon him and his followers in this election year.[17]

The American System was immensely popular throughout the state of Pennsylvania in 1832. The bank had statewide appeal, and Jackson had garnered many enemies by his July veto. In the west internal improvements were emphasized, and Old Hickory's opposition to federally funded and managed internal improvements of an intrastate nature was reflected in his Maysville (Kentucky) Road Veto of May 1830. In the east and around Pittsburgh the highly protective tariff was jealously watched, and Jacksonian promises to lower it in order to meet southern demands brought cries of dismay from Keystone industry. In June 1832, the Harrisburg *Chronicle* editorialized the unflinching enthusiasm of press and politicians of the Commonwealth for the system:

> We avow our adherence to the AMERICAN SYSTEM, sustained as it is by the Constitution, by the sanction of the venerable father of the Republic, by the opinions of a large majority of the people, and by a long successful operation, which has carried our country forward in an unparalleled tide of prosperity and national greatness.

The votes of Pennsylvania congressmen in the Twenty-Second Congress sustained this belief. The bank, of course, had almost unanimous backing. On the issue of internal improvements a bill passed the House (102 to 73) on 4 June and the Senate (26 to 13) on 22 June with the support of the Keystone delegation. Wilkins, as the western senator, voted in the affirmative and while Dallas did not vote, he had backed an appropriation for improvements the same day. In the House the delegation was almost evenly split with thirteen in favor, eleven opposed, and two not voting. Distribution, a Clay measure which meant the dispersal of federal funds to the states on the basis of land sales and was regarded as an accessory to the American System, had overwhelming Pennsylvania support. On 3 July 1832 a distribution bill passed the Senate (26 to 18) with both senators voting with the majority. Backing for the measure was as strong in the House (where the bill was defeated by postponement, 91 to 88), with the Pennsylvanians voting nineteen to seven for the bill. Internal improvements, distribution, and even the bank, did not rank, however, with the all-important issue of the tariff.[18]

Slavery was probably the only issue to rival the tariff in national importance in the first half of the nineteenth century, but for most Pennsylvanians the black problem was secondary. Men of most political, social, and economic views favored the protective tariff. It was considered the lifeblood of the growing coal, iron, and textile industries. While it was naturally claimed by the anti-Jackson supporters of Clay, the tariff had the endorsement of the state's leading Democrats as well. Governor Wolf, in January 1832, told the legislature that protection was a "favorite measure" in the "best interests" of the people of Pennsylvania. George M. Dallas, years before he was elected senator, was considered a staunch protectionist. Although he felt the United States had "tariffed too much and awkwardly," when he learned from Secretary of the Treasury Samuel Ingham that modifications might be enacted in 1831 in accord with the president's promises, and to the deprivation of Pennsylvania, Dallas told a friend, "I am not quite ripe for this." Thomas Cadwalader referred to Dallas as a man with a cool head and warm heart on the subject. This was not the case, however, in 1831. When he received Ingham's information, Dallas signaled a call for a tariff meeting with such friends of the restrictive system as Charles J. Ingersoll and Matthew Carey. Although this early action proved premature, there was no question that the state's interests had an advocate in the Senate in 1832.[19]

In January 1832 presidential aspirant Henry Clay led the crusade for modification of the ultraprotective "Tariff of Abominations" of 1828. Both Pennsylvania senators followed Clay's actions and the progress of his bill with great interest for the next six months. Dallas basically agreed with the Kentuckian's ideas on modest revision, although he became increasingly unhappy with the "defiance, exasperation, and scorn which have characterized Mr. Clay." Wilkins added the warning that while he, too, concurred with the revisions, he "had no idea of abandoning the principle of protection."[20]

Dallas made his tariff debut in a lengthy and impressive speech that consumed all of 27 February and part of the following day. He leveled an attack primarily at southern congressmen who were seeking to blame their distress on protection. There were other causes, Dallas asserted, such as soil-exhausting cotton and degradation of work as fit only for Negroes. Protection was "one of the moving objects of the Revolution, of the Union" and if it was ended, Pennsylvania could "be thrown back a century." Dallas stood opposed to "an unconditional surrender to the Utopian theory of free trade. . . . I am inflexible as to nothing but adequate protection."[21]

After the initial shock waves subsided over the tariff, the Senate settled down to work out the specific provisions of the bill. By April Dallas had privately questioned his February speech and his rigidity on the issue. The very idea of "his old tariff speech" was offensive to him. He told Henry Gilpin, "I feel really ashamed about my tariff harrangue [*sic*]—questioned incessantly and able to do little more than shrug my shoulders." Dallas wondered aloud whether he, as a senator, in compromising on the tariff, could yield to an extent which his own judgment approved, but which he knew would not be acceptable or sanctioned by Pennsylvania. By June he feared that the problem was becoming so bogged down that the Senate might adjourn before coming to any conclusions.[22]

The political skies cleared, however, and on 27 June Dallas informed his wife that he had "counted noses" and the Pennsylvania system would be steadfastly maintained. With the constant backing of the state press throughout, the protectionists moved toward victory in July. On 28 June the House passed the bill (132 to 65)—with the Pennsylvania delegation almost evenly divided (14 to 12)—and sent it on to the Senate, where the Tariff Committee had been chaired by Wilkins himself. Both Dallas and Wilkins joined the majority (32 to 16) to carry the measure on 9 July and proclaim a victory for Jacksonians and the principle of protection. Three days later Dallas reaffirmed his faith in the tariff before the Senate as being essential to the best interests of his state and the nation: "My first rule of proceeding had been to give to domestic manufactures if possible the whole aid of the whole revenue—to reserve all duties on articles which don't compete with us and make their duty free." Dallas was satisfied that the tariff had been adjusted upon "safe and liberal principles," but Wilkins was being assailed by anti-Jacksonians Henry Clay and Daniel Webster as a traitor to the American System for his acceptance of a compromise. Pennsylvania's senators had obeyed the instructions of the legislature and people of the Commonwealth, as well as the president, and had discussed the issue rather than let it be destroyed. Dallas had urged Wilkins to move for what proved to be a successful committee of conference to adjust the differences between the two houses of Congress. Keystone protectionists generally found the Tariff of 1832 acceptable. Most important, iron duties were restored to the adequate level of 1824 (the actual reduction was from an outrageous 50 percent in 1828 to the still very high 40 percent of 1824).

Much to the delight and relief of all citizens, the tariff left the state's interests practically unscathed.[23]

Although the tariff changes had a limited impact in Pennsylvania, the South continued to express its disapproval to Jackson and Congress over the high rates, and extremists in South Carolina again began to promulgate the doctrine of nullification. The president urged Congress in his December 1832 message to lower the duties further and thus alleviate the crisis. The following month the self-styled "Great Compromiser," Henry Clay, brought forward a new, more conciliatory proposal, thus ending the weeks of confrontation and near civil war from November 1832 to February 1833.

Dallas, although a member of the committee that reported the bill to the Senate, arose on the first day of debate (21 February) to voice his grave concern. He declared that the prosperity of his state depended upon the protective tariff. However, he admitted that the needs of the southern states must be recognized and alleviated. Dallas emphasized his interest in the general good and hoped that some compromise could be reached. He would do nothing, however, to sanction the abandonment of protection to aid a particular section of the country. While the Senate debated, the House passed the bill on 26 February by a 119 to 85 margin. The Pennsylvania delegation overwhelmingly opposed it by a 24 to 1 vote. A week of discussion in the Senate produced no drastic changes in Clay's compromise. Its sponsor later asserted that he had conceived the plan while visiting Philadelphia and had submitted it in confidence to a group of economic and political leaders who assented to it. If this were true, the benefits of the proposal so obvious to others remained invisible to Dallas.

On 1 March the frustrated senator again spoke on the so-called healing bill. If there were suffering in the South (and he doubted it), the causes went much deeper than the tariff. Dallas opposed taking a grievance from South Carolina and fastening it upon Pennsylvania. He claimed this measure would result in great economic ruin and discontent in his state with hundreds of thousands of people out of work. The bill heralded the abandonment of the protective system. It provided for a too-rapid cutback in rates over a ten-year period without enough safeguards and securities. Although Dallas was certain the measure would pass, he hoped that the entire issue would be delayed until a more representative Congress convened in the fall.

The tariff could not be postponed, however, and Dallas and Wilkins joined the *minority* in a 29 to 16 vote favoring its passage. The strong reaction of the Pennsylvania press was to be expected. A few pro-

Clay National Republican papers attempted to show the beneficial results of the tariff, but their arguments were weak. Coal and iron duties would be lowered to 20 percent by 1842. The Democratic press was outraged, but the Anti-Masonic *Pennsylvania Telegraph* best expressed the feelings of much of the state. "THE TARIFF IS GONE. To speak in plain terms, it has been most inhumanely murdered by its reputed Father [Clay]. . . . The Bill will be almost a death blow to the prosperity of Pennsylvania."[24]

What angered Dallas, Wilkins, and many other Pennsylvanians was the belief that the Tariff of 1833 was passed because South Carolina had used nullification as a bludgeon. The Philadelphia senator said the bill would not even have made its appearance if the crisis in the fall of 1832 had not arisen. South Carolina had adopted a severe posture on the tariff and Pennsylvania, in response, went to the other extreme. The issues of the tariff and the Union were intertwined for many Keystone citizens who saw their economic prosperity resting on both.[25]

South Carolinians periodically had considered nullifying the Tariff of Abominations ever since its passage in 1828. Dallas expected the state would do so in 1830, when extremist James Hamilton was elected governor. Again, the following summer, Dallas warned Ingham of the mischief of the doctrine and those who "incessantly harp upon it." Even then, Dallas said he was ready to attack at the first overt act with overpowering force. Finally, in the fall of 1832 a popular election was held in the Palmetto State, which resulted in the summoning of a constitutional convention. The convention, meeting on 19 November, declared the tariffs of 1828 and 1832 null and void within the borders of South Carolina. Immediately, the president proclaimed that the Union must be upheld and its laws enforced. Dallas and Wilkins rushed to Jackson's support, attacking Hamilton's "mad message" and assuring the president of the universal backing among his friends and foes alike on this issue. Privately, Dallas was deeply worried over the crisis and confided to his wife that nullification was more "reckless and rife" than he expected. He maintained his confidence in the president, however, and called his address on the problem "the noblest paper the country had witnessed since the Farewell Address of Washington. It ought to make every American a Jackson man."[26]

Dallas declared his views publicly in the Senate on 8 February 1833, when Chairman Wilkins reported a bill out of the Senate Judiciary Committee. The measure would empower the federal government to use force in collecting customs duties, if the customs officers were interfered with in obtaining them. In support of this bill, Dallas argued that Charlestonians could not have free trade while Philadelphians paid duties. Such action, fostered by the doctrine of nullification, was unconstitutional because it impaired the obligation of contracts. In addition, the South Carolina ordinance nullified an immense body of other laws, including the Judiciary Act, which prescribed the mode of appealing from state tribunals to the federal courts. Dallas blamed the illegal actions of South Carolina on a "clique" rather than on the people, who were not permitted to vote on the ordinance. "Nullification is secession in disguise," Dallas said, "with a constitutional mask, partial in its pretension, and covert in its operation." Again he emphasized that the United States was a union from 1776, and when the federal-national government was formed each state surrendered part of its sovereignty. Only amendment or revolution could change the Constitution, and the second course was "wholly and unqualifiedly" wrong. Nullification implied revolution and the Union must be preserved, by the use of force if necessary. Wilkins echoed this fiery nationalism: "The moment we fail to counteract the nullification proceedings of South Carolina, the Union is dissolved; for, in this government of laws, union is obedience and obedience is Union." The Senate agreed. On 20 February 1833 it passed the Revenue Collection Bill by 32 to 1 (with John Tyler of Virginia in opposition). But one week later Congress halted the federal-state duel by adjusting the tariff rates to a level acceptable to South Carolina. A disgruntled Dallas could take comfort only in the fact that South Carolina's senators had supported the new tariff and were thus, in effect, temporarily abandoning nullification. He felt this was perhaps an involuntary but nonetheless decided step forward in national and party unity.[27]

It is doubtful, however, that Dallas really believed Calhoun had abandoned nullification. This was the issue that had divided the two men as early as 1828, and the one that would prevent their political reunion. Calhoun felt nullification was essential to the preservation of the Union; Dallas thought it was a key to its destruction. The South Carolinian's hostility toward the tariffs of 1828 and 1832—both economically vital to Pennsylvania—did nothing to enhance their relationship. In Jackson's first administration Dallas had been forced by Calhoun's position on nullification to seek new political ties. In an effort to secure his own future, the Philadelphian gradually moved farther away from the South Carolinian and closer to Old Hickory. All correspondence between Calhoun and Dallas ceased. The vice-president's deciding vote against Van Buren's mission to England in

January 1832, and his resignation from office at the height of the tariff crisis in December 1832, finalized Dallas's disillusionment with his quondam favorite. He continued throughout his life to respect and admire Calhoun, but he considered him to be misguided. It was impossible for Dallas to support a man who in thought and action threatened both the Democracy and the Union.

If a new Family Party was being formed in 1832 on the Dallas-Wilkins relationship, its actions in the contest for the vice-presidency combined with their views on the American System to cause it to be stillborn. The Pennsylvania Democracy was closely tied to the financial and transportation interests of the state, including the bank and internal improvements (canals and railroads). Both Dallas and Wilkins held bank directorships or stocks at one time. For many years there was a bitter rivalry between Pennsylvania and New York over these issues. The Keystone State began to falter politically in 1832, when it became increasingly evident that the president favored Martin Van Buren for the second slot on the ticket. The New Yorker was an old enemy of the local Democrats, and they were forced to attempt to displace him without damaging Jackson's chances or personally alienating him.

The contest for the favorite-son nomination began in 1831 with Buchanan, Dallas, and Wilkins as the leading contenders. Buchanan, however, did not wish to antagonize the president and wrote him in September 1831 that he would withdraw, leaving Dallas, the leading candidate of the Calhoun men, as the front-runner. Dallas refused to take any active role in securing the nod, resolving to let his friends conduct the political maneuvering for him. Consequently, he did well in the eastern half of the state, but strong exertions were made against him in the western half in favor of Wilkins. It appears that in January–February 1832, Dallas was so involved with the bank struggle that he did not have the time or the inclination to become actively engaged in the contest for the vice-presidency. His major concern was not that he receive the nod, but that Van Buren be stopped. Dallas told Gilpin on 31 January, "My friends are, perhaps without exception, opposed to the further advancement of that gentleman. They don't like him personally or politically, and one of the incurable causes of their dislike is the fact of his being from New York."

By the time of the convention on 5 March Dallas's chances for the nomination were minimal, since the more ambitious Wilkins actively sought the post. After ten ballots at Harrisburg Wilkins prevailed by a vote of 67 to 62 over Dallas. On the final ballot Van Buren received one vote and never exceeded four at any time. The convention adopted a secondary resolution that stated in case Wilkins died or withdrew the state's support would fall to Dallas. In addition they decided by an 80 to 51 margin not to send delegates to Baltimore for the national convention in May.[28]

While these convention antics were obviously aimed at preventing Van Buren from receiving Pennsylvania's votes in any manner, they did not stop young Simon Cameron, an aspiring and unprincipled Democrat, and his followers from attending the Baltimore gathering and casting all of the state's votes for the Little Magician from New York. This move defied popular sentiment and his action was repudiated the following January, when the Keystone electors cast their thirty votes for Wilkins. The ruin of the party, however, did not come from Cameron's moves, but from the obstinacy of the leading politicians to battle Jackson's personal choice. There were rumors that Dallas, and perhaps Wilkins, would be given foreign or cabinet posts to remove them from the New Yorker's path. The president probably did not doubt that both senators had voted in favor of Van Buren's unsuccessful nomination for American minister to England in January 1832, just to get him out of the country. The state's efforts to displace Van Buren, one way or another, failed and at a high cost to the Pennsylvanians. They had further angered the president's heir, and combined with the sensitive bank issue and their rigidity on the tariff and internal improvements issues, brought additional disfavor from Jackson himself.[29]

There is no question that the people of Pennsylvania were disappointed with Jackson by the fall of 1832. He had alienated large segments of the state with his economic policies and his failure to choose a Pennsylvanian for his vice-president, which threatened to turn the state into a political vassal of Van Buren's Albany Regency. While Jackson's personal popularity did not suffer enough to destroy him, he ruined the spirit and credibility of his party in the state. The vote in 1832 reflected the division and disgruntlement within the local Democracy. The president defeated a slate of anti-Jackson electors by a 91,000 to 66,700 margin. This represented a decline from 1828 of 10,000 votes for Jackson and an increase of 16,000 for the opposition. Philadelphia city and county (combined vote totals), which he had carried by a solid two-to-one majority in the previous election, was lost in 1832 by 10,000 to 12,000 votes. The president won Allegheny County, but just barely in 1832 after a striking success in 1828. Nor did Old Hickory help in state races torn by local issues. Governor Wolf was reelected by a slim 3,000 votes over Anti-Mason Joseph

Ritner, in contrast to his 25,000-vote margin over the same candidate in 1829.[30]

The Keystone Democracy still supported Jackson, but its enjoyment for the game of politics was gone. The president no longer liked or trusted the Pennsylvanians. Ingham, who favored the bank and Calhoun, had been dismissed from the Treasury Department; Wilkins, who was both pro-bank and anti-Van Buren, had made himself unacceptable; Dallas had the Calhoun stain and was the sponsor of the bank bill; and Buchanan, because of his old Federalist ties, his alleged connection with the "corrupt bargain" of 1825, and his personality had already been sent into diplomatic exile in Russia. Thus when it became obvious in 1832 that Pennsylvania deserved a cabinet post for its election support, and the Treasury was available, Jackson had great difficulty in finding someone he considered suitable. Finally, William Duane of Philadelphia, a Van Buren man who was not deeply involved in state politics, was chosen.[31]

The Pennsylvania Democrats of the 1830s were astute politicians, but it did not require deep thought on their part to recognize how Jackson regarded their organization. Wilkins and Dallas in particular were aware that they were in trouble. Both men had voted pro-American System and anti-Jackson on many of the major issues of the day. Wolf had been elected by a narrow plurality over Ritner and could not afford to lose the administration's confidence by backing either senator. This situation was especially damaging to Dallas, whose short-term seat was up for reelection in 1833. As the problems mounted for the senator in Washington, so did his disaffection with his situation. In June 1832 he told his wife, "Every hour of my present existence is a drag. My days are wearisome and my nights are wretched. . . . I can endure a great deal in discharge of duties, but such a life as this I would not endure long if I could." Dallas wrote that he had no appetite and no real spirit. He felt like a "lifeless body," and "everything seemed artificial." When he learned that the Senate session would go on into mid-July he moaned, "I shall tear my eyes out and eat my heart up. This is tenfold more than I bargained for."

There can be no doubt of the pressures, political and personal, that had been placed on the Philadelphian during the past two years. Perhaps the damage done to his career was not as severe as the strain placed upon his marriage. This was the first time in their fifteen years together that the Dallases were apart for any extensive period, and George missed his wife and children deeply. He began writing Sophy as soon as he arrived in Washington and they continued an active correspondence over the next eighteen months, interrupted only by her occasional and brief visits to the capital. Dallas complained each time a day passed without a letter from her and urged his wife to encourage the children ("his little pig-tails") to write as soon as they completed their homework. After only one month apart Dallas lamented, "the weather now turns beautiful . . . and I long to see the river running away, and you running towards me. . . . " Anticipating a visit to Washington, he bubbled, "I feel an instinctive inclination, every minute or two, to open my arms, expecting you to run into them." He coyly cautioned, "Bring no servant to worry or be expensive. Come alone and I will be your slave, lacer, hair dresser and packer."

While both husband and wife relished these visits, they could not dissipate Sophy's self-pity over the fact that she had to stay in Philadelphia most of the time while George was playing the role of statesman in Washington. Her letters were filled with complaints of sickness, loneliness, envy, and poverty. Dallas would have had to thrive on bad news to enjoy a report on Susan's scarletina, and her own gloomy state of mind, climaxed by the observation that he did not know what it was like "to be alone these long nights."

Dallas's efforts to cheer her up by reporting on the Washington social scene merely convinced her that he was wallowing in the fleshpots. As his term drew to a close she wrote, "You have not much longer to play the beau, and, I suppose you must take advantage of your present bachelorship." In another letter she exploded in a bitter and cutting harangue, "I think Washington is a despicable place whatever *you* may think to the contrary . . . I think that man and wife if they care for each other are fools to be separated."

Dallas was caught between two worlds because his wife insisted that they were incompatible. He longed for his family while he thrived on the conversation and company of distinguished men. Perhaps he would have found some of them less distinguished if he had stayed around them longer. As it was, his feelings were akin to awe when he encountered the legendary figures in Congress. He personally liked Henry Clay, although he was amused and irritated by his presidential aspirations and constant bids for the attention of the ladies in the galleries of the Senate. Thomas Hart Benton was "a fine, tho' accountable fellow" and Daniel Webster "a remarkable man in every respect, his fund of information is inexhaustible." Congressman William Rives of Virginia, whom Dallas judged to be priggish and conceited, was his greatest disappointment.

The senator enjoyed a good glass of sherry and Havana cigars, as well as a weakness for snuff, and he had all three sent from Philadelphia. He passed his leisure hours in the capital playing whist or chess, riding horseback and dining out often, frequently with Secretary of State Edward Livingston of Louisiana. Meanwhile, Mrs. Dallas eased her loneliness by attending the theater, the opera, parties (generally with George's mother, Mrs. Campbell, or Mrs. Alexander Bache). She also purchased quantities of new clothes, which improved her morale but drove Dallas to the verge of bankruptcy on more than one occasion. He habitually responded to these assaults on his pocket-book with pleas for frugality. His apprehensions were acute at the close of his senatorial term when Sophy reported that the Philadelphia account contained but $67. Yet on this occasion, she pushed ahead with her social responsibilities, heedless of the cost because she was entertaining, among others, the famous Shakespearean actress Fanny Kemble.

It would be folly to underestimate the influence of this remarkable woman on her husband. She was extremely knowledgeable about developments on Capitol Hill, often commented on them, and frequently advised George on a particular course of action. She was especially excited by the events in South Carolina in the winter of 1832/33 and angry when she encountered a lady ignorant of the crisis. "Where can she have kept herself," Sophy wondered, "for it appears to me the very air breathes union and nullification." Other leaders radiate the calm assurance that her husband would remain cool and make the right decisions, irrespective of party. She was proud of his contributions in the Senate, but nonetheless wanted him home and was a decisive factor in his decision not to stand for reelection.[32]

As early as December 1832 the senator told his supporters of his decision. In addition he wrote to General Samuel McKean, a member of the governor's cabinet and Wolf's choice to succeed Dallas, expressing his desire for McKean's success. Dallas undoubtedly knew he was *persona non grata* in Washington and thus resisted requests for a change of position before the spring election. His refusal threw the still-disbelieving state Democrats into a frenzy. Many of them had undoubtedly felt Dallas's statements were mere rhetoric. When he stood by them, the Democracy fell into factional disarray. McKean could not be elected without the support of the Buchanan clique, whose leader was in Russia. Therefore, the legislature adjourned after numerous unsuccessful ballots, to reconvene in December 1833.

Buchanan returned to the United States on 24 November 1833. He hurried to Washington, where a bargain was made with the president to defeat the Dallas-Wilkins faction and the Anti-Masons. Instead of running for the Senate himself, Buchanan supported Wolf's man,

McKean, who won handily on 7 December. The following year, when the session of Congress ended in June, William Wilkins learned that he had been named to replace Buchanan in St. Petersburg. This of course left Wilkins's seat open for Buchanan. A Wolf-Buchanan alliance would be more amenable to Jackson's desires and also would be more willing to support Van Buren in 1836. In December 1834 the election to replace Wilkins was held. The Anti-Masons, the newly formed "Whigs" (the old National Republicans of Henry Clay and John Quincy Adams), and the Dallas-Wilkins clique each ran a candidate against Old Buck. Their opposition was futile, however, since Wolf's backing of Buchanan was enough for victory. In a gesture of defiance to everyone the Dallas men refused to vote for the victor, even when his majority was assured.[33]

The "New Family"—if one had ever really existed—was gone from national politics, and its leaders were disgraced. The Buchanan faction would now face the problems of Dallas and Wilkins: how to maintain the president's favor and follow the wishes of Pennsylvania at the same time. Such concerns, however, would not be the official responsibility of either former senator. For the next ten years—a decade of Democratic presidents—they would remain in virtual exile, far removed from the arenas of political controversy. Many people undoubtedly thought the senatorial transgressions of each man had cost him his political career. Certainly no one could predict the reemergence of both in 1844—Wilkins as John Tyler's secretary of war, and Dallas as vice-president-elect of the United States under James K. Polk, whose nickname was ironically "Young Hickory."

4

State Politics and
The Russian Mission
(1833–1839)

In the summer of 1833 George M. Dallas returned to Philadelphia expecting to retire from public service and go back to his law practice. Undoubtedly he desired a slower pace of life after two years in the Senate, but his future was not to be spent in solitude. In the next five years he would serve in two government positions, witness his state party torn apart, and become involved in a new quarrel over the bank.

Even though Dallas had fallen from favor with the national administration, he remained a powerful force on the county and state levels. He was an active member of the Philadelphia Democracy and worked tirelessly to promote Governor Wolf's regime, which was threatened by a Whig–Anti-Mason coalition and dissident Jacksonians. Patronage was of course a major problem, and Dallas was constantly advising the governor to strengthen his position in the state and the party through the granting of proper appointments.[1] While Dallas was considered for the federal cabinet post of attorney general in 1833 and the United States Senate in 1834, he chose to remain in state politics. He found the Senate "very tempting," but could not afford to support his expansive family on a senator's salary. He told Wolf, "Perhaps at some future day, I may feel the patter of ambition more open to my tread, at this moment, I dare not venture on them [national politics]." Dallas was completely satisfied with an appointment as attorney general of the Commonwealth, which he received on 15 October 1833.

This office placed little pressure on him and permitted the continuance of his private practice: a practice which, not incidentally, had been enhanced by the prestige of almost two years of federal service. While Dallas still argued cases before the local courts, he began to spend more time in the state capital with the state supreme court. This was certainly agreeable to him because it also enabled him to maintain close ties in Harrisburg with state affairs.[2]

The primary problem Dallas encountered in his service as attorney general was a scandal in the Eastern State Penitentiary in Philadelphia. In January 1834 Dallas began to investigate rumors of torture and corruption in the prison. He quickly discovered that reforms were needed to end misuse of state property and brutality to inmates. The attorney general wrote to the governor to inquire what should be done. Wolf was skeptical and indignant about the charges, since his friend Samuel Wood was the warden. However, he instructed Dallas to continue the investigation until he was satisfied and to submit the findings. A month later, on 24 March, Dallas informed the governor that Wood was acting "improperly" and "carousing with a prostitute" inside the prison walls. Dallas pursued the problem throughout the year, uncovering incredible mismanagement. He warned Wolf in September that if the public learned what was occurring in the prison, the administration would be greatly embarrassed. Dallas urged the governor to initiate an inquiry in his own defense. With a stimulus provided by the governor's annual message, an investigation was begun by a committee of the State Assembly. Dallas attended these hearings in December and was impressed, indeed outraged, at the testimony. His sentiments were confirmed: The warden and the board of inspectors were indiscreet, if not dishonest, and should all be replaced. The committee agreed, returning its verdict in late January 1835. Dallas, deeply interested in penal reform and capital punishment, had made a small but significant contribution to the reform movement in Pennsylvania through his long and penetrating inquiry.[3]

George Wolf had alienated many people during his six-year administration. Reasons for the diverse discontent were sectional. Internal improvements, public-school laws, and constitutional revisions were measures supported by the administration, but hardly by all Pennsylvanians. With these issues provoking heated debate, a good opportunity existed to defeat the governor in his bid for a third term. Dallas recognized the seriousness of the challenge in 1834 and urged Wolf to solidify the party as much as possible by a wholesale cleansing of anti-Wolf personnel from county patronage jobs. Unfortunately, Wolf was reluctant to take such harsh action. When an irregular convention met in Harrisburg in March 1835, the governor was renominated by one segment of the party. His opponents then held their own gathering and selected Henry A. Muhlenberg to oppose him. Since both men were strong candidates and nominally tied to the Buchanan faction, both Old Buck and the national administration were perplexed as to whom to support. Washington remained neutral, while Buchanan tried to conciliate both sides and urged a new convention and candidate. His efforts met with failure. Meanwhile, Dallas, who remained an ardent Wolf supporter, grew increasingly dismayed over the stubbornness of both factions. He believed that Jackson backed the governor and that Muhlenberg should yield to the incumbent. By September Dallas and other Democratic leaders recognized that if the split continued, the Whig–Anti-Mason coalition candidate, Joseph Ritner, would win. When the rupture did not heal, Dallas's fears came true. The combined vote of the Democratic candidates was 12,000 more than Ritner's total. However, the Anti-Mason was a landslide victor over both Wolf and Muhlenberg individually. Dallas was bitterly disappointed at the Democrats and angered at the Whigs, whom he attacked as political prostitutes. Within days after the election, Dallas resigned the attorney generalship. He expressed his deep sorrow to Wolf and told him he would use whatever influence he still had in Washington to try to secure a federal appointment for him. Wolf considered Dallas a loyal and kind-hearted friend, but doubted that anything could be done because of the number of enemies the governor had made in Washington. Philadelphia was still the old Family Party leader's bailiwick and Dallas attempted to wrangle the post of collector of the Port of Philadelphia for his comrade. Wolf failed to receive that plum from the president, but eventually he did obtain the post of comptroller of the Treasury. Throughout this traumatic period Dallas was bracing himself for the Anti-Masonic onslaught, which he was sure would come.[4]

The legislative session of December 1835 was a political powder keg. The victorious Anti-Masons moved quickly to secure a special committee to investigate the Masonic Order. With Representative Thaddeus Stevens in control the committee launched its proceedings in January 1836. Dallas never doubted that he would be called to testify. The Philadelphian had joined Franklin Lodge No. 134 upon his return from the peace mission to Europe in 1815. He had risen steadily through the ranks of the order to become the Grand Master of the Pennsylvania Lodge in 1835. In December 1835 Dallas was plotting strategy with Wolf concerning the type of statement that should be prepared in their behalf. The Philadelphian urged rigid preparation focused around a written declaration explaining the Masonic position. In effect, this paper would relate their general knowledge of Masonry, but it would issue a denial to answer "personal and insolent questions." Dallas anticipated that if either he or the former governor were called early to testify, they could set an example of restraint, then silence, for the order. Within a month a host of high state dignitaries, including Wolf, Dallas, Judge Josiah Randall of Philadelphia, and Joseph Chandler, editor of the *United States Gazette,* had been called to Harrisburg.

The Anti-Masons, with solid Whig support, began the inquiry with Chandler. He responded to the questioning in the positive, firm manner Dallas and Wolf had urged. When Dallas was called by the committee on 18 January, he answered and stated his position, but he refused to testify under oath. He later admitted to Sophy that Chairman Stevens was an intimidating personage: "I have never seen such a bold, bad man have such entire ascendancy. Everything is corruptly sacrificed to propitiate him." The entire hearing—if it could be called that—lasted only a few days. No Mason would testify and the committee was thrown into disorder. As a result, all the witnesses were held in Harrisburg while the House debated whether to indict the Masons for contempt or close the investigation. Dallas had no faith in the justice of the "fanatics" (as he labeled the Anti-Masons) or in the Whigs, who were their "vassals." The Masons demanded acquittal or jail and Dallas feared it would be the latter. Dallas was convinced his own courageous stand would eventually help to destroy the Anti-Masonic witch-hunt, but he fretted over the less-than-subtle maneuverings of some "friendly" legislators to compromise the Masonic position. When Philadelphia attorney William B. Read suggested a formal reprimand from the speaker of the House Dallas exploded, "Damn, double damn, the whole race of cowardly skunks!" Fortunately for the Masons, the Whigs had endured enough of the farcical hearings. Public attention had been drawn to them, and work almost stopped in the state government as people crowded in to witness the proceedings. In an effort to avoid further embarrassment to the administration, the Whigs joined with the Democrats to end the fiasco. Dallas, who had threatened to "withdraw from politics absolutely" if the Anti-Masons were upheld by the people, was delighted and urged his Democratic colleagues to take quick political advantage from the affair. There is no doubt that this investigation was the watershed of Anti-Masonry in Pennsylvania.[5]

Closely tied to the Whig–Anti-Mason coalition in Pennsylvania was a move to recharter the Bank of the United States as a state institution. This issue involved Dallas in a heated political debate by the summer of 1836. Since the bank clash of 1832, Dallas had been silent on the issue. When Secretary of the Treasury Roger B. Taney began removing the federal deposits in February 1834, Dallas refused to participate in local anti-bank meetings. He felt the removal was ill-timed and unnecessary, especially since it would damage the finances of Pennsylvania. But the "audacious and insolent attitude" taken by the directors of the "Monster" and its friends justified federal action. Dallas blamed the bank's downfall on the arrogant and ambitious Nicholas Biddle, who ruined a proud and prosperous institution through his policies.[6] With this final phase of the bank war it is not surprising that Biddle looked to Pennsylvania to save his crumbling empire. In January 1836 the Whigs and Anti-Masons in the State Assembly introduced a resolution to charter the Bank of the United States as a state agency. The same month the Democrats in their convention adopted a proposal opposing the recharter. Nevertheless, in the legislature in February eight Democrats crossed over and voted with the Whigs to insure passage of the measure. These traitors were soundly denounced and the factious Democracy began to reunite for a cause—the repeal of the charter. As a reaction to the bank bill, various Democratic committees met around the Commonwealth to determine what could be done. On 15 March a committee in East Smithfield wrote to Dallas to ask his advice. His reply of 6 July would echo in the chambers of the United States Senate. After repeating his feelings about the ill-timed movement for recharter in 1832, Dallas said he had supported it then because of the resolutions of the people of Pennsylvania. But, he noted, a good institution had been perverted by bad directors who had made it a political issue after the veto message of July 1832. Dallas was alienated by this mixing of politics and economics. He viewed the rechartering of the bank in 1836 as an attack on Pennsylvania Democrats, pointing out that the bank directors were the same men who had previously attacked Jackson. However, there was a solution to the problem. Dallas urged that the state constitutional convention be called and the charter of the bank repealed by amendment.[7]

This stunning advocacy of what appeared to be an unconstitutional breach of contract by a state of a federal proviso reverberated throughout the country. Henry Gilpin told presidential nominee Martin Van Buren, "It came like a thunderbolt." The letter made the bank party realize that the Democracy was serious in determining to repeal the charter. Dallas had stated that the bank was essentially public in that it affected the general value of property and exercised powers too broad to be considered private. But whether public or private, the state legislature reserved the right to revoke a franchise, as it had to take private property when public welfare required it. Gilpin regretted that Dallas did not put the argument in the strongest form, but he deemed it "excellent" and "of great service." Philadelphia Democrat Charles J. Ingersoll, an old friend of the bank, denied this. He told the Little Magician that he wished Dallas had consulted his political friends before publishing the letter, which was disapproved of by Ingersoll's associates. He said that Dallas was mistaking privilege for property, that he conceded contract, that he was attributing extravagant power to a constitutional convention, and pain and passion were being placed over reason and right. The opinion of the administration (and perhaps also Van Buren) was reflected in an editorial of the *Washington Globe* on 17 September 1836. The contest was one of popular will versus prerogative monopoly. The "Monster" was still alive. The *Globe* supported Dallas and hoped that he would be called into a "position of trust" so that he could carry out his ideas. Abel P. Upshur, a powerful Virginia politician and future secretary of state, writing under the pseudonym of "Madison," disagreed. In a letter to *Niles' Register* in October, he attacked Dallas's position as destructive of the chartered rights of a corporation. "Madison" questioned the limit of a constitutional convention's power to repeal the charter. He granted that the people might have the power in time to come, but that such action would unconstitutionally annul an obligation the state had previously contracted.[8]

Upshur's argument was reinforced in the Senate by Thomas Morris of Ohio. In the process of discussing items of state constitutional validity regarding the admission of Michigan into the Union in January 1837, Morris asked Buchanan what would happen if a constitutional convention approved Dallas's scheme of repeal by amendment. The Ohioan declared the idea was "incendiary," "revolutionary," and "calculated to excite the people to rise up in rebellion against the laws." It was against the Constitution of the United States and violated the sanctity of contract. Amazingly, Buchanan rushed to Dallas's defense. He first noted that this was a local matter that needed no outside interference. Nevertheless, Buchanan said, Morris was misrepresenting and misquoting Dallas. Although Buchanan admitted he had never been on "intimate terms with Mr. Dallas," he was certain that the Philadelphian did not support nullification of the Constitution, which was political heresy. Buchanan insisted that Dallas expressly referred to the Supreme Court as the tribunal that must decide whether a constitutional convention has the power to repeal a bank charter. The senator agreed with Dallas that a state charter was not a contract and could legally be broken. Dallas responded to this vigorous defense with a burst of thanks and gratitude. He told Buchanan—his enemy for over a decade—that it would give him "pleasure and pride to cultivate a greater intimacy . . . between us." He hoped he could reciprocate such an act of good will. Buchanan quickly responded that he was "not only willing, but anxious to cultivate a greater intimacy . . . between us."[9]

The brief détente that resulted between Dallas and Buchanan was the outcome of one thing only—politics. The bank was a crucial question in Pennsylvania and the Democrats desperately needed to maintain a solid front. The fact that a constitutional convention had been called and would soon vote to "postpone indefinitely" the issue of repealing the bank charter (December 1837) was not the major concern of the Democracy. The bank was a political rather than an economic issue to the party. It united the Democrats in the elections of 1836 and later against the Democratic "traitors" and the Whigs. The Jacksonians had to have an issue that would overcome the factionalism and the colorless, unpopular Van Buren. Unity was the only way the powerful and triumphant Whig–Anti-Mason coalition could be beaten. The state legislature, the president, and a United States senator were to be elected in October, November, and December, respectively. In the state elections the people rebuked the legislature that had chartered the bank. Only 18 out of 133 members were returned to Harrisburg. An incredibly even split of 66 Democrats, 66 Whig–Anti-Masons, and 1 Independent Whig had resulted.

The Little Magician had the greatest difficulty in the Keystone State. He was anathema to the entire populace, even to the Democrats, who supported him only because he was Jackson's choice. The Whigs backed General William Henry Harrison, who they were confident could defeat Van Buren. They were almost correct. Van Buren won by a narrow 4,000-vote margin in a total vote that well surpassed that of 1832. He almost duplicated Old Hickory's performance in the previous election, while Harrison added 20,000 to the anti-Jackson column. In an 18 November letter to the president-elect Buchanan commented on the tough fight he expected in the coming Senate election. He noted that the Bank Whigs and Anti-Masons would prefer any person to him "unless it might be the Devil or George M. Dallas." With surprising ease, however, Buchanan triumphed over perennial Democratic rebel Henry A. Muhlenberg to be elected to his first full six-year term.

Dallas had not been a candidate for any office in 1836, but certainly his bank letter had been instrumental in both arousing and uniting the Democracy. While this was successful, it was not a politically or socially popular move in Philadelphia. Sidney George Fisher, a wealthy Whig dilettante, noted in November 1836 that the pressure in the money market was severe and Dallas's letter had destroyed the confidence of Europeans in the bank's securities; bank stock was unsalable. Fisher, repulsed by the Dallas letter, wished Dallas would receive the execration he deserved from the Democracy. However, Fisher felt sorry for Dallas's family, which he noted was large and poverty-stricken, since Dallas had scarcely any law practice and depended on the hope of receiving an office from Van Buren for sustenance. Fisher's sympathy, however, did not extend to social gatherings. He refused to attend a ball in January 1837, held by the Dallases, although some of his more realistic friends felt it to their advantage to go. One of the few positive personal results to emerge from the bank letter for Dallas was a remunerative request from the Girard Bank of Philadelphia for an endorsement of the stability and integrity of the institution. He originally agreed, but in November decided that it would be unwise to mix banks and politics and thus declined to vouch publicly for it.

While the Democracy was victorious, many Jacksonians in Philadelphia opposed Dallas for his stand on the state bank charter and many others supported the triumphant Buchanan. Dallas was an outcast socially and politically. Even his narrow base in Philadelphia had been threatened by his own actions. As early as February 1836 he expressed interest in obtaining the French mission to escape his uncomfortable predicament. President-elect Van Buren, in an attempt to end state factionalism permanently, offered him the Russian mission in February 1837. Dallas quickly agreed to this self-exile.[10]

Strong pressure had been exerted on Van Buren in the winter of 1836/37 for a cabinet post for Pennsylvania. The Keystone State had been victorious for the Democrat over almost insurmountable odds and many party leaders expected a sizable political reward. Henry Muhlenberg had much support as a cabinet consideration, but Van Buren retained all of the old Jackson men in their posts, except for naming Joel Poinsett, a southerner, as secretary of war. In an attempt to placate his disgruntled followers the president offered Muhlenberg the Russian mission and then the position of secretary of the navy. Muhlenberg felt he could not afford to take either of these posts, however, and waited until 1838, when he was appointed the first minister to Austria. Van Buren then moved to his second choice for the Russian mission. In these circumstances Dallas received the offer and promptly accepted.[11]

On 7 March 1837 Dallas assumed the title of Envoy Extraordinary and Minister Plenipotentiary to Russia. He would hold this post for two and a half years. When he returned to the United States in the fall of 1839, Whig diarist Philip Hone made the following general evaluation of the Russian mission:

> This is an arrangement of the government to pay the stipulated price of duty work performed by some unscrupulous partizan by the office of short duration, long pay and no services. It is the best bone they have for such picking, there is always meat upon it. The Minister to Russia has a $9000 outfit, $9000 salary and I believe half as much for returning. He goes to England and France, figures by virtue of the title Excellency in the salons of London and Paris, makes the tour de Europe en Prince, arrives at length at his post, puts on his diplomatic uniform (exercising all caution to keep the sword from getting between his legs), makes his round of dinners and balls, talks French (if he can) with the Emperor, and has the run of the Palace, and then when the weather is pleasant and the traveling good, receives recall, comes again to Havre or London by another route, and after all this pleasant marching and counter marching at Uncle Sam's expense, the first thing we hear about him since his appointment is the arrival of his excellency so-and-so, who it is understood makes place for some other patriot who desires to make the tour of Europe.[12]

Before he departed for the long voyage ahead, Dallas began to read about diplomacy and the special duties that he would be required to perform in Russia. He told Gilpin that he found diplomacy "pleasanter than law."

The spring was brightened for Dallas by a visit from his brothers, Trevanion and Alexander. The three men had not been together for over fifteen years. By 1837 George's youngest brother had risen to prominence in Allegheny County as a judge of the court of common pleas. Youthful adversity had made his rapid ascent particularly impressive. He had been forced to interrupt his studies at Georgetown when his father died, resuming them later with his brother in Philadelphia. After his sister Matilda moved to Pittsburgh and married influential attorney William Wilkins in 1818, Trevanion followed to study with his new relative. The frontier of western Pennsylvania offered greater opportunity than the Quaker City and after passing his bar exam in 1822, the promising young barrister rose to the judgeship in 1835. His marriage to Wilkins's niece, Jane, had not hindered his career. Physically impressive, dignified yet fun-loving, Trevanion earned the respect of the entire profession in Pittsburgh. When he succumbed to scarlet fever in April 1841, he was an associate judge of the district court. George was stunned by his brother's death, because despite their difference in age and physical separation they had shared a lifelong affection for each other.

On the other hand, George was never really close to his older brother, Alexander. Due perhaps to "the Commodore's" absences at sea or postings at distant naval stations much of his life, the two siblings had developed mutual admiration but not warmth. Alexander had always been a totally dedicated navy officer, having enlisted at the age of fourteen in 1805 during the Tripolitan Wars. By 1810 he had risen to lieutenant and was soon to participate in the controversial *Little Belt* incident, which almost provoked a war prematurely between the United States and Great Britain. As lieutenant-commander in the War of 1812, Dallas served aboard the *President,* which engaged the British ship *Belvidera* commanded by his Aunt Charlotte's husband, Captain George A. Byron. Throughout these early years of his life the young officer drifted away from his family. He was rapidly becoming an arrogant, independent, and solitary figure. Dignified, but not tall, he possessed piercing brown eyes, dark red hair, and a complexion weathered by sun and wind. A graceful dancer and an excellent conversationalist who spoke several languages, he was always in demand at social affairs, despite his fiery temper and outspoken manner. His callousness toward his family was reflected in his refusal to visit them while in Washington in 1815; instead he decided to sail immediately with Stephen Decatur for the Barbary Coast. When he returned Dallas discovered the navy was languishing in its peacetime role. To avoid total boredom Alexander decided upon a commercial venture to China. He took leave of the navy with the rank of captain and signed on a Canton-bound vessel as supercargo. Both he and George saw commercial possibilities in the venture and entered into it as a partnership. But the year-long cruise did not prove to be lucrative. When it was over the captain eagerly rejoined the service. In 1819, while stationed in Philadelphia, he met Henrietta Meade, the eldest daughter of prominent merchant and diplomat Richard Worsam Meade and sister of George Gordon Meade, who would be the victor at Gettysburg. After a whirlwind courtship the couple married in 1821. The captain could not keep his bride in the style to which she had become accustomed, however, and financial problems within the household developed quickly. To alleviate this situation her father backed a new commercial venture, this time to Mexico. Alexander's second effort proved as unfruitful as the first and he returned from Mexico City and Vera Cruz with empty pockets. Throughout the 1820s he served primarily in the Caribbean battling pirates, and took the opportunity on one voyage to visit Jamaica and his cousin Samuel Jackson Dallas, the speaker of the Colonial House of Assembly. In 1830 Captain Dallas was promoted to commodore and ordered to Pensacola to command the new naval station. The lonely and primitive gulf outpost probably contributed to keeping Dallas's disposition on razor's edge. He was a constant irritant to the commander of the Home Squadron and the threat of bad feelings erupting into a duel was always present. Whether because of the tension, the climate, or inadequate medical care, Mrs. Dallas's health failed in Florida, and she died in October 1831.

The couple had lost one child, but a second son was taken to Washington to be raised by a sister-in-law. Meanwhile, the commodore devoted his time to his work, and his efforts were rewarded in 1835, when he was given command of the *Constellation* and the Home Squadron, the largest American fleet at fifteen vessels. The successful and powerful widower constantly fascinated the ladies and he finally remarried in 1836. His choice was the youngest daughter of Colonel Byrd C. Willis of Virginia, an army officer at Pensacola.

In May 1837 Dallas became involved in a controversial encounter between the United States sloop-of-war *Natchez* and the Mexican brig *General Urrea*. The American vessel had brought the *General* into Pensacola for violating the treaty between the two nations regarding trade in the Gulf of Mexico. In an effort to prevent open conflict Dallas sailed for Mexico to negotiate for the release of the ship. After he threatened to leave a force along the coast to prevent further hindrance of American commerce, the Mexicans capitulated.

The commodore made one of his occasional visits north in 1839 and, intending to visit Pittsburgh, decided to steam with his family up the Mississippi and Ohio rivers. In typical fashion, he quarrelled along the way with a riverboat gambler over a card game and escaped violence only through quick action by the ship's captain. Alexander proceeded to Pennsylvania, where he visited with the Wilkinses and his brother Trevanion. He then crossed the Alleghenies to see George, newly returned from Russia, and his nephew, University of Pennsylvania Professor Alexander Dallas Bache. Returning to Florida, the commodore was relieved of command at the naval station in 1842 and at his own request was given the three- to four-year assignment as leader of the Pacific Squadron. In the spring of 1843 he departed for Peru to take command of the fleet, but he could not find Commodore Thomas Jones, whom he was supposed to relieve in Callao. Weeks passed into months and Dallas was driven to distraction by his inability to find the missing squadron. It finally appeared on 3 June 1844 in the Callao harbor, just as the sailors on Dallas's vessel were lowering his ensign. The fifty-three-year-old commander had died of "paralysis." Dallas had been imaginative and resourceful, with a mind for hydrography and an interest in the use of steam. The loss of his experience was a sharp blow to the navy. He was temporarily interred in Peru, but in 1847 the government ordered his body shipped home. In New York the ship was met by his son, now a midshipman, and brother George, who was by this time vice-president of the United States.

When he visited Philadelphia the commodore did not stay with his brother, but rather with his nephew Alexander Dallas Bache. Alexander was the son of Richard Bache (the grandson of Benjamin Franklin) and Sophia Dallas, the officer's sister. The younger Bache had attended West Point at the age of fifteen and was graduated without a demerit at the head of his class. His gentle, friendly, unassuming manner won him many friends and resulted in the offer of a teaching post at the Point after graduation. Thereafter he worked on fortifications at Newport, Rhode Island, where he met and married the daughter of a prominent Newport citizen. Like many of the other Dallases who married within their social but out of their economic class, Alexander was hard pressed to support his wife and to also send money home to sustain his mother and younger brothers and sisters. His dilemma was resolved by the offer of a chair in natural philosophy and chemistry at the University of Pennsylvania. This particularly pleased his mother, who continued to provide him with advice and counsel throughout his life. The portly professor was an instant success. His brilliant research in the area of magnetic forces and his leadership in the Franklin Institute and American Philosophical Society earned him the appointment as president of the newly formed Girard College in 1836. The responsibilities of his new post included a voyage to Europe to study its educational systems. He returned with a mastery of curriculum, which aided in the establishment of the Philadelphia common schools, and with a love of German wines. Meanwhile, the college languished and Bache resigned the presidency in 1842 to return to Pennsylvania. Soon after, however, the government tempted him with the superintendency of the Coastal Survey and he moved to Washington. The wise and likeable professor gathered men of ability around him and made the public aware of the contributions the survey would make to all seagoing Americans. He also assumed the leadership of the Bureau of Weights and Measures and became a regent of the Smithsonian Institution. During the Civil War Bache would be appointed vice-president of the Sanitary Commission and assist in the construction of military defenses for the city of Philadelphia. This task would require long hours in the sun and provoke a migraine condition. The professor's health worsened after this, his once great mind feeble, and he became increasingly withdrawn. Death came quietly in 1867 to one of the great nineteenth-century American men of science.

Bache had been president of Girard College in 1837 when Dallas was preparing for the journey to Russia. It is likely that the popular professor attended the numerous fetes held in his uncle's honor. But the newly appointed diplomat was not idling away all of his time in farewell celebration. In mid-April his friends of the Philadelphia bar presented Dallas with a gold snuffbox. Two days later he, Sophy, and their seven children journeyed to Boston to embark on the U.S.S. *Independence,* which would take them to London. The party arrived in England in June and stayed there for a month to shop and tour the countryside. Finally, they proceeded on to the port of Kronstadt, where they landed on 29 July. The Dallases were quickly "settled and happy" in a "snug house" owned by a Russian count. On 6 August the new American minister and his wife were presented to Emperor Nicholas I and the Empress Alexandra at the Peterhoff Palace. Dallas was impressed with the pleasant and relaxed manner of the royal couple. He felt perfectly at ease with them and enjoyed an informal chat. Dallas attributed this openness to the fact that Americans do not have the "bred in" respect for monarchs and they are thus more convivial with them and vice versa. Dallas no doubt wished that this atmosphere would extend to his professional duties. Upon his arrival the American encountered the rigid Count Nesselrode, the czar's vice-chancellor, who was less than anxious to find a solution to a long-standing diplomatic problem between their nations.[13]

In April 1824 the United States and Russia negotiated a treaty in an attempt to resolve their conflict of interests on the northwest coast of North America. The treaty stipulated: (1) the citizens of the two nations should have unrestricted liberty to frequent and trade with the natives on the unsettled northwestern Pacific coast; (2) citizens of either country could not resort to places where there were settlements of the other without first securing permission from the authorities; (3) Americans could not make further settlements north of 54°40′, and Russians could make none south of the line; (4) for a period of ten years, however, citizens of either country might reciprocally visit "without hindrance whatever, the interior seas, gulfs, harbors, and creeks . . . for the purpose of fishing and trading with the natives of the country"; and (5) trade in liquors, arms, and ammunition was absolutely prohibited.

At the time the document was signed there was apparently no agreement between Count Nesselrode and the American negotiator, Henry Middleton, on the effect of the expiration of Article 4. Nesselrode viewed it as giving Russia sole possession north of 54°40'; in 1834 American rights to go above that would cease without first gaining Russian permission. He considered Articles 1 and 4 together; the expiration of one abrogated the other. The Americans would have unrestricted trade for ten years and no rights after that. The United States had negotiated a compromise for immediate gain. Middleton interpreted the treaty in an entirely different manner. It granted no sovereignty to Russia above 54°40' except at places that were settled. All other points were still to be open to the trade of both nations. When the Russians settled an area, the United States could then seek confirmation of trading rights. The American government soon adopted this posture, which was certain to lead to controversy when the clause expired.

On 17 April 1834, Article 4 was no longer in effect. The Russian government, with constant prodding from the Russian-American Company, which held an economic monopoly in the northwest-coast fur trade, then moved armed ships into the area and informed Washington that unrestricted commerce was no longer permitted north of 54°40'. The United States government made no serious attempt to renew the provision until it learned of the harsh Russian action. Secretary of State John Forsyth may have anticipated a simple renewal of Article 4. In the summer of 1835 he ordered William Wilkins, then minister to Russia, to begin negotiations toward a renewal. In November Wilkins pressed Nesselrode on the article but the count would not be hurried and said he had to discuss the matter with the Russian-American Company. Wilkins, who had never been optimistic about the prospects, recognized these stalling tactics, but could do nothing about them. In April 1836, before a definite reply from Nesselrode arrived, Wilkins received permission to return home. The problem remained in this suspended state until Dallas arrived in St. Petersburg in August 1837.[14]

While Dallas was still in London, however, an additional incident was reported to him that further heightened tensions. In the summer of 1836 an American sea otter hunter, the brig *Loriot,* commanded by

Captain Richard D. Blinn, had hoisted anchor in the Sandwich Islands and sailed for unoccupied Tuckessan Harbor in northwest America, latitude 54°55′. About 19 September an armed ship of the Russian Imperial Navy had boarded the *Loriot* in the harbor and ordered her crew to leave Russian domains. Blinn tried to discuss the matter with the officers for two days, but they remained adamant in their demands. When the *Loriot* delayed sailing for over a week, armed boats were sent on 27 September and the ship was forced to put to sea. While anchored off the harbor of Tateskey, bad weather forced them to seek shelter and the American captain asked the Russian officers if he could enter the port. He was refused. Blinn, unable to seek safety in storms, obtain provisions, or hire a native crew, was obliged to abandon his voyage and return to the Sandwich Islands in November. He promptly filed a complaint to the State Department, entering a claim against the Russian government for lucrative profits he lost because of the actions of the Imperial Navy. This claim was based on violation of Article 1 of the treaty.[15]

The issue to be investigated, according to the Americans, was whether there were settlements at Tuckessan and Tateskey harbors. If there were, American ships could be excluded; if not, American rights had been violated. In London Dallas eagerly sought out charts, maps, or books that might indicate the locations Captain Blinn had visited. The minister thought he had found the harbors on a small island 150 miles off the continental coast, but he would have to investigate further. In the meantime, he was instructed to complain to the Russian Ministry that its vessels had acted in a most "unfriendly manner," particularly since an American request for a map of Russian establishments along the coast had never been answered. If no settlements existed at these two harbors, however, Forsyth ordered Dallas to protest a violation of Article 1 and earnestly press for damages to the *Loriot*. Dallas ultimately had been unable to ascertain positively the location of the two ports during his stay in England. When he arrived in St. Petersburg, he immediately began a "cautious inquiry" with agents of the navy and the Russian-American Company. He wanted to be certain of the status of the harbors before pressing his case with Nesselrode. Dallas envisioned great problems arising from trying to negotiate Article 4. He was confident that Nesselrode would interpret the article—which made no mention of "establishments," settlements, or points already occupied—as protecting the American right to trade in the disputed area for only ten years. This right was granted without limit of time in Article 1. Dallas asked Forsyth why Article 4 was placed in the treaty if it had not been intended to yield power in relation to sections divided by 54°40′ at the end of a decade. Although Middleton undoubtedly did not intend this to be the case, instead seeing Article 4 as an enlargement rather than a restriction of Article 1, it could be easily interpreted the count's way. Dallas judged that the Russians had a good argument for halting all American activity above 54°40′, but he would remain steadfast in protecting American claims until instructed to the contrary by Forsyth.[16]

By the end of August Dallas's inquiries had resulted in some information "from a reliable source" regarding the two harbors. Neither Tuckessan or Tateskey had been settled by the Russians. He immediately wrote to Nesselrode, informing him of the American government's displeasure over Russia's naval actions in an area "yet distinguished by no settlement" and expressing the hope that such moves were not condoned by the Imperial government. The note also included a claim for indemnity for the *Loriot*'s owners.[17]

Months passed and Dallas received no response from the vice-chancellor, although in early December the minister was given additional instructions on procedure from Washington. Finally, on 27 December Nesselrode informed Dallas that after a brief vacation he was now ready to resume his duties in the Bureau of Foreign Affairs. The next day Dallas wrote to him to formally propose the renewal of Article 4 for an indefinite period. Considering the *Loriot* affair, he noted that prompt settlement of the issue, which the United States had been urging since May 1835, was now almost mandatory. The frustrated American officer, unaccustomed to seasonal diplomacy, complained to Nesselrode that he had been in Russia six months, and for five of those the government had been on vacation. Dallas wanted a quick decision by the Russians, so that he could submit any action to Congress before it adjourned in the spring. The vice-chancellor told Dallas that he would consider both Blinn's claim and Article 4 as soon as he could, only to be diverted on the next day by the destruction of the mammoth Winter Palace by fire.[18]

On 23 February 1838, six long months after his initial request, Dallas received an answer from Nesselrode. It was a complete rejection of his demands. The Russian naval commander who boarded Blinn's ship was acting in accordance with instructions given him on the expiration of Article 4. The *Loriot* had the right to sail into any unoccupied harbor along the coast until April 1834. The owners of the ship and the United States government had two years' warning prior to the incident of Imperial sentiments on the subject of rights above and below the 54°40′ line. For this reason the Russian government could not accept responsibility for losses incurred by the ship. There was, of course, no mention of renewing Article 4. Dallas was becoming painfully aware of a growing Russian desire to reinforce exclusive claims over northwest America, as she had prior to 1824. Secretary of State Forsyth also expressed fear that Russia would claim exclusive jurisdiction over the territory. He wrote to Dallas urging him to tell the Russians that the United States would in no way acknowledge absolute Imperial possession above 54°40′, except at settled places. Dallas replied that if the Russians continued to interpret the treaty in a manner harmful to the commercial interest of the United States, strong measures would be taken. Naval protection of American ships in northwest Pacific waters would be an acceptable form of warning. Dallas believed the czar was pressing for advantages on the coast at this time because he felt the United States was in fiscal difficulty, on the eve of civil war and foreign wars with Mexico and Great Britain. The minister urged that these sentiments be promptly dispelled by open and forceful action.[19]

Rather than employing force, Forsyth instructed Dallas in March 1838 to describe again the American position on the treaty to Nesselrode. Dallas complied with a strong note pointing out American disappointment in official Russian policy vis-à-vis the *Loriot* and regarding the "unfriendly act" as a slight to the American flag and commerce. Blinn had interpreted Article 4 as the United States government had—that Russia could claim areas above 54°40′ and occupy but not possess them. Nevertheless, Americans could still land at unoccupied locations and trade in occupied areas. One historian has declared that "notes less strong than this have been known to lead to war," but the United States was most certainly bluffing, hoping that Russia would back down.[20] Nesselrode would not be bullied. A few days later he replied to Dallas's note by saying that Article 4 had not proved beneficial to Russia and that it had been attended by "serious inconveniences." The prosperity of the Russian-American Company had suffered by it, and the Americans had violated Article 5 by trading liquor and guns to the natives. The American government had taken no steps to halt this illicit trade, which was injurious to the company. Therefore, for the safety and economic growth of the region and the company, renewal of Article 4 was undesirable. Nesselrode added that he did not feel guilty about his action because American commerce would not be endangered by the closing of an area to which such a small percentage of their trade was carried.[21]

The United States was thus told in a firm, gentle, but final manner that she was no longer welcome anywhere north of 54°40′. Dallas did not seem to comprehend fully that the Russians were declaring the right of sole possession. He wrote to Nesselrode on 26 March describing his regret over the Imperial decision, but adding that the United States would respect it and hope for success of Russian ventures in the area. However, in an effort to preserve cordial relations between the two nations, he wanted to ascertain Imperial policy regarding admission of American vessels into the harbors and bays along their coast, so that he could inform his government and American shipowners. In a note to Forsyth on 16 April Dallas reiterated his desire for clarification of Russian claims. He admitted that the refusal to renew Article 4 was far from unexpected and suspected that behind it was "the grasping policy of the Fur Company." It did not seem expedient to Dallas to criticize the alleged motives of the czar's government. The main point had been decided and pursuance of detail would only disturb a decision that had been delivered in friendly terms. The American minister felt that the Russians, by their refusal to renew Article 4, were attaining an important object in their northwest colonial policy, while the United States sacrificed "nothing but a series of vague claims, calculated only to embroil and complicate the relations of the two countries." Dallas maintained that the basic problem concerning renewal centered around a definition of "occupied." He urged further talks with the Russians about the nature and range of the act of colonizing in order to determine which nation would control the area. Without this, American commerce in the region would be "probably entirely destroyed by the pretensions of the Russian Fur Company." Dallas deemed it essential to American trade that water and land positions under Russian dominance in the Northwest be defined, since the United States still claimed trade rights with unoccupied areas under Article 4. He wanted instructions from Forsyth that would define how far he should go in pursuing inquiries to the Russian government regarding locations of settlements and claims to trade with unoccupied lands.[22]

Since Dallas obviously missed the point of Nesselrode's previous messages, he tried again on 9 May. The vice-chancellor made his position plain in a brief and terse statement which declared that no American vessels would be permitted on Russian coastal waters or claims (unoccupied or not) north of 54°40', and he added that this would be enforced by the Imperial Navy. In reverse, no Russian ships would sail south of the parallel. The United States government was warned to inform its citizens of the consequences of violating this prohibition. Dallas finally understood and expressed no desire to pursue the subject further. Forsyth, who had a strong case for his nation's rights and was forceful for a time, also chose not to contest

Nesselrode's views. It is unclear whether this was because of more pressing matters in the State Department or because American trade in the area was too minimal to quarrel about. Nevertheless, the Americans quietly surrendered their position. This action in Washington and St. Petersburg did not greatly affect American shippers in the Northwest. They continued their trade with the coast despite repeated official protests by the Russian-American Company. The company never prospered and as early as 1840 had leased a strip of the coast to the British Hudson's Bay Company. This transaction marked the beginning of the end for the Russians, who faded into the background as the British-American rivalry increased in North America, including the Pacific Northwest, in the 1840s and 1850s.[23]

Two aspects of Dallas's private life in St. Petersburg—his attitude toward his official public duties and toward everyday Russian society—are worthy of consideration. When he arrived in the Imperial capital in August 1837 and was received by the czar and his wife, Dallas was struck by the power of the royal family and the seasonal nature of the government. The American minister discovered the true nature of the Russian system within a matter of weeks. It was impossible for him to acquire information on internal conditions and administration of affairs in Russia. He feared that his family was being "vigilantly supervised" and thought perhaps even some of the household servants were secret police. The Dallases became almost paranoid when Sophy lost a letter in which she commented on the Russian government. It was eventually found, but for a time they were concerned for their safety.[24]

Dallas did not hesitate to emphasize the fact that he was representing a democratic nation. Although he felt warmly received by his colleagues in the diplomatic corps, he was totally bound to their world. Russian society was hedged in by so many prejudices and plain ignorance that it was inaccessible to a stranger. Most of the European diplomats engaged in playing politics with their alliances, but Dallas naturally was not involved. He told his sister Maria, "I despise these entanglements. The republican Minister looks about for something like congenial society—but he is absolutely alone in ideas, attitudes, and feelings." Soon after his arrival in Russia he received an invitation to an elaborate dinner given for him by the czar. Dallas appeared in citizen's dress and was promptly told he could not be admitted under any circumstances. The American minister was vexed at the pertinacity of royal etiquette and refused to wear a military-style uniform, thus missing the dinner. The next Sunday Dallas was again invited to the palace and it is probable that he arrived properly attired. The Whiggish *Niles' Register* chastised him for his obstinacy in this affair and urged him to forget his popularity at home and "remember the old adage—when in Rome do as the Romans do."[25]

Dallas managed to draw a fine but definite line between the Russian social system, which he despised, and the czar, whom he respected and admired. As early as December 1837 the minister was saying, "I must stay here a very very long time before I can acquire a relish for the unnatural condition of humanity that exists. It is all very well while we are in the drawing room . . . there is an order, a tranquillity, and a selfishness about military despotism and its system which seem congenial to the idle and degenerate moments of our nature." Nicholas I, whom many historians have viewed in a rather harsh manner, was warmly regarded by Dallas. He saw much of Peter the Great in Nicholas and opined that posterity would in many respects find Nicholas the better man. The sovereign's state policy had led him to do several things inexcusable to enlightened and liberal nations, but Dallas blamed these actions on the form of government and the prevailing European system. On the other hand, the czar tried to ameliorate the plight of the serfs (but was frustrated by his nobles) and was renowned "for his justice, his clemency, industry, and domestic morality." When rumors were circulated in December 1837 that there were plots to kill Nicholas, Dallas discounted them. He correctly realized that any successful scheme must be developed by the nobility and the army, since the masses "are nothing." These two forces had no motive for plotting against the czar. Dallas pondered, "Why remove an able, indefatigable and ambitious chief in order to hasten the reign of his son, who is young, amiable and rather dull. They cannot hope by any possible change to get a sovereign so admirably fitted for Russia in her actual condition, and so capable of pushing onward her European ascendance." While Dallas astutely exposed the base of Imperial power, he was in this case certainly a poor judge of character.[26]

All of polite Russian society focused around the royal family. When the czar returned to the Winter Palace in October, until the following spring, the social season—and the government—was under Nicholas's personal supervision. The court spent the remaining six months of the year traveling and sightseeing. Major diplomatic contacts were made at the continuous round of parties held during the season. Dallas objected to a diplomacy that was practiced at "saloons" [*sic*] and dinner tables rather than in offices. His wife and daughters, however, were eagerly caught up in the social whirl. The court had four or five parties an evening, but for reasons of health, Dallas allowed his girls to attend only two a week. Unlike Sophy, Dallas found Russian society (after the initial shock of opulence) "listless, somber, and indifferent or unexcitable. Time hung heavily in St. Petersburg on the health and spirits of all but the natives, and they were heavier than time itself." Dallas was justifiably bored. He would talk and play chess at endless parties and learn virtually nothing of importance. He was an outsider socially and politically to the majority of his colleagues. Dallas, who had been in politics and law all his life, could not become involved in either one. The problem of poor mail service further isolated him, cutting him off almost totally from events in the United States.[27]

Perhaps Dallas could have endured the cold informality of Russian society and the frustration of his public duties if he had been content in his domestic affairs. The minister and his wife constantly complained about his inadequate salary and the high prices. He told Gilpin in 1838, "The expense of living here exceeds all belief. . . . Food prices and rent are enormously high. . . . I shall remain in St. Petersburg all summer, being unable to afford even the short trip to Moscow." Sophy expressed similar feelings to her mother in 1839. "The expense of this place swallows up everything. . . . I have made up my mind that without an increase in salary we can not brave another winter here. We are very restricted in St. Petersburg and subjected to much inconvenience." Dallas was forced to economize in every way possible. In letters to his sister Maria, he referred to himself as "*poor* George" and complained about the pittance of the salary he received.[28]

Another interpretation of Dallas's situation, in contrast to this bleak portrayal, can be formulated from the facts he presents. As American minister Dallas received $9,000 a year salary, hardly a trifling amount. The family had twelve servants who lived with them and whose total wages were less than $100 per month. Dallas often mentioned in his letters home that "Phil bought two elegant suits" or "the girls' milliner from Paris is shipping them out their winter clothes." The problem the Dallases faced in Russia seemed to be that of social readjustment. The financial resources they possessed and the "hardships" they endured were a greater burden because of the wealth surrounding them. They had made the rapid transition from the upper echelons of Philadelphia society to an obscure and uncontroversial position in St. Petersburg society. While both Dallas and his wife participated in activities of the diplomatic service, they were really never part of the inner circle. Dallas was frustrated, tired, and bored by the parties at which he was a secondary figure who could contribute or learn nothing of diplomatic importance. Sophy remained happy, but she felt increasingly inadequate in a society in which she could be only an attractive but relatively poor ornament. Another factor that displeased both parents about Russian life was the lack of quality educational facilities. Philip, their eldest son, was ready for school, but the only proper institutions were military schools, which required wearing cocked hats and swords. Always the republican, Dallas forbade attendance at such a place and, instead, acquired the services of a tutor. This was, of course, poor preparation for Princeton or even an English boarding school.[29]

After only one year in Russia Dallas bemoaned his decision to leave Philadelphia. He wrote to his mother-in-law, "Dearly have I paid in the relations of domestic life, during the last year for boldly conforming to the dictates of what seemed to me plain and public duty! What would have tempted me abroad, could I have forseen." By December 1838 he had decided to ask for his recall, for reasons "as plentiful as blackberries in July," so he could be home by the following summer. He hastily wrote to his friends and relations informing them of his plans. This action proved premature, since he had not requested official approval to return to the United States. When he realized his error, he was angered and panicked. "I very much fear that I am more of a slave than I had imagined, and that I shall be doomed to a longer banishment than experience makes me relish." Dallas did not think it was necessary to ask officially for a recall and he was obliged to wait until 1 July for an answer. This made him nervous because it was dangerously close to the end of the traveling season to commence such a long journey. He also wanted to "slip out of the enormous expense incident to . . . the marriage of the Emperor's eldest daughter fixed for the first week of the month."[30]

By June Dallas had decided that he was going home the next month, recall or not. If when he arrived in Philadelphia he learned that the president had denied his petition, he would return to St. Petersburg without his family. Fortunately, the letter of recall arrived on 6 July and Dallas immediately proceeded with his plans to leave Russia. He seemed emotionally exhausted and somewhat bitter regarding his recent experiences. Before his departure he wrote to Mrs. Nicklin, Sophy's mother: "I long—deeply and devoutly long—for domestic seclusion, and the absolute independence of domestic love. . . . whatever comes of me, [in the future] I am quite sure that my only real happiness will be at home with you, my relatives and my wife and children." Dallas added that the broad experiences of the last two years had not enamored him of "what is called the world," but, on the contrary, he was now "unblinded" and could see better than ever before the solid contentment of home.[31]

This disillusionment, however, did not imply that Dallas felt he had not performed a service in Russia. He considered himself a dedicated public servant ("the duties of diplomacy are triple more arduous than I had anticipated," he wrote Maria) when the situation warranted his attention. After his final audience with the czar on 23 July Dallas noted in his diary that Nicholas had convinced him he had not lived in Russia without doing public service and thus achieving the reputation he desired. The next day the American minister departed the capital for Kronstadt and then to Le Havre. After a two-month journey the Dallases arrived in New York on 20 October. In only a matter of weeks he had returned to the security and comfort of the Quaker City. His brother Trevanion had written him in March 1839, "Your return to the United States would be a step of certain propriety. Let me know what your intentions are—will you return to practice in Philadelphia or go higher up the political ladder?" This must have been a question that Dallas and many of his friends and foes alike were asking themselves in the fall of 1839.[32]

5

The Road to Washington (1840–1844)

In the autumn of 1839 George M. Dallas returned to his Walnut Street home to practice law. For the next four years he held no elective or appointive public office. He remained, however, an active and eager—if not powerful—force in the national and state Democracy. Dallas was vocal in his support of a variety of candidates for the 1844 presidential contest. He also commented on a number of issues, including the independent treasury, the national bank, and Texas annexation. His views of this last problem of national concern would be a primary factor in catapulting him into the vice-presidency.

By 1839 the Dallas faction of the Pennsylvania Democracy was a narrow, isolated, and, outside the confines of Philadelphia, politically ineffectual body. The blows the old Family Party had sustained at the hands of Jackson, combined with the successive exiles to Russia of Wilkins and Dallas, severely wounded the organization. When Dallas returned from St. Petersburg, he found himself in command of a political machine maintained by loyal friends such as Henry Gilpin and John K. Kane. For the next two decades Dallas tried to recapture the political magic of the 1820s. He failed. Dallas was burdened by a tendency to commit himself on too many pressing state and national issues. This was in sharp contrast to James Buchanan, who by 1840 controlled the state party. As Buchanan's evasiveness made him an increasingly acceptable candidate in a nation torn by slavery and sectionalism, Dallas's usually firm stands alienated many of his former backers and relegated him to the minority role of loyal opposition to Old Buck.

This subordinate position within his own state party did not diminish Dallas's desire to speak out on national issues. In the winter of 1839 President Van Buren sent Dallas a copy of his annual message. At the time the United States was embroiled with Great Britain over Canadian border violations and the president had aimed some subtle barbs at the English. Dallas was deeply impressed with the "discreet coolness" of Van Buren's remarks concerning what he considered to be a tense situation. The Philadelphian compared the brilliance of this message with James Madison's efforts to control national indignation prior to the War of 1812. Dallas felt England was in a state of turmoil. Queen Victoria was unpopular and the people were discontented. The English were "wildly, universally and uncontrollably fanatic" on the issue of slavery, and Dallas feared that the problem was being exacerbated by the radical Daniel O'Connell in Parliament. Dallas declared that to escape her own domestic problems, England might start a war over the northeast boundary with Canada and then turn it into a crusade to destroy "our southern institutions." The large number of regular British forces in Canada always had struck Dallas as disproportionate for suppressing "a paltry, unorganized, ill-directed insurrection." Fortunately for England and the United States, Dallas's suspicions were incorrect. The British Ministry did not panic over O'Connell's raving, and the northeastern boundary question was peacefully settled by the Webster-Ashburton Treaty of 1842.[1]

Dallas corresponded with Van Buren on a number of national and state political matters in the years 1839–44. The Philadelphian remained a loyal and dedicated Pennsylvania ally throughout much of this period. When Attorney General Felix Grundy resigned in December 1839, both the Dallas and Buchanan factions claimed the cabinet post. Van Buren first offered it to Buchanan, who wisely rejected it. The senator, who was closely allied with Democratic Governor David Porter, recommended the governor's brother, James M. Porter, for the position. This would solidify the Buchanan clique with the state administration and indicate Van Buren's approval of the senator. The president, however, rejected Old Buck's suggestion and selected Dallas as his second choice. The Philadelphian told Henry Gilpin in December, "the Attorney-Generalship has not a particle of attraction to me. I view it as I did some six or seven years ago—and I have no doubt about it that my sentiments are perfectly understood." Gilpin did desire the position, however, and Dallas said he would recommend him to the president. Much to the shock and chagrin of Buchanan, Van Buren appointed Gilpin attorney general. The senator was extremely bitter over the rejection of his choice and told Governor Porter that the action would affect his personal relations with the president: "Every avenue to a Cabinet office during Van Buren's administration is closed against any Pennsylvania man [he apparently did not consider Gilpin a Pennsylvanian] and the President's disposition towards myself is proclaimed from the house top." The senator would not quickly forget this affront in a crucial election year. The president had taken sides in a factional dispute and, unfortunately for him, he selected the much weaker clique.

In declining the attorney generalship Dallas explained to Van Buren that he had been absent from his practice for too long and needed to recoup his financial losses. Besides, he could serve his party better in the coming elections by remaining in Pennsylvania. By this time in his career Dallas had generally removed himself from the local courts, except when he was retained by the county of Philadelphia. His cases had grown in size, as had his fees. Undoubtedly the two most significant challenges he encountered in this period involved the defense of Commodore Jesse D. Elliott before a naval court-martial in 1840 (which he lost) and of Nicholas Biddle, now in 1841 former president of the Bank of the United States. Biddle was being harassed by the directors and stockholders of the institution over payment of debts amounting to more than a million dollars (the amount was later reduced to a quarter of the initial sum and a year later Biddle was exonerated of all criminal charges).[2]

As the disagreement over the attorney generalship indicates, the Pennsylvania Democracy was deeply divided in 1840. Not since the 1835 Wolf-Muhlenberg split had the party been in such trouble. The Buchanan Democrats had strong control of the state administration and much of the federal patronage. They were opposed across the state by the supporters of the venerable Henry Muhlenberg. The Dallas faction maintained a powerful but geographically limited influence over Philadelphia. The Democrats of the Quaker City, most of them Van Buren men, were greatly dissatisfied with the patronage policies of Governor Porter. This problem became apparent in 1840 when former governor Wolf, who had finally been appointed collector of the Port of Philadelphia, died in office. A scramble for the lucrative position immediately began among the factions. In March, when Van Buren, apparently in an attempt to placate the irritated Buchanan element, appointed a man from the interior of the state, the Philadelphians were outraged. Dallas had great difficulty in keeping his men under control. Porter rallies in Philadelphia were broken up by Dallas–Van Buren men. Dallas told Gilpin he was trying "to entreat incessantly for forbearance, moderation, and silence." It did little good. The prerogatives, principles, and delegates of the Philadelphia

Democracy had been offended and then trampled upon, first by Harrisburg and then by Washington.

Van Buren's tactic of jumping from one Keystone faction to another and his perennial unpopularity, combined with the disastrous impact of the Panic of 1837 on Pennsylvania industry, lost him the state in November. The Little Magician was defeated by Harrison by 350 votes out of nearly 300,000 cast. Philadelphia was safe for the Democracy—if only barely—but many areas, including Buchanan's home county, which voted two to one for Harrison, went heavily Whig. Dallas wrote to Van Buren after the election and attempted to console him by describing the victory as "a monstrous cheat" as the result of fraudulent suffrage; that "Louis Phillipe has a much fairer title to the crown of France than General Harrison to the Presidency." Although election irregularities may have cost Van Buren some votes, the reasons for his defeat were much more subtle, extending to internal divisions within the party itself.[3]

The forces dividing the state party were the bank and the financial problems resulting from the Panic of 1837. Pennsylvania had an extensive program of internal improvements and the Commonwealth was in severe financial distress because of overexpenditures on them. Dallas urged a rigid and conservative policy focusing on increased taxes, paying debts, and restoring credit. The federal government could possibly help in this situation. Following early opposition (in 1837) to the subtreasury system as being too independent "of the control, needs and desires of the people," Dallas was converted by the panic to the system: "It is the only measure that can save us [Pennsylvania] from the overwhelming power of the commercial emporium." In December 1841, at a Philadelphia rally to discuss the state's finances, Dallas praised Governor Porter's preelection pledge to pay the debt and to recommend that the legislature require resumption "at an early date." A radical group held a rump meeting at approximately the same time and urged repudiation of the debt and sale of the improvements. By January 1842 the state was in its worst financial position since 1837. The governor and the legislature moved to rectify the situation in a responsible manner. Resolutions were passed rejecting repudiation and a banking act was endorsed that provided for gradual resumption of specie payments. By 1842 the state Bank of Pennsylvania was dead, and President John Tyler had vetoed a new national bank. The removal of the bank as an issue and a compromise on resumption of payments of debts helped reunite the factious Democracy. The elimination of the bank and the sweeping Democratic victories in the state in 1841 were a portent of better

things to come. The Jacksonians had rebounded from the shocking
Whig triumphs of 1840 to reelect Porter by a wide margin in November 1841. They now moved cautiously to select a candidate for the
presidential race in 1844.[4]

The 1844 presidential race began when William Henry Harrison
was buried. Tyler, Van Buren, Benton, Calhoun, Buchanan, and
Richard Johnson were all ambitious contenders for the White House.
Dallas was asked in 1841 by a Philadelphia committee whether it was
advisable to discuss the presidential question at so early a date. The
Philadelphian replied that it was not in the least premature and, in
fact, it might prove beneficial. Judging by the Democracy's loss in
1840, it might take two or three years to find a leader who appealed to
all Democrats. An open, friendly expression of ideas about the right
man would be helpful to the party.

It is difficult to determine exactly whom Dallas supported for the
nomination by May 1844. Late in 1842 the backers of General Lewis
Cass urged him to join their camp with promises of appropriate reward if they were successful. Henry Gilpin wrote to Van Buren that
Dallas had a "decided predilection" in favor of the New Yorker and
that Dallas "estimated Cass' *democracy* at its true value." While
Dallas was not ambitious for political office himself—preferring to
prosper in his private profession—he would come out for Van Buren
at the appropriate time. Gilpin also reported that Dallas had received
overtures from Tyler men, but "he would have nothing to do with
them." Ultimately, Dallas proved his loyalty to Van Buren at a most
crucial hour. In January 1843 Buchanan had been reelected to the
Senate and immediately began a campaign for a favorite-son endorsement. Old Buck made rapid progress against the weak opposition of
the Van Buren forces from the interior of the state in the competition
to win delegate support. Then in the spring Van Buren's candidacy
began to develop in other states and he moved closer to the national
nomination. In April the Little Magician's past appointees to office in
Philadelphia—Dallas, Gilpin, Henry Horn, John Kane, and others—
took the lead in reactivating the "Old Hickory Club." The Van Buren
men were too weak in the central and western parts of the Commonwealth to retrieve the state from Buchanan, but they were in a position of some strength and could afford to wait. Buchanan's support
outside Pennsylvania never materialized and in December he withdrew from the race. This did not throw the state into the Van Buren
camp (barely half of the Keystone delegation that would go to the
Baltimore convention could be called Van Buren men), but Buchanan
was eliminated from the contest and this was Dallas's primary goal. If

Van Buren received the nomination and won in November, Dallas would gain control of the state Democracy. Buchanan had taken a large gamble and lost. He no longer controlled the state administration, Philadelphia was totally independent, and only a fraction of the party was committed to him. Buchanan remained a regular, however, and vowed to support Van Buren to avoid a party split, even though he felt the New Yorker would lose.[5]

Buchanan was not the only Democrat to withdraw in December 1843. John C. Calhoun also decided to quit the contest, just at the time his friends were in Washington joining the other anti-Van Buren forces. Only Richard Johnson and Lewis Cass remained as serious challengers to Van Buren. In December Dallas began his break from the New Yorker. The Philadelphian was strongly allied with a congressional cadre headed by Robert John Walker of Mississippi and Aaron Brown of Tennessee that supported Van Buren and the "reannexation of Texas."

Few people would have identified Walker as the linchpin in this bold band. The Mississippian closely resembled a pygmy. Atop his diminutive body (5 feet, 2 inches and 100 pounds) rested a massive head and dyed black hair. Perhaps because of his size, he developed a defensive nature and hair-trigger temper, which frequently embroiled him in personal duels. Combined with his boundless energy and fiery ambition for wealth and honor, Walker was a likely candidate for success in frontier politics. He broke from his conservative Whig-Federalist Pennsylvania family to campaign for Jackson in 1824. After the general's defeat, he decided to take his young bride, the niece of George M. Dallas, and make his fortune in Natchez, Mississippi. By 1836 his talents as politician and land speculator were evident; he was elected a United States senator and headed the Jacksonian "Mississippi Regency."

Walker began his campaign by publishing a pamphlet early in 1844 justifying the need for American annexation of Texas. Dallas read the tract eagerly. He wrote Walker, "It is comprehensive, clear, argumentative and eloquent . . . my head has been running on this topic for some months and your admirable brochure comes to me like manna in the way of starved people." Walker followed his publication with a fervent and impassioned plea in May 1844, in favor of the treaty for annexing Texas at a secret session of the Senate. The Mississippian offered a variety of reasons (most of which appeared in his publication) for the necessity of such action, including Manifest Destiny, the inferiority of the Mexicans, and a nationalistic desire to expel "English intrigue" from Texas. His speech was a futile effort, since the treaty was defeated by a large margin in the Senate on 8 June. Henry Clay, who had declared himself opposed to immediate annexation in April, joined the majority in voting against it. This of course only increased the likelihood that Texas would be a key campaign issue. As Sidney George Fisher noted, "Conquest, extension of territory, war—these will be the topics urged during the contest, topics always exciting and captivating to the people." Dallas had begun to prove the validity of Fisher's remarks in December 1843. At that time he spoke to a Democratic rally in favor of annexation and caught the attention of party leaders. Approximately one year later he wrote to a Pittsburgh committee which had invited him to speak at a Jackson Day gathering:

> To me the incorporation of Texas into the Federal Union seems not only the opening of a natural and almost exhaustless resource for the fabrics and goods of the east, agricultural products of the west, etc.—but it assumed the aspect of a just and necessary consequence upon the genius and maxims of our confederated system.

Texas, independent since 1836, desired to become a state, and a sizable body of congressmen, mostly expansionist-minded southerners, wanted immediate annexation. This group was becoming increasingly skeptical about the Little Magician's position on Texas. They began to investigate the possibilities of another candidate in the event that Van Buren committed himself against annexation before the convention. Between December and May Dallas flirted with a variety of candidates. In December he was in Washington campaigning for the Cass men at the party caucus to select officers of the House of Representatives. Lewis Cass was by far the strongest alternative to Van Buren. Throughout the spring of 1844 Walker advised the Michigan veteran about the posture he should assume on Texas. Meanwhile, Walker's Pennsylvania allies in the Dallas clique began a boom for their fellow Philadelphian, Commodore Charles Stewart. Thus the pro-Texas men bounced back and forth among a multiplicity of candidates trying to locate a suitable alternative to the uncommitted Van Buren. On 27 April 1844, one month before the convention, the New Yorker took his stand. A letter against the Tyler-Calhoun Treaty and immediate annexation was published in the *Washington Globe*. The views contained in this note ruined Van Buren's presidential hopes, which only days before had been almost assured of success. The crisis that Walker, Dallas, and the other pro-Texas men had feared had come to pass. They now moved to block Van Buren and select a man they could trust.[6]

On 27 May 1844 the Democratic Convention opened in Baltimore. The anti-Van Buren–pro-Texas forces immediately proceeded to halt the New Yorker by moving that a two-thirds vote was needed for nomination. This placed the Pennsylvania delegation in a quandry. They had been instructed to vote for Van Buren. Many of the delegates—especially a strong contingent from the Philadelphia area—would do so, but others from the interior could still be swayed. The delegation was divided among supporters of Cass, Tyler, Buchanan, and Johnson. An intelligent politician could probably have manipulated this leaderless group. Because of the split in the state delegation, half of them voted for the two-thirds rule, which killed Van Buren's hopes of victory. They then turned around and voted for him *en masse* on the first ballot. On 28 May the battle for the presidential nomination continued between Van Buren and Cass, with the Keystone delegation switching over to Buchanan. Between the eighth and ninth ballots Van Buren withdrew, opening the way for the nomination of "dark horse" candidate James K. Polk of Tennessee, a former speaker of the House and a Texas annexationist.[7]

Once Polk had been nominated, the pro-Texas men, led by Walker, moved to quiet the disgruntled Van Buren supporters. Walker himself placed Van Buren's loyal follower, Senator Silas Wright, in nomination for the vice-presidency. This would, of course, placate the New Yorkers and win them to the ticket. No one was placed in opposition to Wright and on the first ballot he was selected. With their work finished the delegates then prepared to leave Baltimore. They were disappointed to learn that Wright declined the nomination, even after a committee of five was sent to persuade him to change his mind. After the way the convention had treated their champion no Van Burenite from New York would accept the post. On 30 May the convention again began the task of choosing a vice-presidential candidate. A man from New England or Pennsylvania was needed as a geographical offset to Polk. The Maine delegation promptly responded by naming James Buchanan, but a Keystone contingent (acting under Buchanan's orders) withdrew his name. Then Levi Woodbury of New Hampshire, Marcus Morton of Massachusetts, Governor John Fairfield of Maine, General Cass, and Colonel Johnson were nominated. Governor Fairfield was a solid leader (106 votes) on the first ballot, but he was short of a majority. Some Pennsylvania men turned to George M. Dallas, who garnered thirteen votes. Immediately, Walker gained the floor and spoke in Dallas's behalf. He specifically referred to Dallas's views on the bank and Texas, which were in accord with Polk's. Dallas was not in Baltimore and had kept his pre-convention activities against Van Buren so quiet that he was still acceptable to Van Buren's followers. The Philadelphian was identified with eastern Pennsylvania and the commercial classes, where he could secure a large segment of the state Democracy. He also would guard the northern protective tariff against any southern onslaughts. The convention was stampeded and on the second ballot Dallas was selected by a large majority (220 to 30) over Fairfield. The governor, a strong candidate, probably would have been nominated, but his views on Texas were feared and his stand on the Webster-Ashburton Treaty did not help his popularity in the South.[8]

When Dallas's nomination was confirmed on 30 May, Walker jubilantly left Baltimore for Philadelphia to inform his relative. He was joined by a formal Democratic committee, led by Fairfield, that arrived in the Quaker City at about three o'clock in the morning. Loud knocks on the front door brought Dallas to the chamber window. He recognized Walker at the door and fearing that his daughter, who was in Washington, was ill, he hastened down the stairs, half-dressed and in his slippers. Sixty men, two by two, marched past the amazed Dallas into his front parlor, all maintaining absolute silence. Dallas, who had no idea what was taking place, stood thunderstruck. Led by Walker into the back parlor, Dallas nervously asked what was happening. After waiting a moment the folding doors between the two parlors were thrown open and Dallas was greeted by a semicircle of applauding men. Governor Fairfield then stepped forward and informed Dallas of the convention's action. The surprised candidate recovered quickly and thanked the committee, promising to reply more formally to the offer. Dallas then opened his sideboard and everyone joined in pledging success to the ticket, as the elated and tipsy Walker whooped through a war dance in the parlor.[9]

Dallas's nomination was met with a wide variety of reactions in and out of the Democracy. Polk was promptly informed about Dallas from a number of personal and political friends. Cave Johnson told the Tennessean that Dallas will "perhaps [be] a *better Vice* than Wright and will add more to our strength." Gideon Pillow traveled to Philadelphia and after a conference with Dallas wrote Polk, "He is very talented and popular and most captivating in his address." George Crockett eagerly declared, "Dallas seems to be more acceptable than Wright and places Pennsylvania beyond a doubt." This attitude was commonplace among Polk's correspondents. Most of them seemed pleased with the selection of Dallas, especially because of his posture on Texas. There are no letters indicating the Philadelphian was a poor choice.[10] Other Democrats who viewed the situation in national terms were equally pleased. John Fairfield reported that the nominations of both Polk and Dallas were received with enthusiasm in Maine. John C. Calhoun reportedly thought the nomination of Polk was the best that could be made under the circumstances. He was pleased because the party was at last freed from the tyranny of the New York dynasty: "I was much gratified with Mr. Dallas's nomination. My friends everywhere will give the ticket a hearty support."[11]

There were, of course, those who were disappointed or resentful over the selection of the candidates. Some New York politicians feared that the failure to place Wright on the ticket would cost them the state and perhaps the election. Van Buren undoubtedly realized the attitude of his followers was not one that would promote party harmony, and he soon began to write letters to his backers urging that they remain loyal. Besides the obvious problems in New York, there were also difficulties in Pennsylvania. Many Buchanan supporters, unsuccessful in attaining the presidency for their leader, also had to swallow the bitter pill of the vice-presidency for George M. Dallas. Robert Letcher wrote to Buchanan in July, "Polk! Great God, what a nomination! I do really think the Democratic convention ought to be damned to all eternity for this villainous business." Senator William King of Alabama, then in Paris, confided to Old Buck, "I have the opinion that Polk and Dallas were bad selections. Dallas brings no strength to the ticket," and neither candidate had the influence that the party's candidates ought to have. John W. Forney, Pennsylvania editor and Buchanan's liaison man in Washington, said that a "considerable feeling against Dallas is manifested," but that this was lost in the general joy of the deliverance of the party from Van Buren. Dallas's nomination was "one of those things which could not be prevented" after Wright's impolitic refusal. Forney felt that Dallas was not strong in the Keystone State, and that his course on the bank issue made him a questionable Jacksonian and a possible hindrance to the national ticket. "Nothing can save him but the union and enthusiasm which now pervades the Party."[12]

The Whigs viewed Dallas's nomination with disdain. Their ticket of the venerable Henry Clay and Theodore Frelinghuysen of New Jersey seemed assured of defeating the two nationally unknown Democrats. Philadelphia Whig Sidney George Fisher smugly noted in his diary:

> Polk is a fourth rate partizan politician, of ordinary abilities, no eminence or reputation and chiefly distinguished for being a suc-

cessful stump orator in Tennessee. . . . Mr. Dallas is a gentleman by birth and education, amiable in private life, very bland and courteous in manner, too much so indeed, or rather too indiscriminately so, to give one an impression of sincerity and truth, a reckless partizan totally devoid of principle and capable of upholding or relinquishing and opinions whenever his own or his party's interests require it. His talents are very moderate, his acquirements scanty, he has an inferior position at the bar, no one would give a dollar for his opinion and his practice is for the most part jury cases unless when political influence introduces him into an important case.

The Whig newspapers were less harsh than Fisher, but nevertheless they considered Dallas's nomination to be a bad political joke played on the American public. The *National Intelligencer* judged Dallas an average politician, a lawyer with fair talents, and fit company for Polk on the Democratic ticket. Dallas was the "chosen victim" to run with the Tennessean solely because of their identical views on Texas annexation. The *New York Tribune* was equally confident that Clay would be victorious in November. It regarded Polk as a "third-rate partizan" and "a buffoon." Dallas was denounced as "a very Jacobinic, loose-principled, Texas Locofoco." Since Wright declined the nomination, some Whigs were guessing that Dallas might also. But the *Tribune* said, "Dallas is not too large to run so—he *must* run. If the Locos can't make him stand, the Whigs must send a Committee and train him. We are not to be cheated out of a contest." The Whigs were delighted with the Democratic ticket. Polk was a mystery to some elements of his own party, and Dallas was a lackluster partisan who had voted more like a Whig than a Democrat in his one brief term in the Senate. How could the Whigs lose?[13]

Dallas reacted to his own nomination with both amazement and indifference. He told Henry Muhlenberg that the convention's action took him totally by surprise, "but the compliment came in a shape that could not be repulsed." Had it involved an unkindness to Van Buren, Calhoun, Cass, Buchanan, or Johnson, he might have declined. Dallas said he had been too happy during the past five years in private life to entertain the smallest wish to be transformed into a public official. He was not wealthy and was surrounded by such a large family that he could not indulge ambition without second thoughts. Dallas repeated these sentiments in a letter to Van Buren in which he thanked him for the support of his forces at the convention. He wrote the Little Magician of his reluctance to engage in public life, which was founded "upon dictates of domestic prudence." Late in June Dallas confided to Thomas Ritchie, the father of the Virginia Democracy, "Personally, I assure you, I would prefer being permitted to stay at home and make hay at the bar, while the sun shines, but having put by foot on the ice, I can't help hoping that it may be strong enough to bear me." Dallas ran for the vice-presidency because he loved politics—and certainly he possessed some personal ambition, particularly in the state Democracy—but primarily he ran because of loyalty to his party and his country. He told a number of people, including Polk, that if he ever at any time and owing to any cause, just or unjust, became a burden to the presidential nominee "pray cut me loose instantly and resolutely. Personally I have not the slightest wish to quit the pursuits of private life." Dallas undoubtedly realized that he was being used by his party. He had not been chosen for his political record or his abilities but because he happened to agree with Polk on the major national issue of the day—Texas—and because he came from Pennsylvania. He was willing to jeopardize his practice and comfortable family life in a contest in which the Democracy's chances were, at best, slim. Dallas recognized the political feebleness of the vice-presidency, but he was willing to endure it for the good of the party. He described his position to Polk as "a bobtail annexed to the great kite." Yet Dallas was hardly, as Sidney George Fisher characterized him, just a "reckless partizan."[14]

The campaign of 1844 focused upon issues as much as personalities. While character assassination was prominent in the party press of the nineteenth century, the bank, Texas, and the tariff were problems that had to be discussed or properly evaded. Naturally, the importance of each of these varied in every state or section of the country, but Dallas, in trying to capture Pennsylvania for the Democracy, was forced to deal with all three.

The bank issue always came back to haunt Dallas. The Whig press continually pointed to the fact that he had sponsored and spoken for the recharter of the Second Bank of the United States in 1832. Dallas tried to minimize the significance of his stand by insisting that he had supported the bank only in deference to instructions from the Pennsylvania legislature. The Whigs countered by quoting directly from his instructions in 1832, which were less rigid than Dallas claimed. If the opposition papers did not attack him for his disloyalty to Jacksonian principles, they did try to make an issue of the Bradford Committee letter of 1836. Also referred to as the "Draco Letter," it provided ammunition for the contention that Dallas's anti-bank views were unrepublican as well as unconstitutional.[15]

Certainly the bank was an important issue in the election in Pennsylvania. The Democratic platform declared opposition to the institution on the grounds that it was unconstitutional and inexpedient. The party aroused many people by claiming that the Whigs desired to recharter the "Monster" as a method of regaining economic and political control of the nation and the state. The primary problem remained, however, to convince the Democrats that their vice-presidential candidate was not pro-bank. Dallas received numerous letters throughout the summer of 1844 asking for information on his position vis-à-vis rechartering a new bank. He replied that he was opposed to a third bank; he had supported the Biddle bank because he had a "representative obligation to obey the instructions from his legislature." When these responsibilities ended he adopted a position "decidedly and openly hostile to the Bank." Dallas told an inquirer, "The principles and policies of Andrew Jackson are of more value to the United States than the Bank in its purest form." There is no way to discern how successful such rhetoric was in convincing doubting Jacksonians that Dallas was a sincere opponent of the bank. Quite probably, his energetic and positive stand on the issues of the tariff and Texas offset their fears.[16]

The Democratic Convention, held in Baltimore in May of 1844, had selected Dallas for the second spot on the ticket because, like Polk, he favored annexation of Texas. Months before Dallas stepped onto his porch on 31 May to exhort a crowd in favor of "Polk, Texas, and Oregon," he had made his position clear as a member of the expansionist coterie headed by Senator Walker of Mississippi. The close relationship between them proved to be extremely valuable in swinging elements of the Pennsylvania Democracy to the side of annexation. Through Dallas the *Philadelphia Pennsylvanian,* the leading Van Buren organ in the state, was persuaded to espouse the cause. Dallas was probably influential in recruiting Philadelphia aristocrat Charles J. Ingersoll, chairman of the House Committee on Foreign Affairs, for the Texas clique. William Wilkins, secretary of war in Tyler's cabinet, was also brought into the fold by his brother-in-law Dallas.

Texas annexation, however, did not seem to have been a crucial issue to the people of Pennsylvania. The press of both parties gave it considerable attention, but the critical problem for Pennsylvania and Dallas during the campaign of 1844 was the protective tariff. In dealing with it, Dallas was to make his greatest contribution and ultimately his greatest sacrifice.[17]

Nobody was in doubt about where he stood, but Polk's record was ambiguous and Dallas had to make the most of it. As a southern congressman, Polk had voted against the high Tariff of Abominations of 1828 and for the reduced rates of 1832. He would have preferred to hide behind the murky tariff plank of the Democratic platform of 1844, "which meant everything to everybody," but evasion was a perilous tactic in Pennsylvania, as even an outsider like Senator Walker recognized on the eve of the campaign. Instructing the candidate about the facts of political life, Walker reminded the Tennessean that he would have to represent the Union and therefore would be obliged to stretch his principles far enough to endorse "incidental protection." Walker conceded that such a stand would be unpopular in the South but mandatory in Pennsylvania, where the inroads of a recent depression had made a protectionist policy even more popular. He discounted the risk by arguing that Polk's enthusiasm for Texas would more than counterbalance any losses that he might sustain below the Mason-Dixon Line because of his equivocation on the tariff.[18]

Dallas, if not Polk, knew that Walker was right, and his conviction was reinforced by the agitation for a statement about protection on the morrow of the convention. Henry Muhlenberg was but one of the correspondents reminding Dallas that there was almost universal sentiment for the tariff in Pennsylvania. Dallas relayed the information to Polk through Andrew Jackson Donelson. Donelson spoke plainly, reminding the candidate that a lobby would be organized against him on the tariff and urging him to give the enemy "no advantage which can be avoided." He went on to say that success is certain "if your ground on the tariff is wisely chosen. Do not be in a hurry in taking it." Polk got the same advice directly from Pennsylvania Democrats. A Harrisburg correspondent warned Polk, "Much will depend . . . on the position you can occupy on the tariff question. This is the only question that can give us any trouble in the state." Another demanded an explicit pledge in behalf of a *revenue tariff,* "so adjusted as to afford protection to our iron, coal, and manufacturing."[19]

Polk had always favored reducing the duties, but he had never gone on record against the tariff per se. Although this prudence facilitated a rapprochement with the high-tariff Pennsylvanians, Dallas and others demanded a statement from the candidate. Polk finally yielded on 19 June. His pronouncement took the form of a letter to John K. Kane, a Philadelphia associate of Dallas. In it, Polk opposed tariff for protection only, but he endorsed discriminatory duties that would produce needed revenue and at the same time offer reasonable shelter for home industries. Polk added a cover letter to Kane, in which he expressed misgivings about publicizing his views "unless . . . absolutely necessary." "Young Hickory" later wrote to Dallas informing him that he would issue no more public letters, or make any public appearance whatever: "It will comport best with propriety and the dignity of my position to remain quietly at home." It would also avoid further controversy. After additional thought, Polk ordered Kane on 2 July to withhold the tariff letter entirely, but the Democrats had already published it alongside a Henry Clay letter that indicated a similar position. The Pennsylvanians were relieved and happy over Polk's statement. Upon reading the nominee's opinions Dallas immediately wrote him to express his satisfaction: "I think your doctrine on the tariff will impair your strength here very little if at all, and perhaps it is the matter on which brevity would be the soul of wit." After the letter's publication Dallas reported its success to Polk: "The Democracy of Pennsylvania has never been so united and cordial. . . . Your Tariff letter has proven to be exactly what I predicted . . . and has given entire satisfaction." The middle-of-the-road policy would serve its purpose. Polk was proclaimed throughout Pennsylvania and the Northeast as a friend of protection.[20]

His statement came none too soon to counter the propaganda of the Whigs. Their press made earnest efforts to emphasize the divergent positions of Clay and Polk, to the detriment of the latter. The *Pennsylvania Telegraph* quoted from the lengthy Polk speech against the protective system in 1832 and dubbed the candidate a "free trader." The *New York Tribune* printed portions of a pamphlet published by Polk in 1843 in his unsuccessful campaign for governor of Tennessee. His most damaging statement was that he did not regard the high tariff of 1842 to be a revenue measure but "highly protective and oppressive in its character." He went on to endorse the lower rates of the Compromise Act of 1833, which Dallas had vociferously opposed in the Senate. On other issues, such as the bank, land distribution, and internal improvements, Dallas had such a Whiglike record that the opposition focused upon Polk as the major recipient of their literary barbs.[21]

The Democrats of Pennsylvania were not listening to—or even reading—the embarrassing Whig exposé of Polk's tariff record. The Jacksonian press flooded the state with reprints of the Kane letter, challenging "the most skillful logicians to point out a shade of difference" between Clay and Polk on protection. The *Harrisburg Democratic Union* cited the votes of Democratic senators and representatives to prove they were the true friends of the protective tariff of 1842. It chided Clay for being absent at the time of the crucial role call and charged the Whigs with efforts to make the bill more objectionable to President Tyler. Democratic editors also repeatedly singled out Polk as a "special friend" of the coal and iron interests; and they also warned the voters to "beware of Federal lies," forecasting scare stories on the eve of the election, to the effect that "Mr. Polk is dead, has declared himself opposed to the tariff, or has done some other horrible thing."[22] Whether these transparently partisan claims changed many votes is uncertain, but they kept the morale of the faithful high throughout the campaign.

The Democrats encountered a number of severe internal and external problems in 1844 that threatened their chances for victory. The pro-Van Buren–pro-Benton *Washington Globe,* edited by Francis P. Blair, was laggard in supporting the ticket and was actually promoting disunity in its columns. A Maryland correspondent informed Dallas in June that the recalcitrance of the *Globe*—which was obviously a continuance of the bitter Van Buren experience at the convention—was working in behalf of the Whig cause. The Philadelphian complained to Polk about the paper's policies and the reluctance in some quarters of the party openly to back the nominees. Dallas considered the attitudes of Buchanan, Cass, and Van Buren (who had urged his friends to remain loyal) to be correct and proper. However, the same could not be said for Benton and Wright. Dallas feared the potentially serious consequences in New York. These two were disgruntled because they believed the Baltimore nominations were a conspiracy against their favorite and that the results were successful treason to the principles and practices of the Democracy. Dallas urged Polk to ponder how he would handle these rebels, before and after the election. The feud assumed a more personal nature by October, when Van Buren heard rumors that Dallas had insulted both Van Buren and Wright. Henry Gilpin wrote twice to the Little Magician in an attempt to explain that Dallas had been misquoted and that he personally denied having said anything against the New Yorkers. Gilpin claimed that certain disappointed men were trying to portray Van Buren's friends and supporters as anti-Polk and Dallas. Gilpin was shocked at the intrigues that had begun at the Baltimore gathering and were still disrupting the Democracy in the fall. He fretted about what he regarded as the complacency at the top of the ticket: "I do not think that these things have made any impression on Mr. Dallas, he knows the world too well, he knows . . . the real ferocity of the men around him." Ultimately the rebellious Democrats fell into line. By September Dallas had reported to Polk that New York was safe for the Democracy, in large part because of "the recent and most effective exertions of Mr. Wright."[23]

The Democrats faced a more serious problem in Pennsylvania, or at least it seemed so to Dallas. Anti-immigrant political forces were powerful in his own area of Philadelphia and in southeastern Pennsylvania as well. Thus caution was called for when he received letters in the summer of 1844 from groups of German Democrats soliciting his views on immigration. The fact that Dallas received a kindred query from a committee of naturalized New York citizens made him suspicious that the Whigs were trying to force him into a stand that would offend either the nativists or the foreign born. The issue was especially difficult in Philadelphia, a city containing a large number of immigrants. Dallas told Polk that he would say nothing on the topic of nativism unless the Tennessean approved. If forced to make a statement, Dallas said he would attack the nativists as "misled by ignorant or angry passions or by a baser impulse of proscriptive bigotry." The Philadelphian was very concerned about a coalition of Whigs and nativists in his city, which could defeat the local Democrats and cut into party strength elsewhere in the Northeast. He distrusted the abolitionists for the same reason and expected them to work hand in glove with the Clay forces.[24] He had expressed these fears, which were later published by the *Richmond Enquirer,* to John Willis, a representative to the Virginia convention in 1840. Dallas felt the election of General Harrison would open the door for the abolitionists, whom he strenuously opposed because they sought unconstitutionally to violate the rights and domestic institutions of the southern states. At that time Dallas claimed abolitionists were the "ruling cabal" and the "master spirits" of the Whig Party and "the Presidential candidate is notoriously their nominee." The motive for Dallas's letter was undoubtedly political, but he certainly believed his own rhetoric. He hoped to frighten the slave-holding Virginians into remaining firm for Van Buren so as to halt the "threat of abolitionism." It was the Keystone State, however, not the Old Dominion, that failed the New Yorker in 1840. Again in 1844 Dallas cried out against such a coalition. This time he predicted a union of abolitionists and nativists that would merge with the Whigs in the East and North before the 4 March 1845 inauguration. The common designation of this combination would be the Liberty Party. "It is their inevitable tendency and termination," Dallas said. The increase in the number of abolitionists had outstripped his apprehensions and the fanatic hostility to papal power by the nativists had grown immeasurably since 1840. When an alliance was formed among them, they could use the Whig Party as a vehicle to their purposes. Dallas hesitated to admit it publicly in 1844, but he was at least a fellow-traveler in his anti-Catholicism. As far back as 1823 Dallas had been in the vanguard of the movement within the Democratic Party that had warned of the power of Rome in local elections. Dallas had later turned his pen to the subject when he questioned whether a Catholic cross would ever adorn the steeple of St. Peter's (Episcopal) Church:

> It is not fit—we may not dare
> This altar to deform
> By mingling arts of popish glare
> With Protestant reform
> Our fathers struggled long to make
> Their worship pure and plain
> Let Rome retain—we must not take
> Its gaudy garb again.

Dallas warned Polk that while the Democracy would still win in November, the president would have to face a potential confederacy on issues like Texas, naturalization laws, and slavery in the near future. The Pennsylvanian encouraged Polk to placate southern Democrats on the tariff, so that both wings of the party might unite to deal with what he considered to be the greater danger of abolitionism. Dallas viewed its proponents as fanatics and a threat to the Constitution and urged the Tennessean to "postpone the tariff question until the country is secured against the alarming strides of abolition." On 8 October Dallas cautioned Polk that abolitionism was a great issue in the 1844 race. If the South went Whig, the northern Democrats would be alienated. If the South went Democratic the abolitionists would rapidly lose momentum and disappear. In his letter to Polk Dallas stated that "in very truth, the great question of union and disunion is at issue, though not in the shape it is put by some hot partizans in South Carolina."[25]

Dallas never doubted that Pennsylvania would vote Democratic in November, although he showed concern over the possible narrow margin of victory. He was equally confident of the party's chances in the gubernatorial contest in October, although this election caused the Democracy some difficulty when poor Henry Muhlenberg, on the eve of his sure election as governor, died of apoplexy. Dallas did not think, however, that his death would hurt the Jacksonian cause against Whig candidate Joseph Markle. The state leaders immediately recalled the convention and on 3 September in Harrisburg selected Muhlenberg's old rival, Francis R. Shunk of Pittsburgh, the secretary of the Commonwealth and a leading political strategist in the Porter administration. Dallas commented to Polk that although he liked

Muhlenberg, he felt Shunk would be a stronger candidate. Whatever the comparative strengths of the two men, the important fact was that Shunk triumphed in the 8 October election. His margin of victory, however, was only 4,000 votes out of 316,000 votes cast. Philadelphia, led by the anti-Catholic, anti-immigrant Native American Party, went heavily Whig because Shunk had been identified with the Catholic interests. The coalition of nativists and Whigs created a "Waterloo of defeat to the Democrats" in the Philadelphia congressional elections. The alliance swept all but the fourth district—held by Charles J. Ingersoll—in destroying the Democracy. However, across the Commonwealth five more Democrats were added to Congress and the state legislature gained about twenty Jacksonians. Thus Dallas declared in mid-October that the Whigs had been shaken by their statewide defeats, and he predicted that Polk would do well in Pennsylvania—except for his demoralized county—emerging with a plurality of 1,000 votes.[26]

In the first week of November Americans went to the polls to select a president. Dallas wrote to Polk each day, reflecting his nervousness in fluctuating voting estimates, but also emphasizing unflinching confidence in their eventual triumph. On 6 November Dallas received word that New York City and the state of Virginia had voted Democratic. The overjoyed and optimistic Philadelphian exclaimed, "Are we still to invoke our philosophy to be prepared for defeat? Not a jot of it!" But the cautious Tennessean was not quite as certain of his home state. Aware of the strength of the Whigs, Polk warned, "I think our chances to carry the state are best, but in so close a contest . . . there must still be doubt." He feared, too, for Pennsylvania, noting, "you may have been overwhelmed by the many and the corrupt means . . . which have been employed by your unscrupulous adversaries." Tennessee fell to the enemy, but the Keystone State held. When the final ballots were tabulated, the Polk-Dallas ticket enjoyed a solid electoral lead (170 to 105), capturing fifteen states to eleven for the Clay-Freylinghuysen slate, although the Democrats' popular-vote margin was only 37,000 out of 2.7 million votes cast. Democratic strength was prevalent in the West and Southwest, while the Whigs were strong in New England and parts of the old South. Polk's victory in New York and Pennsylvania was the key to his success. His margin in the Keystone decision was as narrow as the national one: 6,382 out of a total of 328,000 votes. He lost both Pittsburgh and Philadelphia decisively. Party divisions in the rural counties formed no discernible patterns, nor did they justify the claim that the legendary Jacksonian agrarians elected Polk. Counties that

voted for Van Buren in 1836 voted for Polk in 1844, with little deviation. Whig balloting was likewise similar in both elections. Apparently
the addition of Dallas to the ticket made little difference in terms of
the number of voters who turned out in Pennsylvania, although it is
impossible to judge the state and national effects of his views on the
tariff and Texas.[27]

The Whigs were extremely bitter over their defeat in Pennsylvania.
The *National Intelligencer* commented, "These returns clearly indicate, we think that the state has studied her interests so well as to
have given her vote for a man directly and inveterately opposed to
them—a species of political wisdom for which Pennsylvania has distinguished herself on former occasions." The Democrats were of
course elated and declared that the victory had "settled forever" the
questions of a national bank and land distribution, and that it provided a mandate for the United States to "re-annex" Texas and "re-
occupy" all of Oregon up to 54°40'. There was no mention of the
tariff. The *Philadelphia North American,* a nativist paper that was
anti-Texas and pro-tariff, did not ignore the protection issue. The
paper claimed that the state had been "swindled by a cabal of as
desperate demagogues as ever clutched the public purse." The Democracy had lied to the people of the Commonwealth by arguing that
a free trader was a protectionist. The editors predicted that soon
Pennsylvania and the state Democracy would regret that they had
supported the banner of "James K. Polk and the Tariff of 1842."[28]

George M. Dallas was now vice-president-elect of the United
States. As he prepared for his departure from Philadelphia in the
winter of 1844/45, Dallas must have given serious thought to the problems facing him as presiding officer of the Senate and to the future of
his party and the nation. The tariff, Texas, Oregon, and a restructur-
ing of the Democracy were all pressing problems that the new administration would encounter in the next four years. Polk had pledged
himself to one term in office. Thus Dallas's actions in Washington,
and the power he could gain and assert as vice-president on state and
national leaders, might place him in a prominent position as one of the
dominant figures of a new Democracy.

6

Vice-President:
Patronage and Protection
(1845–1846)

The first two years of the Polk administration were extremely significant for the nation and for the political career of Vice-President George M. Dallas. During this period Dallas began to think about the presidency and, displaying unusual ambition, made conscious efforts toward reaching the White House. To attain this end, he had to defeat the challenge of Pennsylvania's other factional leader, James Buchanan. Dallas also had to solidify and expand his position in his native state, since he was strong only in the urban eastern half. Therefore, he could not afford to alienate the voters on any issue—such as the tariff—crucial to the state's interests. Ultimately Dallas failed to win control of the Pennsylvania Democracy or to rally the support of the general populace to his side by positive national action. The events of 1845–46 forever doomed Dallas's chances of attaining the presidency.

The president-elect was an unknown quantity to many members of his party, including the vice-president-elect. Dallas hoped, however, to become a powerful influence in the Polk administration. He implemented his strategy early in order to reach his goal. In mid-November he wrote to the Tennessean encouraging him to stop in Philadelphia for a few days on his way to Washington for the inauguration. This would give the two men an opportunity to become acquainted, as well as present Dallas with a chance to express his feelings on a number of political matters. The Philadelphian was already thinking about the cabinet selections and urged Polk to dismiss Tyler's men, even though they might be good Democrats. A fresh start had to be made, beginning with Polk's cabinet. Although Dallas firmly believed every-one in the present cabinet should be released, he was particularly adamant about John C. Calhoun, the secretary of state. Calhoun might do endless mischief in the administration. He was the head of his own political faction, a free trader, and had erred in his diplomacy (presumably over the defeat of the Texas annexation treaty). Dallas suggested that Calhoun be replaced by the energetic Robert John Walker of Mississippi. He also listed C. C. Cambreleng or William Marcy of New York for the Treasury; Andrew Stevenson of Virginia for the Navy; Ralph Ingersoll of Connecticut for attorney general; and "a Pennsylvania man" (Dallas would submit names if requested) for the Post Office. He had no preference for the War Department.[1]

The election of Dallas was a hard blow for the Buchanan faction, but they did recover, and in an attempt to checkmate the Philadel-phian they began to promote Old Buck for the cabinet. Buchanan launched an early campaign for the State Department by having the Pennsylvania electors recommend him at the same time they cast their ballots for the president. Dallas responded angrily to this action by his fellow citizens. He wrote to Walker, "A more grotesque and humiliating movement could not well be made." A meeting was held in Philadelphia to denounce the electors "for their precipitous inter-meddling," but Dallas urged Henry Horn to attend it and attempt to prevent further disunity. To Walker, the vice-president-elect ex-pressed a strong and realistic outlook:

> I have become Vice President willy-nilly, and anticipate the ne-cessity of enduring heavy and painful and protracted sacrifices, as the consequence. Well!—I am not, in the bargain, disposed to be considered a cypher! on the contrary, I am resolved that no one shall be taken from Pennsylvania in a cabinet office who is notori-ously hostile to the Vice President. If such a choice be made, my relations with the administration are at once at an end.

Dallas adopted this resolute attitude because he was well aware that he was involved in a political life-and-death struggle for the presiden-tial nomination in 1848. Dallas believed the Pennsylvania Democracy would never be content to have as its exclusive representative and candidate "the distinguished gentleman so prematurely and arro-gantly foisted upon Mr. Polk." The vice-president-elect had high hopes that his "upright, sagacious firm and true-hearted" chief would make the right appointment to the State Department; and that, of course, would be Walker.[2]

On 13 February Polk met Dallas a few miles west of Baltimore at the Relay House, where the Cumberland line joined the Baltimore-Washington Railroad. Dallas took advantage of the train ride to the capital to make his sentiments on the cabinet known. Once in the city the Philadelphian "hung to the President-elect like a leech," staying at the same hotel and constantly reminding him of the dangers of Buchanan's influence. Walker, in contrast to his Uncle (by marriage) George, was not particularly concerned about Buchanan's challenge. In late January the Mississippian had informed Dallas that he expected Calhoun to be retained in the State Department temporarily, and perhaps for the entire term. Therefore he was following the advice of his friends and competing for the Treasury Department, where he felt he could deal with the problems of currency and the tariff. He had urged Dallas to hurry to Washington to aid him in his fight.

When Dallas arrived, he quickly entered the fray in Walker's behalf, but he apparently still had the State Department in mind. After a week in Washington Dallas remained confident that "Mr. Polk will meet the expectations of the country and his friends." But, he noted, "One false step may do permanent mischief." On 20 February, however, Dallas confided to Sophy that matters were not proceeding as well as he had desired. There were "symptoms" that he did not like. Nevertheless, the results were uncertain and he continued to hope for the best. The situation rapidly unfolded within the next few days. On 21 February Dallas commented that "external indications all point to the appointment of Buchanan as Secretary of State." His disappointment in Polk was reflected in the same letter, which evidenced misgivings about the quality and quantity of resolution and judgment of the president-elect. By 23 February news of Buchanan's selection had been made public. Dallas deemed it "a most dangerous choice." Dallas found the remainder of Polk's nominees to be right and proper, but he predicted that the secretary of state would involve the Tennessean in great difficulties. Dallas feared strong discord within the party, which could have been avoided by putting Walker in the State Department and appointing a Calhoun man from Virginia attorney general.[3]

Dallas had previously pledged to Walker that he would divorce himself from the administration if Polk appointed an anti-Dallas man to the cabinet. He had done so with the selection of Buchanan. Rather than resign or sulk, however, the Philadelphian redoubled his efforts to secure a post for Walker and thus neutralize Buchanan. The Mississippian enlisted the aid of the unscrupulous Simon Cameron, who had his sights set on Old Buck's Senate seat, to help him win the

Treasury. Walker had been offered the attorney generalship, but on the advice of Dallas and others had refused it. He would now accept the Treasury Department or he would remain in the Senate. Walker had the support of the South and the Cass men in the Northwest, as well as Dallas's Pennsylvanians. By early March Polk realized that he had thoroughly irritated his vice-president and to placate him—and the deep South—Walker would have to be appointed. His selection was a balm to the wounded Dallas men. It was not as much as they had hoped for, but they were generally satisfied. In many other areas there was disgruntlement over Walker. Andrew Jackson regretted Polk's choice. Old Hickory felt the Mississippian had talent and was honest, but that he was surrounded by too many debts and broken speculators to be a good secretary of the treasury. He also pointed out that Walker was aligned with Dallas (whose group was the "real old Democratic party of Pennsylvania"), and friction between them and Buchanan was likely to develop. There were also those Democrats, some in the cabinet itself, who merely felt Walker was "a weak link."[4]

In the first week of March Polk completed the formation of his cabinet and made the list public. The treasury post was given to the loyal Walker, while a fellow Tennessean, Cave Johnson, was appointed postmaster general. Polk's desire for a balanced cabinet was reflected in the appointments of Buchanan and Marcy to the State and War departments, respectively, George Bancroft of Massachusetts to the Department of the Navy, and John Young Mason of Virginia as attorney general. The president never left any doubt as to who would run the administration. When he offered Buchanan the top position in the State Department he told him, "I desire to select men who agree with me and who will cordially cooperate with me in carrying out my principles and policy." Polk reiterated his determination to be master by insisting that any cabinet officer who became active in the presidential race would immediately resign.

President Polk had carefully chosen his cabinet for geographical and political reasons. Mason and Johnson were personal friends of his. Bancroft was from New England and had led the movement to introduce Polk's name to the Baltimore convention. Marcy was a special problem. He was an old Jacksonian and a member of the economically and politically conservative "Hunker" faction in New York, which was anti-Van Buren. Empire State politics evidenced deep divisions, and the selection of Marcy alienated many Van Burenites, who felt the president had sold out to Buchanan, Cass, and Walker. Polk was certainly not to blame for this loss of support. Soon after his election the president, who generally kept his own counsel, determined that Silas Wright would be offered the Treasury—"the most important of departments." Wright was still governor of New York, however, and was reluctant to sacrifice his position. Whether residual bitterness from the 1844 convention entered into Polk's calculations is impossible to ascertain. Nor can we be certain whether he realized the governor would refuse his offer and merely made it to free him from any pledges to select a Van Buren man. Whatever his motives, Polk's strategy was unsuccessful and the selection of a loyal "Hunker" only further alienated the already disaffected more liberal, often anti-slave New York "Barnburners."

The choice of Buchanan was the result of a similar factional dispute. Dallas's nomination as vice-president made it wise for Polk to name the leader of the other state faction as a cabinet member. The Tennessean would not make the mistake Van Buren had made and omit a Pennsylvanian from his staff of advisors. While the selection of Buchanan met with expected hostility from the Dallas men (many of whom were Van Burenites), it also was opposed by Jackson, who had never trusted Old Buck. Nevertheless, Polk had made his choice and it would stand. He had intended that his cabinet would serve both as loyal advisors and servants, even though some were selected to reward members of other factions for their support. The president was wrong in both instances. He chose talented but ambitious men, some of whom were to disrupt the party and his administration. In seeking to satisfy the political needs of the Democracy on issues such as patronage, he had only heightened the existing tensions and frictions. Pennsylvania was a prime example.[5]

The inauguration of George M. Dallas on that rainy 4 March 1845 only formalized a struggle for state power and patronage that had existed for months. Since the election both Dallas and Buchanan had been besieged by office-seekers who thirsted for power after a four-year political drought. The president by his cabinet appointments had seriously confused the patronage problem. Pennsylvania was represented in Washington by the Dallas-Walker and Buchanan factions. New York was also divided between the "in" Hunkers, who controlled the state (represented by Marcy), and the "out" Barnburners (represented by no one), led by Van Buren and Wright. It was mandatory that Polk placate all these factions, so that these states would be secure for the Democracy. Distrust was rampant as the factions struggled with each other and the president in an effort to gain the federal patronage and state domination. Party unity was of course shattered in these two states. Buchanan reported to Governor Francis Shunk that "Philadelphia is now in a state of office-hunting excitement never before known." Every Democrat had the idea that the vice-president could procure for them all the offices they desired. Dallas's primary problem was to respond to the demands of the Philadelphia Jacksonians, whom he was supposed to represent. If he could not meet their political demands, they would most likely desert him for someone else who could, such as James Buchanan. Dallas did not enjoy the patronage game. It wearied and frustrated him, but he realized the necessity of playing if he wanted to maintain and expand his presidential chances.[6]

The patronage feud in Pennsylvania was further complicated by the election of a successor to replace James Buchanan in the Senate. In March the Democratic caucus selected George Woodward, an eminent, well-qualified judge from Wilkes-Barre, but rebellious Simon Cameron refused to accept this verdict. He garnered enough support from the Whigs in the state legislature to get himself elected. This action outraged the state party and was a blow to Buchanan, Dallas, and the administration. Infuriated Democrats across the Commonwealth wrote to Dallas and Buchanan urging them to aid in condemning Cameron's revolt and to pressure him out of the party. Dallas was in a difficult position as presiding officer of the Senate. He tactfully responded to the committee that had requested his censure of Cameron by saying that he frowned on such a breach of party loyalty. He agreed with the committee in principle, but as vice-president he felt he could not overstep the bounds of propriety and had to remain "a free and fair public functionary." Nevertheless, Dallas added, "such principles of double-dealing and craft do not belong in the Democratic Party." The ever-cautious Buchanan replied to the same committee on 31 March in a more reserved manner. He refused to censure Cameron and carefully avoided criticism of the legislature. Buchanan thought that any further action in the matter would only cause more dissension. Dallas's supporters were somewhat more critical of Buchanan's attitude. John K. Kane told Dallas that the selection of Cameron, an early Buchanan backer, would give the secretary of state "no pangs"; that Buchanan might resent the manner in which the opportunistic Cameron attained office, but it was doubtful if he opposed his presence there. Cameron's election, however, added a new dimension to the patronage scramble and provided further evidence of the chaotic state of the Pennsylvania Democracy.[7]

With the battle lines drawn, the patronage struggle began in earnest in March 1845. Buchanan, aligned with Governor Shunk, dueled with Dallas, supported by the Philadelphia Jacksonians (Horn, Gilpin, and

Kane) and Congressman Andrew Beaumont from northern Pennsylvania. Cameron was not in a competitive position and accepted what he could get from any source. One prize political plum still to be won was the collectorship of Philadelphia. Dallas backed his old friend Richard Rush, Buchanan supported George F. Lehman, and Shunk favored Henry Welsh (also a friend of Buchanan), while Henry Horn and party veteran Hendrick B. Wright staged their own campaigns. Polk's first choice was Horn, but Buchanan opposed him and the president yielded. Dallas acted as an intermediary and spoke with Horn, who said he would gracefully bow out of the competition with the promise of perhaps the treasurership of the Philadelphia Mint, if someone politically trustworthy received the collectorship. In the middle of the quarrel came Cameron's election to the Senate. Buchanan's reluctance to criticize his conduct killed Lehman's chances for the collectorship and ingratiated Dallas and Horn with Polk. Meanwhile in Pennsylvania, the factional split widened when a Dallas meeting on the Oregon question was disrupted by Buchanan men. The administration was scandalized by this Philadelphia affair and the actions of the two factions in Washington. Polk tried to avoid further embarrassment to the party by compromising on patronage. Horn would get the collectorship, Welsh the Second Customs House, and Lehman the postmastership of Philadelphia. A neutral man would be selected as district attorney for Philadelphia.[8]

Polk's appointments angered everyone. Dallas was so furious that friendly intercourse ceased between him and the president. In August the Chief Executive tried to mollify his vice-president by apologizing for not writing to him recently. He said he would be gratified to confer with Dallas occasionally on matters of public affairs and that he could benefit from his experience and opinions. The president evoked old memories of their unexpected nominations, of similar political principles, and of Texas annexation. He told Dallas that he would replace the incumbent treasurer of the Philadelphia Mint with Richard Rush, if Dallas so desired. Polk placated him in his letter of 23 August 1845: "I would have been pleased to explain to you some of the circumstances attending the appointments at Philadelphia which were made some time ago, but no opportunity for that purpose has occurred. When I shall have the pleasure to see you I will do it." The flattery was somewhat overdone and Dallas was not to be cajoled by the acceptance of the last major Philadelphia patronage post. He coldly responded to Polk's letter on 3 September by refusing to comment on Rush, "in as much as you have not been able to gratify the few requests I have previously made."

Dallas's failures were also reflected in his hostility to Buchanan. The secretary of state had attempted to use his influence to have John M. Read of Philadelphia nominated to the Supreme Court. The vice-president immediately identified Read with the Buchanan faction and informed Walker of the political—although not personal—animosity between himself and Read. Walker was alert to this not-so-subtle hint and led the successful fight to have Read rejected. Buchanan responded in kind. When Henry Horn's nomination for collector of Philadelphia reached the Senate in the spring of 1846, Buchanan was instrumental in having it defeated. Horn was indignant at Dallas for not pushing it through. The extreme bitterness that resulted from this failure divided the Dallas faction and certainly did not increase the Philadelphian's chances for the presidency.[9]

By the summer of 1845 Dallas had been defeated in the patronage war. His loss was the result of a combination of intertwined factors: he commanded a small faction with a narrow geographical base; he was not influential with the state administration; his efforts to become a confidant of Polk's had failed; and he was typically unaggressive in seeking patronage posts. His friends urged him to act more forcefully with the president. They worried that Dallas was "too honorable and too trusting"; that he should "make war, play rough and trust no one." Such actions were not consistent with a Philadelphia gentleman who, while politically astute and active, considered patronage a dirty business to be settled quickly. He told Polk late in March that "the tariff and Oregon are both problems of extreme interest. I wish with all my heart that you were quit of the perplexities of choosing men and had got into the wise and noble field of measures." This attitude quickly led Dallas into boredom and disillusionment regarding the patronage issue. He resented the fact that his nominees were challenged and that the problem had dragged on into the next year. It is no surprise that the more persistent and politically hardened Buchanan emerged victorious. Early in March Henry Simpson explained the plight of a Philadelphia Van Buren–Dallas man in attempting to gain a post. Simpson felt that Polk had turned to Buchanan, his "Prime Minister," in an effort to destroy Dallas as a second-term rival. There was no doubt that Buchanan was "the reigning star of the administration."[10]

Buchanan's patronage triumph did not end the factional struggle in Pennsylvania. Men continued to change sides, depending upon who could procure them an office. In Philadelphia a running battle was launched between Robert Vaux of the *Keystone,* representing Dallas, and John Forney of the *Pennsylvanian,* for Buchanan. The *Keystone* expressed Dallas's disillusionment with the administration in June

1845, in an article dissociating him from the president, the cabinet, and all the measures they formulated. Forney judged that this "sensational" article was evidence that Dallas, who was "below mediocre as a public man," had soured on both Polk and Buchanan and was trying to revenge himself in this way. Perhaps the vice-president would have found some consolation had he known Polk was equally upset over the patronage problem and factionalism within the party. In addition to alienating Dallas, Buchanan had made an enemy of William Marcy through his attempts to gain support from certain Van Burenites. By October 1846 Polk admitted that he had given too many appointments to his secretary of state and that this had resulted in trouble in Pennsylvania and New York. He conceded, "I am now satisfied that I ought not to have done so, and that my administration was greatly weakened by it." Polk would later regret that he lost a loyal Commonwealth congressman because of patronage priorities. David Wilmot of Bradford County would not forget this rebuff. The president realized his failure in the Keystone State and intimated to John S. Barbour of Virginia that he regarded Dallas and Buchanan as too feeble to injure others or help themselves. The patronage struggle did not help the president or the Democracy. Polk's attempts at equal justice for all factions met with failure. Indeed, Van Buren, Dallas, Buchanan, Marcy, and Calhoun had been disappointed by his policies at one time or another. The vice-president hoped to escape this situation by occupying himself with the Senate and its committees, while Buchanan contemplated flight to the Supreme Court.[11]

Dallas avoided some of the patronage quarrels by dedicating himself to the settlement of congressional problems. Whenever a new party succeeded to the control of the White House and the Senate in the same year, as it did in 1845, the Senate met in two sessions. One extra session gathered briefly in March to inaugurate the president; the second, the regular session, met in December. Usually the March session did not legislate (the House was absent) but concerned itself with executive affairs, such as approval of cabinet nominations. Standing committees were therefore not selected. The December session set up these committees, acting through a president pro tempore elected by the majority party. The vice-president was an outsider and rarely took part in these proceedings.

In 1845 the old traditions were broken. The Democracy was shattered into factions on the basis of sections, leaders, and issues. Some of the divisiveness was the result of the Baltimore convention, but new issues, such as the settlement of the Oregon question, also splintered the party. At the March Senate session the Democratic majority leaders decided to select standing committees and keep the vice-president in the chair in order that no president pro tempore could be chosen. One of the major concerns of the administration leaders was that solidly pro-Oregon men should control the important Foreign Relations Committee. Dallas, an avowed 54°40′ man, would name the members. His appointments of William Allen (Ohio Democrat) as chairman and Lewis Cass (Michigan Democrat) and Charles Atherton (New Hampshire Democrat) as associates fulfilled all their expectations. All three were extreme 54°40′ men and would dominate the five-man committee. This of course was totally out of proportion to their true strength in the Senate. Nevertheless, this committee and others, which served for only ten days, endowed the extremists with committee seniority for the regular session.

In December the Oregon men were prepared to repeat their achievements of March. Dallas steadied himself for the battle, but he noted that the administration leaders would resort to these tactics because of the weakness of their position. He told his son Philip that "I just opened the Senate for a session which, as I anticipate, will be one of the most important, disturbed and protracted in the history of the country." Dallas was active in scouting for the administration before the session began. He tried to determine how archenemies Thomas Hart Benton, a powerful western Democrat, and John C. Calhoun, the leader of the southern Democrats, would approach the issue of committee appointments. By 1 December Dallas realized how bad the situation had become.[12]

On 4 December the administration men, bolstered by Polk's annual message urging the settlement of the Oregon question, made their move to allow Dallas to name the standing committees. Benton and his southern followers, Arthur Bagby (Alabama Democrat), William Haywood (North Carolina Democrat), and James Westcott (Florida Democrat) rebelled, joined the Whigs, and defeated the motion by a 21-to-20 vote. This was a great crisis for the administration. The Senate would now ballot for committees and there was a danger of having to work with disaffected or hostile committee chairmen. Dallas denounced the four rebel Democrats and declared they would "have to answer for it," claiming he was personally "indifferent—or rather relieved from responsibility which is sure to cause ill-feeling in some quarters." He then retired, leaving the chair to Senator Ambrose Sevier of Arkansas as president pro tempore. The western Democrats, who formed the majority of the extremists, summoned a caucus, which was an entirely new way of establishing standing committees. Allen and the other administration men appointed in March demanded their old positions on the basis of seniority and these slates were pushed through the Senate. Benton, Bagby, and Haywood refused to attend the caucus, however, when they selected Senate officers, secretary, sergeant-at-arms, and doorkeeper. The candidates for these patronage-bearing posts were defeated by a Benton-Whig coalition.[13]

By April 1846 it was evident that the Democratic Party was in factional shambles. After four months in session the only action taken by Congress had been the prompt admission of Texas. The president's four-point program, which he confided to Bancroft in December 1845, lay dormant: settlement of the Oregon question, establishment of a subtreasury, tariff reductions, and the acquisition of California. It appeared the administration had completely lost control of Congress. Dallas told Richard Rush:

> Parties are in a wretched condition in both houses of Congress and are likely to get worse and worse. It can hardly be said that the administration has a majority in the Representative chamber. In the Senate on all measures beyond mere form, it is in a decided minority. The Triumvirate of Benton, Calhoun and Webster—of men whose greatness has been achieved by hostility to each other—is too powerful to be resisted by Cass, Allen and Dix.

The party had been prostrated by the factional disputes over patronage and the Oregon issue. Dallas had served the administration well in the Senate, and the vice-president had taken advantage of every opportunity to ingratiate himself with the president. The vacancy on the Supreme Court offered him yet another chance.[14]

By the fall of 1845 it was only a matter of time before Polk's desire for tariff reductions would be transformed into a concrete proposal by Secretary of the Treasury Walker. In an effort to avoid the coming protection war Buchanan sought escape in a Supreme Court appointment. The court seat allotted to the middle states was vacant and the secretary of state asked the president in September for the appointment. Buchanan's friends unknowingly blamed Dallas and his allies for trying to remove Old Buck from power. For a variety of reasons, however, mainly focusing on Oregon, Buchanan decided to remain in the cabinet. He nominated John M. Read, an old Philadelphia Federalist, for the bench in his place. The anti-Buchanan men lined up behind Pittsburgh judge Robert C. Grier. Thus in December, while the two candidates for the court destroyed each other, Polk sought out his own man. Dallas had wisely remained aloof from this phase of the struggle and now he and Walker began cautiously to promote the selection of George Woodward. As Woodward had only recently been the caucus candidate Simon Cameron had defeated for the Senate, the appointment of Grier would be a rebuff to the Cameron-Buchanan element. On 23 December Polk sent Woodward's nomination to the Senate, without consulting his secretary of state. The following month a coalition of Whigs and dissident Democrats, led by Cameron, defeated the nomination. Buchanan was so outraged at the president's action that he considered resigning. Many Democrats were equally angered at the secretary for aiding in Woodward's defeat. Dallas felt the only thing that kept Buchanan in office was the critical posture of foreign relations.[15]

The Supreme Court confrontation aided in reconciling Dallas with the president. The alienation the Philadelphian had suffered over the patronage battles was now discounted, as Dallas superseded Buchanan temporarily in presidential confidence. Dallas wrote Richard Rush in December 1845, "My relations with the President are just now of the kindest and *most* confidential nature. How long to continue so I cannot venture to guess as the foible of instability on some matters is, I fear radical." These sentiments were repeated to Sophy that same month. John Forney reported Dallas's strong influence to Buchanan in February 1846.[16] Over the months, however, the vice-president had cautiously grown to regard Polk as "unstable" and daily expected to receive "the cold shoulder." Dallas said, "I shall not, however, give him the cause, and of course, if it occurs will care little about it." Thus he realized that although he might be in favor with the president at the moment, it was a tenuous relationship at best and one which could be sundered by the slightest incident. This flexibility in advisors that the president maintained frustrated and angered Dallas. Several times the Philadelphian was called to discuss "a most important communication" with Polk only to realize "the President . . . has the faculty of making mountains out of mole hills. I am heartily sick of factitious importance." In spite of this Dallas demonstrated unswerving loyalty to his chief and his party. After the patronage battle, unlike Buchanan, he took great pains not to agitate the president. His devotion never received a stronger test than in the debate over the tariff bill of 1846.[17]

George M. Dallas was an important man in the plans of the Polk administration in 1846. Senators loyal to the president were in the minority and the casting vote of the vice-president in the Senate could be crucial on a number of issues. Therefore, late in 1845 and early in

1846 Polk was careful to mollify Dallas and win his support, but without deliberately placing him in a position of power or authority within the administration. A good example of this can be found late in November 1845, when Polk wrote his annual message, which, most significantly for Pennsylvania, contained suggested reductions in the tariff. On 28 November the president confidentially called in Dallas and gave him a preview of the message. The vice-president was flattered: "You have made me very happy tonight," he told Polk, "I will go home and sleep sound." Dallas did not know that Thomas Ritchie was in another room and was being similarly cajoled that same evening. Although the Philadelphian was pleased with Polk's trust, he was understandably skeptical of the reactions of the Keystone State. He wrote to Sophy on 2 December, "The message has produced a strong sensation, but whether on the whole and durably, it will be a beneficial one remains in doubt. Our Pennsylvania men are struck with despair and I do not see how they are to survive the free trade batter which Walker will assail them with in his annual report tomorrow." Dallas made similar observations in a letter to Richard Rush on 4 December. He particularly feared the reactions of the coal and iron industry to the reductions.[18]

The McKay Bill was framed largely by Secretary of the Treasury Walker. It said that "no duty should be placed on any article above the rate which would produce the maximum revenue" and that *ad valorem* would replace specific duties. Polk considered the tariff the most important measure of his administration, but many Pennsylvania coal and iron businessmen thought it would mean the destruction of all home industry. Solid opposition to the proposed tariff quickly developed in the Commonwealth. While the national party organ, the *Washington Union,* launched its campaign against the tariff of 1842, most Democratic papers, such as the *Harrisburg Union,* defended it. The state legislature in the spring of 1846 urged the Pennsylvania representatives and senators in the capital to oppose the tariff reductions. Democratic committees and conventions throughout the state denounced this attempt to destroy the protective system.[19]

Action on the tariff measure was delayed in the spring of 1846 by problems over Texas and Oregon. Finally, on 14 April, Chairman James McKay reported the bill out of committee to the House. During the last two weeks of June it was earnestly debated in the committee of the whole. Keystone congressmen spoke loudly against the tariff, but they were in the minority when it was approved 114 to 95 on 3 July. The only Pennsylvanian to favor it was David Wilmot, the representative of an agricultural district, who felt the Tariff of 1842 was oppressive to American industry. On 6 July the Senate received the bill and promptly began two weeks of debate on it. Dallas's state was wholeheartedly opposed to the tariff, but the resolutions of the Baltimore convention, under which the vice-president was elected, and the Polk administration were committed to altering the tariff. If he remained loyal to his party and sacrificed his state's interests, he would be committing political suicide. Dallas was well aware of the situation in which he might be placed and he thought out his position clearly in case the undesirable occurred. On 3 July he wrote to his legal colleague, Henry Phillips, in Philadelphia, "I am determined whenever the casting vote is elicited that it shall conform as closely as I can make it to the resolutions of the Baltimore Convention. . . . I can not bear to falsify my promise to those who elected me as their representative." The convention had taken a strong stand favoring executive action, and the vice-president felt that in voluntarily assuming the duties of his office he could equate his casting vote power with that of the presidential veto. Dallas was committed by the convention's resolutions to represent the whole of the American people, as well as the executive branch of government. If the need arose to cast his vote, he would do so. He would study the situation daily, and if he judged that the nation and the party would benefit from a lower tariff, the Commonwealth would have to suffer. This stance was in exact accord with the position Richard Rush urged him to assume after the November election. At that time Rush advised:

> Pennsylvania politicians are small men. . . . You are not of their race and they left you. The *union* put you where you are, and can keep you there and do more. . . . Pennsylvania cannot lead, she can only follow and bellow. You cannot repudiate the state, you must love her openly, and your notion of elevating her in the scale of the union is noble, and may *begin* to come about five years hence, but at present the union is your element and platform.[20]

Dallas was under constant pressure in July from forces against and in favor of the tariff. Letters, newspapers, and personal visits were used to persuade the vice-president. His enemies in the Buchanan camp observed the proceedings with great delight. Forney commented to Buchanan, "It would be fun if Dallas had to untie the tariff knot. Rare fun." Dallas witnessed the Senate debates with growing apprehension. On 13 July he told Sophy that he did not think he would cast the deciding vote on the tariff, since it would probably receive a majority of two. After that the situation began to degenerate steadily. Dallas reported, "The tariff and its fate keep all the restless mortals on earth in perpetual movement." He suspected that Senator Haywood was defecting from the administration, thus leaving either a tie or a one-vote majority for the president.[21] Simon Cameron made Dallas additionally nervous by his powerful Senate speech on 22 July in behalf of the Tariff of 1842. Cameron quoted from Dallas's speech in favor of the Tariff of 1832 and said that Pennsylvania would not have supported candidates committed to any downward revision of the protective system. The following day Dallas remarked, "These tariff speeches are as vapid as [they are] inexhaustible." The vice-president, however, still did not believe that he would have to cast the decisive vote. Dallas was tireless in trying to arrange a compromise that would satisfy both his state and the administration. Walker and the vice-president approached Polk with a measure to reduce gradually the duties over a ten-year period to the levels now proposed. Polk did not encourage it, however, "fearing it might produce confusion and be the means of losing the bill." An exhausted and frustrated Dallas complained to Phillips:

> I labored night and day to bring about a compromise, and had a dozen shapes for it, any one of which I made no hesitation to declare should commend the casting vote of the Vice President. The Whigs . . . would not listen to any terms. . . . Cameron and Sturgeon might at one time have accomplished it, but they shrank from the responsibility.[22]

The situation approached a climax on 25 July, when Senator Haywood resigned rather than obey the instructions of his legislature and vote for the bill. Three days later, after much political maneuvering, the bill was recalled from committee and brought to a third reading. The pressure now fell on Senator Spencer Jarnagin of Tennessee. Jarnagin, a Whig who favored protection but had been instructed by the Democratic legislature of his state to vote for the tariff, refused to vote on the third reading, leaving the Senate in a 27 to 27 tie (27 Democrats in favor, 24 Whigs and 3 Democrats opposed). The moment Dallas dreaded had arrived, but he was well prepared. He told the senators that he had analyzed the vote and determined it was not on a sectional basis. The House had expressed the opinion of a majority of Americans in a similar way earlier in the month. Dallas felt therefore that most Americans desired to change the system of assessing the duties on foreign imports. Certainly there were provisions in the bill of which he did not personally approve, but overall it was more equal and just than the Tariff of 1842. Because of the obvious sentiments of his native state, his decision was more difficult and painful. As a representative of all the people he was obliged to vote for the tariff. The vote on the passage of the tariff itself was anticlimactic. Jarnagin, following the instructions of his legislature, decided to vote for the measure, thus insuring its victory, 28 to 27, without the casting vote of the vice-president. On 29 July it was sent back to the House with an amendment. By a vote of 115 to 92 the bill was passed and sent to the president. Polk quickly signed it on 30 July and the Tariff of 1846—the Walker Tariff—became law.[23]

Dallas was quite conscious that his stand had placed him in an unenviable position in Pennsylvania. He told Henry Phillips on 28 July that he had received (and probably would receive) a "torrent of abuse," but that these attacks only convinced him that he was on the right side. Dallas wrote to Sophy that he would most likely be "exalted to the skies by one side and sent heartily to the opposite place by the other side." But no matter what might be said or done, "I know and feel that I should have made myself justly despicable if I had shrunk from the duty." Nevertheless, Dallas feared the reactions of his fellow Philadelphians and urged Sophy to "pack up and bring the whole brood to Washington" if there were indications of a riot over the tariff. Dallas knew that bitterness on the part of all monopolists, especially the Pennsylvania miners and manufacturers, would result over his casting vote. Yet he was sure of his convictions and obligations to the "national constituency" and steadfast in his loyalty to the president and the party. It might be noted, cynically, that Dallas had much to gain in the low-tariff South and West from his vote, but this gain would hardly compensate the sacrifice of support in his native state and the potential backing of the more populous Northeast.[24]

The reactions to the passage of the tariff were predictable. The morning after the news of the bill reached Philadelphia, Dallas was hanged in effigy from the telegraph wires of a main street. The Pennsylvania Democracy on the eve of state elections was thrown into a violent struggle between Dallas-Buchanan elements, who had favored modification, and Cameron men, who had backed the Tariff of 1842. On the floor of the Senate Cameron entered a solemn declaration that *REPEAL* would now be the word among Democrats of the North and they would not cease until it had triumphed. Whig writers and editors echoed these feelings. Diarist Philip Hone mourned that "Polk, Dallas and the Tariff of '42" was the banner inscription that had carried the

Democrats to victory in Pennsylvania in 1844. But this "faithless, corrupt administration" had destroyed the tariff and laid domestic industry at the feet of foreign competition, hence sacrificing national prosperity to party discipline. "Long may their names [Polk and Dallas] be recorded on the same page with those scourges of mankind, war, pestilence, and famine, and the measure they have accomplished be included in the category of small pox, cholera and yellow fever."[25]

Numerous Keystone papers reprinted Dallas's statement in 1844 that the Tariff of 1842 was a Democratic measure and would be safe in the hands of James K. Polk. Led by the *Philadelphia North American,* probably the most rabid tariff sheet in the nation, cries of repeal blended with vitriolic attacks on Dallas. The *North American* launched daily barrages at the vice-president for single-handedly destroying his state for a chance at the presidential nomination in 1848. He had sold himself to the slave drivers of the South, but "they will laugh at his credulity, and despise his heartless and inhuman treason." Dallas was further lambasted as a "dough face of the North" and an "abject tool of Southern intrigue." The editors felt that Dallas really favored the Tariff of 1842 and had voted against his conscience and his convictions. His obligation as a national official was not to vote as his party desired, but as his conscience dictated. The Philadelphia *Spirit of the Times* continued the bitter invective. The vice-president was labeled "treacherous" and an "assassin": "His fame shall be immortal to execration, immortal to infamy." The *Harrisburg Pennsylvania Telegraph* and *Pittsburgh Daily Gazette* joined the attack. The *Gazette* noted: "It is said that Dallas shed tears when he gave his casting vote against the welfare and industry of his native state. Out upon the vile Crocodile!" A variety of out-of-state Whig journals, including the *New York Tribune* and *Niles' Register,* condemned the tariff and Dallas.[26]

Many of these papers referred to the Walker Tariff as "the British Bill." The *Baltimore Clipper* hinted that there was a strong connection between an amicable settlement of the Oregon question and the destruction of the protective Tariff of 1842. There were widespread reports of chaos, panic, unemployment, and collapse of domestic industry as a result of "free trade." Polk and Dallas had betrayed not only their own party but the nation.[27]

Administration journals in Pennsylvania had great difficulty defending the new tariff. Virtually no Democratic paper favored the tariff before its passage, and all were deeply disappointed by its success. The *Harrisburg Democratic Union* reflected this political embarrassment and declared that Dallas's part in the matter was to be "deeply regretted." The editors urged that the tariff be repealed or modified at the earliest possible date. By September the paper had tempered its views for political purposes in an election year, but the bill was still obviously unpalatable. The *Pittsburgh Daily Morning Post* tried to blame the tariff on individuals rather than on the Democracy. While Dallas's argument for favoring the measure was "very plausible," he should have voted against it, as did the Keystone senators and repre- sentatives. The *Post* reminded Democrats that R. M. Johnson—not Dallas—had been their choice for vice-president in 1844. The editors wrote that this new tariff was probably superior to the Clay Compro- mise of 1833 (which Dallas had opposed). Outside the Commonwealth it was considerably easier to praise Dallas. The *Washington Union* of course was in the forefront, commending the vice-president for his courage and firm principles. The editors took every opportunity to publish similar reports from New York and southern papers in Dal- las's behalf. All of these lauded the Philadelphian for placing the value of his nation over section or state and promised that the De- mocracy would not soon forget him.[28]

Perhaps the most accurate evaluation of the tariff came from the columns of the nonpartisan Philadelphia *Public Ledger*. This paper, generally nativist in its politics, favored an extension of the natural- ization period for foreigners, while opposing slavery extension and immediate Texas annexation. The editors praised both the vice- president and the congressional representatives from Pennsylvania for voting as their conscience dictated. The paper noted that the tariff was not a "free trade" measure, but was actually moderate. Closer examination proved that the *Public Ledger* was correct. When the political rhetoric was cleared from around the tariff, it was far from a free-trade document. Certainly the iron manufacturers, for example, were prospering under the Tariff of 1842 and therefore rejected the new measure, which might injure their recovery from the Panic of 1837. The *ad valorem* duties on coal and iron (30 per- cent) represented about a 25 percent reduction from the specific 40 percent duties of 1842. This was hardly free trade. In fact the free- trade list under the Walker Tariff was shorter than any other tariff act between 1828 and 1900, with the exception of the Morrill Tariff during the Civil War. Iron manufacturers did not feel the effects of the Tariff of 1846 until 1848 because the price abroad remained so high that the *ad valorem* duty was sufficient protection against for- eign importations. A slight recession had set in, but the industries recovered by 1852. The lower tariff rates actually aided domestic consumption and foreign importation, which helped the United States in a period of expansion.[29]

The tariff was as much a political as an economic issue. For years Pennsylvania politicians had used protection as a means to attain office. Its importance in the campaign of 1844 was evident. Dallas took an active part in convincing Pennsylvanians that "Polk, Dallas, and the Tariff of '42" would provide a safeguard for their industries. Why then did Dallas vote for the reduced rates in 1846? Only one month after the passage of the bill the vice-president responded to a laudatory letter by a Maryland committee:

> No act of general policy, as it appears to me, was ever more distinctly condemned by the suffrages of the great body of the American people than the Tariff duties on imports passed by the Whig Congress of 1842. . . . Fraudulent principles of assessment, and its exorbitant exactions, could be defended, even plausibly, by no one; and its repeal or modification, openly proclaimed as a leading object of Democratic reform, became an essential part of the issue involved by the animated election of 1844. . . . A change of the Tariff was involved, directly and unequivocally, in the popular verdict rendered in favor of James K. Polk.

While Dallas was probably correct in judging tariff reform to be a part of the Democratic platform, it was equally certain that he participated in the deception of his native state on this issue to insure its vote. Tariff reform was built up sectionally in the South and West and played down in the Northeast. Pennsylvania papers delighted in challenging voters to find the differences between Clay's and Polk's protectionist views. The vice-president was instrumental in this campaign, which was at best equivocal and at worst fraudulent.

Dallas undoubtedly supported the Tariff of 1846 because it was an administration measure and it enhanced his chances for the White House. There had been no guarantee that the Philadelphian would have had to take a stand on the measure before that fateful afternoon of 28 July, but he had already made his sentiments known to a number of correspondents. Because of his close contact with Walker, Dallas realized that although the tariff would not be well received in Pennsylvania, it was not free trade and would not destroy domestic industry. Politically, of course, he gained respect from southern and western Democrats for his firm stand for his party and the nation. He must have known this would help him in the campaign for the presidency, even though he had alienated his own state. Dallas believed devoutly in the Union and the Democracy and in good conscience could vote for a measure he deemed to be for the betterment of both. The vice-president relied upon his tariff position, as well as his stand on foreign affairs, to carry him to the White House in 1848. However, just as his tariff vote ruined him in Pennsylvania, so did his extreme views on Oregon and the Mexican War blunt his campaign efforts in the remainder of the nation.[30]

7

Vice-President: Expansionism and the Election of 1848

By 1846 Vice-President George M. Dallas was well aware of his precarious political position. He had grown bitter and frustrated over the patronage battles with Buchanan. While he had not been totally excluded from Polk's favor, Dallas was agitated over the manner in which such political struggles overshadowed what he considered the more pressing national problems of Oregon and Texas. The vice-president had not gained control of the state Democracy through the patronage and, in fact, had lost ground to the secretary of state. His casting vote on the tariff had seriously damaged Dallas's presidential hopes in his native state, while it had enhanced those of his archrival. The only avenues remaining for public attention and achievement were in the field of foreign relations. The vice-president was an expansionist and a nationalist who believed in an aggressive foreign policy. That he should capitalize on this in hope of winning public favor was natural, especially after his disappointments in domestic affairs.

Dallas had deep fears and suspicions about England, which probably originated with his experiences in the War of 1812. He was a firm believer in the Monroe Doctrine, regarding it as a splendid document which contained the noble and beneficial principles that kept the Western Hemisphere an American preserve. Dallas particularly feared Great Britain's naval and economic might as a potential rival to America's. Consequently, he was eager to halt any real or imagined English advance in the region, whether it was in Texas, Oregon, or

Cuba. He was perennially anxious about Cuba because of the weakness of Spanish authority. Dallas dreaded the "oven heat of emancipation" which could strike the island if Spain allied with England, and he continually hoped that the "pear would ripen and fall into our lap." The vice-president expressed the constant but unfulfilled hope that the United States would be able to eliminate the potential problem by purchasing the island. He judged that $100 million was not too great a price to pay.[1]

However, a more troublesome matter in 1846 was the northwest boundary with Canada. Dallas had been actively involved with this issue over the 54°40' line during his two years in Russia. While the Philadelphian had reluctantly conceded Imperial control above the line, he was consistently adamant in pressing American claims below it. Dallas felt that the United States should control as much of North America as possible. While he believed in Anglo-Saxon superiority, he also felt that a spirit of Manifest Destiny guided the country to this goal of continental dominance. Such expansion would advance the Union as a world political and economic power by the addition of natural resources and coastline. It would also contribute to a reunion of the factious Democracy by adding valuable lands both north and south of 36°30'. The vice-president viewed Great Britain—and the Royal Navy—as the main obstacle to success. The English had to be cajoled or bludgeoned into surrendering their interests in North America.

The initial American offer to the British in 1845 of a 49° boundary dividing Oregon had been shunned by British Minister Richard Packenham. By early March, Dallas believed that England would rather fight the United States than accept the parallel. This opinion was corroborated by accounts of British intrigues in Mexico "to get at the accursed Americans." The vice-president did not mind a war in a good cause against a single adversary, but he was concerned about two simultaneous conflicts. If they came, however, Dallas expected the nation could survive the onslaught. The British navy might destroy the capital and many of the cities and towns on the Atlantic seaboard, but they could not reach the great interior heartland of America. Economically, the United States, and particularly Pennsylvania, would benefit from a war with England. The Commonwealth alone would be relieved forever of $1.3 million in annual remittances to British creditors. Dallas optimistically noted that there was some consolation to be found in any great calamity.[2]

To the vice-president, an avowed 54°40' man, a 49° settlement would be a national disgrace. He followed closely the interchange of messages between the two governments over Oregon and predicted virtual national disintegration and chaos for the United States, especially if the Columbia River was conceded. Political parties would be broken or destroyed, sectional hostility would rise sharply, the national government would be transferred to Missouri, and the navy would become a "useless piece of embroidery." This would be destructive to the interests and growth of the far West and could not be forgotten until it was revenged. On 20 March Dallas confided to Richard Rush that "rather than wound the spirit of the country and incur such consequences, I prefer the hazards of war—a war that will purify us of too much trade and that will bind the West indissolubly to the East." If Dallas made such extreme statements in hope of recouping his recent political losses, or perhaps building western support, his efforts were not wasted on either the public or his rival. Through editor John Forney, Buchanan was alerted to each succeeding move by Dallas and was determined to reap whatever popularity he could from jingoism. Therefore, he toughened his position on Oregon, mindful that a war over the issue would probably stall downward revision of the tariff, which he opposed. The president was no more interested in enhancing the political appeal of Buchanan than Dallas was. Caught in a withering crossfire between the jingoists and fellow Democrats who had little stomach for a war over Oregon, Polk instructed Buchanan to formally notify the British government that it would henceforth be obliged to assume the initiative in any further negotiations on the subject.

By the end of April the bellicosity of Dallas toward Great Britain had subsided and he began to urge a diplomatic solution. Dallas believed that Sir Robert Peel, having launched his great experiment in free trade, would want to give it a fair chance of success and, therefore, avoid war with the United States at any sacrifice. Dallas told Rush that he remained a thoroughgoing 54°40′ advocate and would go to war with England before surrendering one good harbor on the Pacific coast to the British. This, he said, was his own "peculiar and unalterable position." He was not naive, however, and realized that the administration had submitted a 49° offer to the English in the summer of 1845 and was honor bound to accept it, if the ministry were to agree. Moreover, Dallas was aware of the anxiety and readiness within the administration to close the controversy as soon as possible, and he was not in a position to alter this desire. Since he also doubted that Peel would take the initiative, the vice-president urged Polk to do so on 23 April. Dallas wanted the United States to adopt a conciliatory posture, adding that if war became necessary, "let us be sure to have the opinions and sympathies of the enlightened republicans everywhere. . . . I wish to put Sir Robert Peel in the wrong." In the same vein he noted that Peel had not sustained British Minister Packenham's hasty rejection of 49° and recommended that the offer be revived. Dallas thought a second rejection would put London in a bad light, whereas an acceptance would open the door to the negotiations and a settlement along the lines the administration desired. In either case, as Dallas pointed out, nothing would be sacrificed but "a cobweb of pride." In abandoning his previous posture as a saber-rattler, Dallas argued that the public would do the same. He left the door open for retreat by adding that he indeed favored 54°40' and would not be unhappy if Polk spurned his plan.

The president ignored the advice and demanded in effect that the British assume the initiative. Fortunately for the United States Dallas was correct in his assumption that Peel and his foreign secretary, Lord Aberdeen, wanted peace (although he was wrong in thinking they would delay their response). The British soon offered 49° and this was approved by the Senate on 15 June. By that time Dallas had come to accept the settlement line. Indeed, he was upset over the hostility it created among the ultras, the 54°40' Democrats in Congress, because he wanted the United States to concentrate on the war with Mexico, which had commenced in May.[3]

From the outset Dallas adopted a cold but realistic attitude toward American difficulties with Mexico. While he respected the English and was fearful of the damage they might inflict on the United States in a war over Oregon, he was contemptuous of the Mexicans and saw no risks in a bellicose policy. His one concern was to avoid fighting both states simultaneously. As the danger of a head-on collision with the British receded in May, he told Sophy with elation that the sentiment in Baltimore and Washington for war with Mexico far exceeded his expectations. The reports that General Zachary Taylor had been attacked by an enemy force only added to Dallas's excitement: "The spirit of the whole South is roused in the finest possible tone . . . the entire national sentiment was exhibited yesterday [12 May] in the House of Representatives where in effect war was declared." Dallas was joyous over the outpouring of national fervor and its unifying effect on the Democratic Party. When war was declared on 13 May, the Philadelphian exulted, "Congress has acted as becomes a great nation—conscious of its power. . . . The people will sustain us gallantly." It was an accurate forecast.[4]

The vice-president was an aggressive expansionist and nationalist who supported what has euphemistically been labeled Manifest Destiny. The more land and economic and political power the United

States possessed the happier Dallas was. With an eye toward the election of 1848, the Philadelphian was also aware that embracing such "destiny" would endear him to sizable segments of the Democracy. His plans for the future of Mexico were well formulated before the war. On 19 February 1846 he confided to Rush the hope that finally everything which had at first been "topsy-turvy" would soon be part of the United States. He made his position more explicit on 19 and 20 May in letters to Sophy, in which he declared that after Taylor defeated the Mexicans he should "proceed to release all the Northern states of Mexico from the tyranny of Paredes [the military dictator] and to achieve a complete revolution in favor of the 'great Northern union'. . . . I hope we shall not halt in our progress until we get fresh redress, produce the downfall of the military usurper Paredes, and prepare all the northern departments of Mexico for annexation to the United States."

As the war progressed into 1847, Dallas contemplated urging the president to call twenty-thousand more volunteers to end the conflict, but he relented when Walker complained about the additional cost. While supporting a firm military prosecution of the war, Dallas also remained one of its staunchest political defenders. When presidential aspirant Justice John McLean published a letter in the *Cincinnati Gazette* attacking the war as miserable, unnecessary, and unconstitutional, the vice-president hurried to present the administration's position. He claimed that the war was justified because the United States had done nothing more than defend Texas from Mexican invasion. He was less convincing on the constitutional question; arguing on the one hand that the war had been preceded by all of the legal steps required of the executive and Congress, and on the other that a show of force in disputed territory was not a declaration of war. The conflict, he went on to say, "was not miserable, but glorious." In retrospect he concluded that it had demonstrated American strength, "created a bevy of American heroes, astonished the Europeans, brought victory to the United States and humbled an audacious and perfidious nation."[5]

The peace plan of Dallas went further than the annexation of Mexico's northern provinces. From the early days of the war he had hoped to secure American rights of transit across the southern peninsula. On 19 April he floated a trial balloon in the obscure, semiliterary Philadelphia journal *Spirit of the Times,* proposing a canal across the Isthmus of Tehuantepec. His article was promptly reprinted in the influential *Washington Union* on 26 April, and later in Democratic papers throughout the nation. It argued that any treaty with Mexico should include the irrevocable cession of a strip of land across the isthmus for a canal and/or railroad. He noted that the British had previously investigated such a project, and he emphasized its feasibility as well as its subsequent value to the United States and the entire world. Dallas pointed out that a canal could be cheaply and easily constructed at a cost of $25 million spent over five years. Mexico would also benefit from such an enterprise, the more so because she lacked the economic resources to undertake it herself. Striking a self-righteous theme, he added, "Mexico in sober truth should not be permitted to be the dog in the manger—to keep selfishly useless that which without injury to her, may be converted into the means of bringing closely together, of improving and of enriching the whole human family."[6]

It turned out that Dallas was behind rather than ahead of the more enthusiastic land grabbers. In fact by the fall of 1847 there was substantial sentiment for swallowing all of Mexico. The agitation reached its peak in January and February of 1848. Moreover, it was obvious to the contenders for the White House that Mexico would be the dominant issue of the coming campaign. At the time it seemed that the winner would be a man who advocated the total absorption of Mexico. Buchanan edged toward this position, asserting that if an honorable peace were not available the United States would have to "fulfill that destiny which Providence may have in store for both countries." Not to be outdone, Dallas in a public letter urged his fellow countrymen to advance "the great objects of civilization." More specifically, the vice-president declared:

> This war, in my judgment, can have but one wise, natural and legitimate end—peace or subjugation. . . . Opposed as I am to receive permanently into the family of American freemen those who are unwilling to enter it, I can yet discover in our noble constitution of government no thing not perfectly equal to the vast task which may be assigned to it by the resistless force of events—guardianship of a crowded and confederated continent.[7]

The president, however, resisted the extreme demands of the expansionists and maintained his moderate initial desire for New Mexico and California. If the war had continued longer perhaps Polk would have capitulated to the advocates of annexation. As it was many Democrats—with the notable exceptions of the Calhoun faction and a few New Englanders—subscribed to such a policy. Time, however, ran out on the ultras. They had argued that Mexico must be taken by the United States to fulfill Manifest Destiny, to acquire valuable economic assets, and to forestall the possibility of Mexico or her possessions serving as a base for European intervention. In taking this stand they had assumed that the Mexicans would never sign a treaty parting with New Mexico and California. Polk, however, did not accept this assumption and submitted Nicholas Trist's comparatively mild treaty to the Senate on 19 February. The introduction of the measure sounded a death knell to the expansionists' schemes. On 10 March the Senate approved Trist's handiwork and the national movement for absorption died. Dallas did not relinquish his dreams of national glory easily, however, and continued to hope for annexation.

In October 1848 he told correspondent W. W. Chew that it was repugnant to him to bring in "the hordes of ignorant, degraded, tawny, black, brown and semi-barbarous beings" (the Mexicans) as equal partners in the Union at that time. Dallas emphasized the "wholesale and unmeasured" attitude of contempt which most Americans held for Latins; that "we set them down as a rude and vicious people." But, after all, he magnanimously declared, "they are *our* barbarians," lower in the sociocultural scale than some Indian tribes, but not so degraded as "the creeping and cadaverous root-diggers." The Mexicans were victims of misrule, and while government was not to act in place of private charity or reform, "we may not fear contamination from them and, in fact, by our contact uplifting them and they may imitate us." Dallas prophetically feared the chaos of Mexican politics and the possibility of a European monarch dispatching a scion to take over the government. If this became probable, Dallas felt "it would have been better to expunge the name of Mexico from the map forever." The revolution in 1855 in Mexico caused the Philadelphian to comment that "the door of peaceful annexation ought never to be shut." Nevertheless, it had been closed, and with it were extinguished the last hopes for the presidency for George M. Dallas. He was a man who by 1848 had been humbled by his archrival, Buchanan, discredited in his native state, and deprived of what he regarded as a winning issue. In spite of these handicaps, he chose to challenge the secretary of state in 1848 frontally by seeking the designation of favorite son in Pennsylvania. The sequel was a futile and pathetic campaign that embittered Dallas and removed him from the national scene for eight years.[8]

The spotlight shifted to others, and the presidential hopefuls were numerous because Polk had announced in 1844 that he would not seek renomination. Those struck with "presidential fever" included Wright (who died in 1847), Cass, and Buchanan. Before the Dallas boom was deflated, he tried to outmaneuver his more famous rivals.

In 1845 Dallas Clubs were formed, which held a series of dinners and rallies for the vice-president. In Kentucky one county board had nominated him for the presidency, and Indiana correspondents expressed confidence in his stand on internal improvements. In the South they cheered his position on the tariff and the Missouri Compromise. The Philadelphia *Daily Keystone* was established to combat the local Buchanan journal, edited by John Forney, who reported that the Dallas rallies were failures. The vice-president conceded to nothing publicly but admitted privately that he lacked the friends to keep the *Keystone* on a sound financial basis.[9]

Nonetheless, it appeared for a time as if Dallas possessed enough strength to block Buchanan. At the very least, he was able to create the impression that the secretary of state lacked control of his own state. As an old Jacksonian, polished and gracious, as well as socially active in the Philadelphia elite, Dallas exercised real authority in eastern Pennsylvania. He had powerful friends in Washington and Harrisburg and a lifelong career in politics and diplomacy. His weaknesses, however, were obvious. He had a negligible following outside Philadelphia and Allegheny counties. His tariff vote and his opposition to Cameron's election as senator had also cost him support in segments of the party. Most importantly, Dallas did not have the drive and zeal for politics that mark a winner. This deficiency was evident in the patronage battle with Buchanan. The vice-president testified to his weakness and frustration in a letter of 3 September 1845 to Polk: "I fear another failure, another complete checkmate and I am not willing to incur again the chances of the game." By recoiling from the clash over patronage, Dallas not only damaged his influence in the state but also hurt the morale of his campaigners in Philadelphia.[10]

Forney repeatedly emphasized to Buchanan in 1846–47 that the vice-president was not a serious contender. "Dallas is cold and out," he told him. "He is shelved." This pessimism was not as evident in the Dallas faction in 1847. Supporters of both Buchanan and Dallas contemplated introducing a resolution to sustain their respective candidates at the Harrisburg gubernatorial convention in March, but a five-hour struggle ended in a draw. The partisans on each side after this contest retired for the summer, while a boom for Zachary Taylor was begun by both parties. By September the Democrats realized that the general was not willing to be their candidate and the duel between Dallas and Buchanan was resumed.[11]

Certainly one of the major issues in the campaign was the Mexican War and the ultimate status of slavery in the territories. The Wilmot Proviso of 1846 provided one controversial solution to the problem, although it was unlikely the successful Democratic candidate would adopt it. Southerners opposed the proviso because they feared that all territory taken from the Mexicans would enter the Union as free states. Northern expansionists had to put forth a position that would satisfy southern concern and yet assure their Yankee brethren that the rigid tenets of the proviso should not be a *sine qua non* for addition of territory. Late in the summer of 1847 the candidates began to declare publicly their sentiments on the measure. All the contenders had carefully gauged northern public opinion and decided that they could now safely come out in opposition to slavery agitation and for expansion without committing political suicide. Buchanan, for example, suggested on 25 August that the Missouri Compromise line be extended to the Pacific Coast. Cass quickly followed with a statement noting that Mexican territory was not suited for slavery and that the local residents should decide the issue. Thus, while both Buchanan and Cass opposed the proviso and personally regarded the extension of slavery as unlikely, their positions were intended as a concession to southern opinion.

Dallas presented his views in a speech at Pittsburgh on 18 September. The vice-president began his address by defending the Tariff of 1846 (as a revenue, not a free-trade, measure) and the war (which was initiated by the Mexicans). He then turned to the proviso and slavery in the territories. Dallas rejected Buchanan's plan of compromise, noting that "I am of that old school of Democrats who will never compromise the constitution of my country." Dallas had opposed the original Missouri Compromise of 1820 as unconstitutional because Congress could not legislate on slavery for the territories. Instead, "the very best thing which can be done . . . will be to let it alone entirely—leaving to the people of the territory to be acquired the business of settling the matter for themselves." Dallas believed that whether or not Congress legislated on the subject, it would exist or not only by the will of the local populace.

The appeal of Dallas's popular sovereignty doctrine lay in its ambiguity. Almost every Democratic politician recognized the right of the residents of a territory to decide the slavery question when they were admitted into the Union as a state. What was uncertain in Dallas's message was exactly when slavery should be voted on by the people. Many Calhounites interpreted the speech as indistinguishable from the position of the South Carolinian in guaranteeing slavery anywhere. Numerous Yankees, including David Wilmot, felt it was essentially a free-soil speech, allowing for the prohibition of the institution before it was even established. Even New York's hostile Barnburners preferred it to Buchanan's proposal to extend the Missouri Compromise. Many Democrats realized that Dallas's stand was compatible with radical interpretations on both sides. Dallas undoubtedly hoped an equivocal stance would win him both northern and southern support.[12]

Much of the press reaction to the Pittsburgh speech lacked Dallas's ambivalence. The *Pittsburgh Daily Gazette* attacked it as filled with untruths and exaggerations. Dallas had "dodged" and "skulked" on issues. "A Machiavel [*sic*] would have been ashamed of shuffling like this." The vice-president was branded an unprincipled opportunist without self-respect. The local Democratic *Daily Morning Post* rebuffed this Whiggish attack, but it carefully avoided comment on Dallas's position on the proviso. The administration organ, *The Washington Union,* openly rejected Dallas's opinions on the concept of compromise, declaring that it would be the best way to preserve sectional harmony.[13]

While the press and politicians throughout the nation debated the merits of the various candidates' positions on the proviso, the Dallas and Buchanan men launched their fight to the finish for control of the Commonwealth convention. Supporters of the vice-president conceded defeat in the interior of the state, so the contest was waged mainly inside the confines of Philadelphia. A victory in the city and county would make Buchanan's nomination a certainty. But success in the Quaker City would be difficult because the local party machinery had hitherto been responsive to the wishes of Dallas. For this reason, Buchanan complained to Polk about federal appointees actively working in Dallas's behalf in the city. The president refused, however, to take any part in the contest. Lacking organization the secretary of state had to rely on John Forney's *Pennsylvanian* and "an incongruous band, united by a mutual desire to overcome the traditional Democratic leadership."[14]

Rallies were held throughout the fall as the movement to garner delegate strength heightened. Dallas and his followers pressed the Buchanan men in all areas of the state where they thought they had a fighting chance, but outside Philadelphia their efforts were futile. The secretary's lieutenants reported to him regularly on the relative strength of the vice-president in the various counties. Forney considered Dallas a dangerous nuisance, stating to Buchanan, for one, that "he can only do you harm, his chances are I think utterly hopeless." This did not discourage the Dallas men from holding a massive demonstration of five-thousand persons at the Chinese Museum in Philadelphia on 1 December. A week later, when both factions attempted to organize a rally at the same time, a free-for-all resulted. Finally, on 18 December, the Buchanan faction held their meeting at the museum, in spite of a last-minute diversionary gathering of Dallas backers held simultaneously at Commissioner's Hall.[15]

On 2 January 1848 the election was held for the 85 Philadelphia delegates to the state convention. In the city Dallas won 47 delegates to Buchanan's 38. The popular vote gave Dallas the victory by a 1,391 to 1,267 margin. The county returns indicated a similar margin for the vice-president, although he lost his own ward and congressional district. The Buchanan men charged their opponents with bribery, patronage frauds, stuffing ballot boxes, and even importing voters from New Jersey. In spite of these allegations, the Dallas forces had emerged from the contest with a narrow victory, too narrow to prevent Buchanan from sweeping the interior in the next few weeks. Reading the returns, the state Democratic legislators, who met in caucus on 1 February, endorsed the secretary of state. Sentiment for Buchanan was so overwhelming that Dallas supporters could obtain only fifteen signatures on a petition denouncing the action of the caucus.

The outcome of the state convention that met on 4 March was almost a foregone conclusion. After two hectic days Buchanan received a commitment from a majority of the delegates to the national convention, who also adopted the unit rule. Nevertheless, the minority delegates loyal to Dallas and Cass were a source of weakness to Buchanan. The convention also rejected their candidate's proposed major resolution to endorse an extension of the Missouri Compromise line. Instead, it substituted one complimentary to Cass and Dallas. The two affronts did not destroy Buchanan's obviously powerful position in the Commonwealth, but they certainly damaged his bargaining position at the national convention.[16]

The outcome of the Pennsylvania elections for delegates dampened but did not eliminate Dallas's presidential hopes. The Buchanan men were bitter over the divisive activities of the convention. While they claimed that Dallas had no popular support in Pennsylvania, they realized the division within the state party aided the vice-president's chances in other areas. Anti-Buchanan J. I. Abert, in April 1848, wrote to Lewis Coryell, a close friend of Dallas, that the vice-president was still in a strong position for the nomination. The South and the West were for him. The only question mark was Pennsylvania herself. Abert believed that Buchanan would have meager support outside the Keystone State. Unless her Democracy yielded to Dallas at the national convention, the presidential mantle would probably fall upon Cass. Abert was partly correct in his assumptions.[17]

While Dallas possessed appeal to politicians of the Democracy, he also had certain disadvantages. Some Calhoun men considered him too ambitious and distrusted him because of his close contacts with the tarnished president. Others admired the vice-president but feared that he was too closely identified with the southern interests. He could never compete with the extremely popular General Taylor in the South and his popular-sovereignty doctrine had alienated many northerners. Nevertheless, Dallas's name was frequently mentioned throughout the South at state conventions in the early months of 1848. The Mississippi (Walker's home state) convention met on 8 January and an unsuccessful attempt was made to make Dallas the official nominee. The same week the Arkansas convention announced that it was prepared to back Cass, Buchanan, Dallas, or Levi Woodbury of New Hampshire. Woodbury, a former senator and presently a Supreme Court justice, was the favorite of the dynamic William L. Yancey of Alabama and was an especially powerful force in the deep South. In addition to some strong competition Dallas's strength was weakened when Cass's Nicholson Letter was spread through the South in January 1848. This document was almost a repetition of Dallas's Pittsburgh position on popular sovereignty, and it won the senator support in the West and among unpledged delegates in the South. Thus, as the national convention approached, Dallas's chances for success had sharply diminished. His own state was committed for Buchanan; the Northeast was alienated by his opposition to the protective tariff, his speech against the Wilmot Proviso, and alignment with the South; the West was not opposed to him, but it backed its sectional favorite, Lewis Cass; and the South was factionalized and divided over a number of candidates. The outlook appeared bleak for the Dallas forces, but they persevered, perhaps anticipating another convention of 1844.[18]

The Democratic Convention of 1848 was held in Baltimore in May. In the weeks immediately preceding the gathering Dallas's name was frequently mentioned in correspondence to Democratic leaders such as John Van Buren and William Marcy. Dallas's only hope was that a two-thirds rule in the convention would probably wreck the prospects of the front-runner, Lewis Cass. Buchanan was the second choice, but he lacked national support and could not present a solid delegation in his native state. In the event that their man should become the logical alternative, "crowds" of Dallas's friends had traveled to Baltimore to speak, coax, and cajole delegates. The long Buchanan-Dallas duel and the efforts of the rivals in other states were fruitless, however, since Cass was swept to a comparatively easy victory on the fourth ballot.

The factionalism within the Democracy that had been evident before and during the convention on both the state and national levels became a major factor in the campaign. Dallas was active in behalf of the nominee, but the challenge was overwhelming. The popular Taylor would undoubtedly draw some Democrats to his camp, while Martin Van Buren on the Free-Soil ticket appealed to elements in the northern tier of Commonwealth counties. The Pennsylvanians were influenced by New York–New England contacts and had been sympathetic with the Wilmot Proviso. They disliked the positions of both Buchanan and Dallas on the issue of slavery in the territories and looked toward Van Buren's leadership. The election results confirmed any fears the Democrats had. The Whig candidate for governor won the October election by 300 votes out of 337,000 cast. Cass's defeat was much more decisive. He received 172,000 votes to 186,000 for "Old Rough and Ready." Van Buren garnered only 11,000 votes, not enough to change the result of the contest. In a lackluster election, in which the major issue of free soil had been avoided, Cass lost New York, Pennsylvania, and the presidential race by a wide margin. The vice-president, more disappointed over the fate of the party than over his personal failures, now turned his attentions to Congress, the proviso, and his future in the Democracy.[19]

Dallas returned to Congress in December 1848 with a new outlook on politics. He realized that he was now a lame-duck vice-president, and consequently he became more outspoken and corrosive in his comments on events and personalities. The Wilmot Proviso, of course, and the problem of slavery in the territories was the major issue at this session of Congress. Dallas was certain that the proviso would be accepted and that the president would not veto it. Polk had favored the extension of the Missouri Compromise line, but he was convinced that slavery could not exist in the Southwest. The vice-president feared that Calhoun had again gotten "the crotchet of disunion and Southern independence into his head," and that he would use Wilmot's measure as a hatchet to split the Union. Calhoun would then place himself at the head of a separate southern confederacy. Even though Calhoun was "teeming with revolution," the Philadelphian still held him in the highest regard. When the South Carolinian fell ill in January 1849, Dallas after visiting him remarked, "such is the close of an exalted, tho' erratic career of a really great mind, after near forty years of continuous service." Dallas felt that Calhoun's illness and the divisions in Congress further prepared the way for the success of the proviso. "The abolitionists have a clear field for operations, and if they push resolutely forward, cannot fail of entire success. The game is up as far as the new territories are concerned." The vice-president was, of course, wrong in his assumptions about Calhoun's immediate retirement and of the passage of the proviso. In these months Dallas seems to have grown closer in sympathy, if not in theory, with the proviso supporters. Perhaps he was angered over the willingness of certain southerners to disrupt the Union and their reluctance to accept the proposition that slavery should be banned in territories where it would be nonprofitable in any case. On the other hand, later he would frown upon the Compromise of 1850, regarding it as an insufficient and illegal attempt at a solution.[20]

In December 1848 the vice-president was an interested, if not influential, observer of the national political scene. He believed that "there is a perfect fog in national politics" and no man, Whig or Democrat, was really certain in what direction the ship of state would sail. Dallas felt that with Taylor at the helm, "she will be put on an ultra Whig tack and her rudder lashed down. . . . [The Whigs] are waging exterminating war." Yet the Philadelphian had thought highly of Taylor throughout the war and now predicted that he would make a fine president. In his eyes Taylor was a man of destiny, an observant and thoughtful individual, possessing vast diplomatic knowledge. The general was not a Washington or a Jackson, but he had the opportunity to be greater than either of them by disregarding all party alliances and restoring the Republic to its primitive simplicity, purity, and integrity. Buchanan disagreed with the vice-president and told him Taylor was ignorant and would make a poor Chief Executive. Dallas noted that this was evidence of political bitterness on Buchanan's part, since Taylor was vastly superior to the secretary of state in natural talents and in service to the Union. This lofty view of Taylor did not survive a meeting with the general in March 1849, however. Dallas was totally disappointed because his man on a white horse lacked the appearance and self-assurance that he had expected of a war hero. Dallas added that "if he has any intellectual greatness physiognomy is a cheat."[21]

Dallas's relations with Polk had declined steadily during the years of the war. The vice-president's views on expansion had been ignored and his suggestions for military appointments rejected. By 1849 the two men were rarely on speaking terms. When the Philadelphian was not immediately invited to a presidential dinner in December 1848, he felt snubbed and contemplated refusing a later invitation. When Dallas was requested to attend a dinner at the White House in January, he again thought of refusing, but decided it would be wiser to go. In February Polk asked Dallas if he and his family would visit him in

Nashville for a week or two in the fall. The vice-president officially declined, pleading professional commitments. His private response, expressed in a letter to Sophy, was simply, "Bah!" Dallas took particular delight in the fiasco that resulted from the attempted use of gaslights for the first time in the White House in January 1849. A soiree had been scheduled and as the evening progressed and the lights grew brighter, the odor grew stronger, eventually gassing everyone out onto the front lawn. The final negative judgment on the president was a comparison of Polk and Charles I of England, which Dallas confided to his diary. He found a phenomenal similarity in the defects of both men. He cited numerous examples of presidential deviousness, faulting him for the chronic habit of saying one thing and doing another. Unless compassion asserted itself at the eleventh hour, it is unlikely that Dallas shed any tears when the Tennessean died in June 1849.[22]

The vice-president's greatest pleasure during the Polk administration had been his position as presiding officer of the Senate. He enjoyed the activity and took pride—bordering on arrogance—in asserting his prerogatives. He told Henry Phillips, a Philadelphia lawyer and politician, before the tariff vote, on 12 April 1846:

> My unalterable determination is not to allow the party to warp my judgment a hairs breadth as presiding officer and I am absolutely sure of being able to carry this determination into execution, no doubt I shall make a great many mistakes . . . but I defy a thousand Websters to make me dishonest or to alarm me out of my known duty. As to my political friends, when they ask me to do wrong I quit them preemptorily. I have too many children to look in the face, to be able to spare a spark of my integrity.

The experiences and disappointments of the campaign and election of 1848 removed the excitement and enjoyment from many of Dallas's duties. In July 1848 he remarked that "never was a poor fellow so tired of a congressional session as I am of this." Only the importance of several leading questions prohibited him from deserting the capital before his term expired. It appeared to him as though both parties were trying to do nothing during the lame-duck session, leaving all of the explosive issues to the Taylor administration. Thus, the Philadelphian was anxious for Congress to adjourn so that he could go home. His family wrote him frequently, urging him to return as soon as possible. In January 1849 he told Sophy with an air of relief that in only one month they could begin spending the rest of their lives in welcome domestic obscurity. In spite of his attitude there was already some talk of Dallas's candidacy in 1852, but the vice-president did not like or approve of such rumors. It smacked too much of premature nomination and made him open to undesired political attack. "The Presidency is fast getting out of my head," he noted in his diary, "and I don't want my mind diverted from a steady and exclusive pursuit of professional practice." The vice-president was tired of the sacrifices, both personal and financial, of public life and longed for his retirement on Walnut Street.[23]

The nation's second highest office had taken its toll, physically and emotionally, on the Philadelphian. Sophy, who had never cared to live in Washington during his two-year senatorial term, was no more agreeable to the idea during his vice-presidency, although she had visited him frequently. Public service again placed Dallas in a shaky financial position and Sophy compounded the problem by urging him to take the family on a European tour! Dallas not only watched the family purse strings carefully, but he was also the guardian of its morality. When George discovered that his wife had purchased a copy of Alexander Dumas's *Memoirs of a Physician,* he declared the work to be full of vileness. It was denounced as not "fit to light cigars with" and "Parisian trash." His family would be better advised to read William MacAuley's *History of England,* which he had devoured with no offense to his sensibilities.

While he was in office Dallas lived a fairly Spartan existence, first residing with Senator Lewis Cass and later moving into a room by himself on Capitol Hill. One of the few luxuries Dallas afforded himself was a black coachman, whom he delighted in dressing in a black hat with a broad band and steel buckle, and relishing the praise the youth received for his flair and style. The weather in the capital apparently did not agree with Dallas and he was often ill. He continually complained of "the bile," drank a good amount of magnesia, and bathed his feet in hot water and mustard or cayenne pepper. The vice-president generally dined out, often with the Robert John Walkers or his nephew, Alexander Dallas Bache, who was now with the Coastal Survey.

In an effort to supplement his salary as vice-president Dallas had maintained his law practice throughout the four-year term. Undoubtedly the prestige of high public office added to the importance of the cases he received. In 1846 he joined with Charles J. Ingersoll in rendering an opinion for the Commonwealth of Pennsylvania regarding the manipulation of funds under the charter of the Mine Hill and Schuylkill Haven Railroad. The following year Dallas became involved in what he considered to be "the most important and interesting case of professional practice I have ever been engaged in." It involved the land claims of Charles Sibbald of Philadelphia against the federal government. Sibbald owned several parcels of Florida land, originally under grants from Spain in 1816, which had been transferred when the United States assumed ownership. The government later charged that Sibbald had not maintained the property by operating a sawmill as he had promised, and it challenged his claim. In 1838, after lengthy litigation, the Supreme Court found in Sibbald's favor and awarded him compensation of $78,000. He rejected this paltry sum, however, and employing Dallas, Daniel Webster, and Henry Gilpin, filed claims with the Treasury Department for over $15 million. The final decision would be rendered by the secretary and, Dallas guessed, "unless Walker has lost his intelligence and fairness, it [the case] will be a lucrative one." Apparently Walker did misplace these attributes, because after weighing the decision for weeks, the judgment went against Sibbald, and angry Uncle George noticeably cooled for months in his relations with the secretary.

Probably the most sensational of Dallas's cases during this period was the Pierce Butler divorce. Butler was the handsome, well-born, rich Philadelphian who had married Shakespearean actress Fanny Kemble in 1834. The unhappy marriage was torn apart by temper and tension and Fanny finally left Butler. In 1847 he filed for divorce on the grounds of desertion. Two of the best Philadelphia lawyers were obtained in his behalf, John Cadwalader, soon to become a judge, and George M. Dallas. Given the popularity of his wife, Butler feared the verdict of a jury. Fanny had already hired Rufus Choate, a Massachusetts Whig, as her counsel, but her husband worried about the possible addition of Daniel Webster to her staff. To eliminate this threat he employed Webster himself and, for insurance, two dynamic young New York lawyers, Charles O'Conor and John Duer. Cadwalader, who had not been consulted on this matter, considered this professional overkill and, despite Butler's pleadings, withdrew from the case. Dallas, equally outraged, viewed "the importation of foreign lawyers into Philadelphia as cheapening and depreciating the domestic article, and derogatory to its character." Money triumphed over integrity, however, and Dallas remained on the case for a $1,000 fee.

The vice-president's deep involvement in his practice brought him under heavy attack from the Whig press for dereliction of his official duties. Ignoring these charges, the Philadelphian was carefully planning for his return to private life. Dallas hoped to capitalize on his now-national reputation by entering into full-time practice with his son Philip, who had recently passed the bar examination. Perhaps the most accurate reflection of Dallas's rise in personal and professional stature was his nomination to membership in the prestigious Philadelphia Club. He had never been totally accepted into the upper echelon of Quaker City society. In fact, the only club of import that Dallas belonged to was the Society of the Sons of St. George, incorporated in 1813 "for the advice and assistance of Englishmen in distress." So, when he was informed of his selection he reacted with surprise, telling his friend Henry Phillips, "I should as soon have expected to be enrolled in a conclave of cardinals or a troop of strolling players." Dallas had no intention of accepting such belated recognition. He told Phillips to remove his name from consideration.[24]

On 2 March Dallas made his eloquent farewell address to the Senate. That body responded with a standing ovation and a resolution praising the vice-president's impartiality and ability over the past four years in discharging his duties. Dallas noted in his diary that his farewell message to the Senate was probably the last scene in his public career, and he believed it was an honorable, if not triumphant, termination of his vice-presidency. Since Dallas believed that this was his final departure from the capital, he expressed in his diary opinions and observations garnered from over thirty years of political experience. Undoubtedly some of his comments were the products of the bitterness of defeat: "There is no such thing as greatness"; "Lying is inseparable from oratory"; "Public men have flatterers and abusers, but neither friends nor enemies"; "Sincerity is perhaps the only virtue which public men cannot under any circumstances practice"; and "The press is conservative of liberty, but destructive of independence." Other remarks reflect his feelings toward the nation or himself in 1849. Dallas feared the results of territorial gain from the Mexican War, but he was certain the United States would survive. He perceptively commented on the blacks in bondage: "Much is said about the irreconcilable characters of slave labor and free labor, mere words—if the slaves were white the irreconcilability would vanish. It is antipathy of color, not condition." Dallas revealed some of his own sentiments on politics in the following quotes: "None of the great qualities are necessary to make successful public men—a combination of the minor ones [are] far more certain"; and "Truth, courage, candour, wisdom, firmness, honor and religion. Many by accident now and then [may] be serviceable, but a steady perseverance in them leads invariably to private life."

The vice-president no doubt also considered his career when he noted: "Altho[ugh] everybody knows that American public life is full of annoyances and leads almost invariably to poverty and repentance, yet nobody believes you when you disclaim a wish to enter it or express satisfaction at getting out of it. The thought always is the grapes are sour.''

While there were many politicians in Washington who took a more optimistic view of his usefulness than Dallas, he was wearily and eagerly awaiting the opportunity to rest and to collect his thoughts. After retiring to his private practice, Dallas remained active in state and local politics. He also spoke out frequently on various national issues. As it turned out, he was to wait seven years for his party to call him back into national service.[25]

8

The Quiet Years (1850–1856)

George M. Dallas—senator, minister to Russia, and vice-president of the United States—retired to private life and the practice of law in 1849. The Philadelphian relished the opportunity to spend time in the courtroom and with his family, and to expound on the major issues of the day as an ordinary citizen.

During this six-year period Dallas reached his zenith as a lawyer. The quality and importance of his practice had increased appreciably over the past quarter century. Almost totally abandoning the local courts, he argued effectively on the state and national levels. One of the few Philadelphia cases he handled was the 1850 divorce of trage-dian Edwin Forrest. His state cases often involved a defense of the rights of businesses, such as railroads to merge, expand, or use public lands (*Sharpless* v. *Philadelphia*, 1853). Sophy received letters fre-quently from her husband in Harrisburg or Washington, where he would often spend several weeks pleading a case. Staying at Gadsby's or the National Hotel, he delighted in renewing old congressional acquaintances and dining with the Baches or the Walkers. Certainly one of the most tragic incidents—Dallas recalled it as "a painful expe-rience"—was witnessing a final performance of the fading Secretary of State Daniel Webster before a standing-room-only Supreme Court in 1852. The great man spoke haltingly and ineffectively for about an hour, then dawdled, and finally was totally embarrassed as his mind went blank. At this point in their respective careers both Webster and Dallas received about the same attention for national office. Although his name was often mentioned for the Democratic presidential nomi-nation in 1852 and again in 1856, Dallas was not a serious challenger. He remained loyal to the party, campaigning for the Democracy at every occasion. His vigor in politics as a private individual, however, kept him in the public eye throughout this period and was a factor in his receiving the appointment as minister to England in 1856.

The measure that drew most of Dallas's attention and evoked the greatest response from him was the Compromise of 1850. His sentiments on the constitutionality of compromise were well known, especially when the issue involved slavery in the territories. He made his feelings known again repeatedly in the early 1850s, when numerous committees and individuals requested his opinion of the bill. In a letter to Senator Henry S. Foote of Mississippi in May 1850, Dallas reiterated the idea that the Constitution was the bulwark of southern rights and their only breakwater against abolitionism. He went on to say that southern statesmen were making a grave error in helping demolish "their true citadel" by conceding to Congress the power to legislate on slavery. Dallas did not distinguish between the states and the territories on the matter of slavery; he believed each should legislate for itself without federal interference. If Congress was permitted to legislate in favor of slavery, it could also pass laws against it and the floodgates would then be opened. He predicted that southern property would then not be safe one year. The Philadelphian was bitter over the increasing sectionalism and disunion in the country. He was particularly vexed over the tendency of southern leaders to place all northerners in the same category as enemies. Many Yankees (obviously referring to himself), he assured Foote, were working earnestly and successfully to vindicate and reassert southern rights under the Constitution. The southerners were making the task more difficult each day by rejecting all intercourse with their northern friends.

Dallas repeated these feelings in a Fourth of July letter in 1850 and at a November Union meeting in Philadelphia. In this public letter he again appealed to the Constitution as the only rescue and shelter from the problem of slavery. Dallas believed the essence of the federal Constitution was its abstinence from all interference with states' rights or local sovereignty. The general government was not to do what the local community could do for itself. The Constitution provided for slavery and it was basically and unalterably a matter of local concern. At the meeting Dallas referred to the Union as a glorious confederacy formed of sovereign republican states. He pointed out that the Constitution guaranteed protection for slavery and the federal government was not given the privilege to interfere with state or local institutions. If a challenge to the Constitution arose, for example, through a conflicting law in the newly acquired Mexican territories, this should be left to the judiciary to decide, not the legislature.[1] Thus while Dallas was opposed to the slave trade, boasting in 1835 that "we have nearly purged our soil [Pennsylvania] of every vestige of this pestilent opprobrium [which was] among the worst, the vilest and meanest of crimes." He consistently refused to view the question of slavery itself in moral terms.

The most publicized remarks Dallas made on the compromise resulted from a July 1851 letter to a Texas correspondent. In this letter Dallas noted the compromise had failed because of the collapse of the Fugitive Slave Law. The basic problem, however, went deeper than that particular code. The Philadelphian emphasized that the difficulty was with the Union in its political sense. *Union* was the direct opposite of *consolidation* and many of the present problems in the United States were due to the habitual tendencies of statesmen to consolidate. Dallas saw the trend at work in the propensity to view the United States as a *nation* rather than a union. According to Dallas, the label "nation" was plausible and innocuous in the sphere of foreign relations, but "full of insinuations and pernicious encroachments" when applied to domestic relations. While the term *nation* found no place in the structure framed by the Constitutional Convention of 1787, Dallas was not so unfair as to question the motives of those who disagreed with him. He simply regarded them as misled by the belief that patriotism required creation of a unitary state. Dallas said he desired nothing more than the safety of the Union, hoping to place it beyond the striking distance of fanatical abolitionism. To the Philadelphian no such thing as southern rights existed as a separate entity since all states were equal. Therefore the rights of all states regarding slavery should be protected, perhaps best through a positive and prohibitory amendment to the Constitution, which would end forever the debates and struggles over interpretations of the revered document. Dallas believed that twenty-four of the thirty-one states would pull together in forming an amendment to preserve the Union. Although Dallas requested that the letter not be released to the press, it was published by the *New York Times* in October. The *Times* was sensible in its editorial response to Dallas's ideas. It declared that the Philadelphian was assuming the ground that Calhoun used to defend—that the Republic was a confederacy, not a nation. The editors recognized that Dallas was not proposing anything equivalent to the South Carolinian's concurrent majority as a solution. The paper rejected as hopeless, however, Dallas's optimism that three-fourths of the states would support an amendment protecting slavery. The scheme was far too utopian to succeed. If any new amendments were passed, the editors predicted they would be against rather than for southern slavery. Nevertheless, the *Times* commended Dallas's bold style and provocative ideas and urged that his letter be read.[2]

Throughout the years 1850 and 1851 Dallas wrote and spoke on behalf of the Fugitive Slave Law. He called it just and expedient to the fugitive, the claimant, and the public. Any violation of the code was considered a part of a vast movement to break down the law and the institutions of the country. Quakers and abolitionists were in the same illegal camp, according to Dallas, because they aided fugitive slaves and abetted sectional hatred. The Philadelphian's stand on the compromise, and especially the fugitive slave provision, won him growing support in the South and caused his name to be mentioned more frequently for the nomination in 1852.[3]

Despite numerous political soundings regarding his own candidacy, Dallas devoted most of his efforts to stopping Buchanan's nomination. Senator Stephen A. Douglas of Illinois was a promising contender, but Dallas backed Michigan veteran Lewis Cass, ostensibly because of his experience and organization. Dallas's political heart, however, certainly beat symbiotically with that of the "Little Giant." Douglas was the leader of the "Young America" movement. This crusade, politically established in 1852, urged an aggressive American foreign and domestic policy. Its loci of power were in the planters of the South, land speculators of the Southwest, and railroad men, merchants, and new immigrants of the Northwest. The group was highly nationalistic and opposed the raising of the issue of slavery as a divisive sectional problem. The Young Americans extended their sympathy to nationalistic movements abroad and backed Louis Kossuth in Hungary and the other revolutionaries of 1848. In foreign policy they cried out for Caribbean expansion, especially with regard to Cuba.

If Dallas were ever to attain the presidency, he would be dependent upon a similar ideology and electorate as the basis for support. He, too, looked toward the South and the West for votes, as indicated by his stand on the Tariff of 1846. He consistently catered to the Germans and Irish immigrants of eastern Pennsylvania, who sympathized with the European revolutions. Dallas was an extreme nationalist, but he believed that slavery in the territories should be decided by constitutional amendment, not by Congress. Sectionalism had to be suppressed for the good of the Union. His activity in Philadelphia in 1851 in relation to Kossuth's visit to the city illustrated his support of the foreign republican movements. Dallas perfectly fit the Young America mold in foreign affairs. His belief in Manifest Destiny and the Monroe Doctrine was firmly established before 1850, and it was reflected in his continued advocacy of the purchase of Cuba beginning in 1848.

Dallas, then sixty years old, was a Young American mentally, but not physically. He belonged to the politically corrupt and debauched generation of Cass and Marcy, whom the Young Americans labeled "Old Fogys." The issues and geographic regions Dallas had tried to claim for the 1848 race were now used and wooed by the younger Douglas. The Philadelphian, perhaps hoping the Little Giant's political collapse at the convention would throw the movement into his arms, remained steadfast in his support of the uninspiring Cass. If this was his strategy, it was doomed to failure.

At the Democratic Convention in May some politicians desired a Pennsylvanian for president, but one more flexible than Buchanan. They brought out Dallas's name and circulated his views on the compromise and the merits of constitutional amendment. Slight mention was made of his similarity to the Young America position. But Cass, Douglas, and Dallas all lacked the needed support at the conclave and booms in their behalf only served to weaken Buchanan's position, while failing to enhance their own. Such tactics ruined the chances for nomination of the leading figures and resulted in the selection of unsung General Franklin Pierce of New Hampshire.[4]

Dallas pursued his normal course as a loyal Democrat and actively campaigned in 1852 for the unknown Pierce. The general had a particular problem in Pennsylvania, which Dallas took an important part in alleviating. A rumor was circulated that Pierce, as a member of the New Hampshire constitutional convention, was opposed to the amendment abolishing the Catholic Test—a provision that prohibited Catholics from occupying a seat in the state legislature or from becoming governor. An amended constitution was submitted to the voters of New Hampshire, but it was twice defeated. Pierce's supporters were forced to explain the actions of the Democratic nominee in the contest and why the measure had not been repealed. This was especially vital in Pennsylvania, where a large number of Catholics voted Democratic. At a massive ratification meeting in Philadelphia on 7 June Dallas spoke in defense of Pierce. He labeled the Whig attack on the nominee "a weak invention of a frightened enemy." Pierce, he said, was active in trying to get the amendment passed, while a coalition of Whigs and abolitionists (Dallas's old bugaboo) was successful in defeating it. It is interesting that Dallas wrote to Pierce after the 7 June address asking him to corroborate his statements! If they were in error, the Philadelphian promised to correct them. In spite of Dallas's efforts to improve Pierce's image, he felt that the Commonwealth was in a weak position in the Democratic column for November. Anti-Democratic Quakers, Germans, and Catholics would probably vote for the Whig candidate, General Winfield Scott.[5]

Fortunately for Pierce and the Democrats, Dallas's pessimism was largely unfounded and the party was victorious in Pennsylvania and the nation in the presidential election. Because both the Buchanan and Dallas factions had been instrumental in dispelling rumors about Pierce, he captured the Catholic vote. Consequently, the supporters of each leader urged the president-elect to grant their man a cabinet post. Pierce wisely realized that Buchanan was in the stronger position in the Commonwealth and probably would challenge him in 1856. To avoid this, he sent him to London, appointing him minister to England. As consolation, James Campbell, a Buchanan man, was selected as postmaster general. Dallas was understandably unhappy over the absence of presidential favor toward his faction. Worse yet, his friends were rejecting Pierce's appointments. Dallas complained to his son-in-law David Tucker in 1853, when Senator Robert M. T. Hunter of Virginia declined a cabinet position: "His going into the cabinet gave me an assurance that we might stand a chance of being in a measure relieved from the superfluous quantity of mere political scheming and demoralization afloat. . . . I am apprehensive that, having heard who were to be his colleagues, he cannot swallow the dose, or link his fame and fate with men to whom he objects. If this be so, we are doomed to a wretched state of distraction."[6]

The closest Dallas got to public service in this period was in 1854. At that time Pierce was anxious to purchase Cuba. The American minister to Madrid, Pierre Soulé, had fallen into disfavor with the Spanish and the president contemplated sending Dallas and Howell Cobb of Georgia to add some force and dignity to the negotiations. Soulé preferred to work alone, however, and this plan was abandoned before the two men were even officially appointed. Such a mission probably would not have satisfied Dallas anyway. The Philadelphian was never happy with Pierce's patronage policies and was growing to dislike his entire administration. In 1854 Dallas refused to interfere in behalf of a man he judged unfit and unworthy for a federal post, even though "the executive taste is for that sort of garbage and if it be deprived of this one, it will seek another of the same kind."[7]

Dallas's disgust with Pierce increased with the passage of the inflammatory Kansas-Nebraska Bill, which reopened the slavery question in the territories. While the popular sovereignty aspect of the legislation was not opposed by the Philadelphian, he still considered this type of congressional measure anathema. Dallas felt this rekindled the sectional controversy and signaled the collapse of the administration and the Democracy. After visiting Washington in early 1855 he wrote to Richard Rush: "We have no administration—the men fill the offices, but do not constitute a government—they are felt no where, talked of no where, thought of no where. . . . It is debatable whether there is a policy at all. The situation is deplorable." Dallas characterized Congress as sullen and factionalized on almost every major issue and the cabinet as a group of men who simply shrugged their shoulders and dragged the country down. In a letter to A. Dudley Mann some months later he attacked the "miserable management" of the Kansas-Nebraska Bill and Pierce's ability as a leader. He claimed the president was "utterly stripped of adherents, absolutely denuded of his own infirmity of purpose and primary disloyalty to principle." Pierce lacked a solitary political prop, except the needy and dependent, and he blindly followed a most fatal principle—free soil. Dallas declared that the free-soil doctrine was a "demon . . . which like chloroform masters all [Pierce's] faculties. . . . Sooner or later [it] explodes . . . scattering fire and stench throughout the house."[8]

Pierce's bungling policies made some impact on Dallas's decision to be available for the Democratic nomination in 1856. The president had alienated large segments of his own party: Cass was already a loser, Douglas was tarnished by Kansas-Nebraska, and Buchanan was still in England. Therefore, as early as 1854 some of Dallas's friends were planning for the Cincinnati convention. "Constitutional Clubs" were formed in Pennsylvania and received hearty endorsements in several southern states. It was clear that these front-groups were championing the state rights Unionist. Although the potential candidate himself refused to take any role in promoting his own nomination, he did little to discourage his supporters. John Forney commented to Buchanan in July 1855 that the presidential campaign had already begun in earnest. Dallas was one of the men the editor frequently cited as a likely opponent of the minister, at least in Pennsylvania. A short time after the Democrats swept to victory in the October elections in Philadelphia, a meeting was held at the Falstaff Hotel which adopted resolutions to secure the nomination of George M. Dallas for president.[9]

Dallas's response to the action of this gathering was characterized by concern and amusement. He was worried about the party's future and told Richard Rush that if the Democracy was not defeated in 1856 it would be because God withheld the chastisement the Democracy richly deserved. In 1854 Dallas believed, in reference to the Kansas-Nebraska Act, that some moral honesty and energy might have halted the growing tide of downward degeneracy. It now had made great strides forward. Dallas wryly questioned the resolutions that labeled him as a man for the times. The times were as bad as they could possibly be, Dallas said, and he asked, "Why am I a regular rowdy? Do I frequent tap-rooms? brawl at street corners? . . . bargain, reach and unscrupulously lie? These are the times—the political times: and, if I know myself at all, I am uncurably unfit for them. . . . The prevailing morals, manners, and maxims disqualify integrity for public [service]." Dallas felt that only Providence could rescue the United States from a dynasty of corrupt and debauched politicians. He expressed slim hopes for the Union, the Democracy, or himself: "Blessed are they who expect nothing," he said, "for they shall not be disappointed."[10]

Despite Dallas's depression, his friends continued to push his candidacy in Pennsylvania. Late in 1855 it appeared that the battle for the delegates in the Commonwealth would be between Pierce and Dallas. Buchanan, still in London, refused to run and his enemies were making capital out of this by offering Dallas as an alternative. The heated contest in the Keystone State forced the Buchanan men to make their move and bring their candidate into the open to preserve their domination of the state machinery. Old Buck had of course made plans long before his return to the United States, which occurred just prior to the convention. His arrival, the announcement of his candidacy, and his Pennsylvania convention victory in March made him the solid front-runner for the Cincinnati nomination.

Undoubtedly Pierce, in an attempt to eliminate one rival at Cincinnati, decided to give Dallas the London mission in January 1856. This offer placed the Philadelphian and his supporters in a quandary. If he accepted the appointment, would it be considered a withdrawal of his name as a candidate for president? Dallas thought not, and in a carefully worded letter to one of his lieutenants, Joel Jones, he repeated his belief that the presidential office was neither to be courted nor avoided. He claimed that he was taking the English assignment as a patriotic duty because of the critical posture of Anglo-American relations. But, he emphasized, his departure was not intended to have and should not have any bearing or influence on the popular choice of a candidate for the presidency. Therefore, Dallas's backers decided to wait until the proper moment in Cincinnati to inform the convention of the availability of their man. Unfortunately, the time never came, as the powerful Buchanan—unstained after all by Kansas-Nebraska—swept to an easy victory. The Lancastrian repeated his triumph in November over Republican John C. Fremont and "Know-Nothing" Millard Fillmore. Dallas greeted the news of Buchanan's success with satisfaction and relief, because Old Buck was a Democrat and because he had saved the United States from discord and shame. The

Philadelphian viewed the emergence of the northern-based Republican Party as a threat to the Union. This new political force, founded in 1854 on Douglas's treachery of the Kansas-Nebraska Act, propounded its antislavery doctrine and agitated a growing sectional friction. Although its politics were not unconstitutional, Dallas disliked what he deemed its alliance with radical abolitionists and the potential danger to the Union its success would bring. Therefore he welcomed the triumph of his old enemy in 1856.

Buchanan's victory marked the end of an era. For thirty years some Americans—especially Pennsylvanians—had rallied to Dallas not because they favored him, but because he was the strongest opponent of Buchanan. Since 1826 the two leaders had challenged each other for control of the Keystone Democracy. Although Dallas had assumed a markedly minority position in the 1830s, the struggle continued until Buchanan reached the White House. George M. Dallas realized that his political death knell had sounded. He informed a correspondent that his "own chapter of politics closed with the dead silence at the Cincinnati Convention." By the time of the election of 1856, however, the Philadelphian had already been in London for over six months. He had just completed the negotiations of a Central American Treaty, which he judged to be the zenith of his public career. He thought that his departure from the United States in March had removed him from the whirligig of national politics. Unfortunately, old political enemies would be a dominant factor in determining the successes and failures of Dallas's British mission.[11]

9

The Court of St. James's: Crimea and Central America (1856–1857)

When George M. Dallas agreed to accept the British mission in January 1856, he abandoned any hopes of becoming president, but his acceptance commenced the most active and exciting segment of his long public career. The Philadelphian served for five years under two presidents, encountering a multitude of differences with Great Britain over Central America, the slave trade, the northwest boundary between the two countries, the treatment of the southern secessionists, and the interpretation of the right of search and seizure. While these issues took on an aura of earthshaking importance to Dallas, they remained a virtual sideshow to the politicians and a populace embroiled in the sectional controversies of the era. The new minister never fully appreciated the domestic crises thousands of miles away, and entertained occasional fantasies about potential Anglo-American conflict and a self-martyrdom that would attain him his place in history. Dallas journeyed to England under the impression that he was to settle a smoldering dispute over American rights in Central America and return home immediately thereafter. So his extended tenure came as a surprise, the more so since he could not have anticipated retention by his archrival, James Buchanan.

Less concerned than in the past by his professional financial and political sacrifices, he departed from the United States on 1 March 1856; two weeks later he arrived in London with his wife, his sister, three unmarried daughters, and a son who would serve as secretary of the legation. The ordinarily hostile Buchanan, whom he was replacing, displayed an indecent geniality, prompted less by a disposition to bury the hatchet with Dallas than by the prospect of release from irksome diplomatic responsibilities. Buchanan's good will lasted through a short continental vacation, but it evaporated once he had put the Atlantic between them. He reverted to form with a sneer that Dallas and his entourage would turn the mission into a "family party."[1]

Dallas promptly began to establish a reputation for himself in British political circles. For three weeks he attended a host of dinners, parties, and other social functions. He enjoyed the hospitality, but he also wanted to take advantage of the lull in the serious Central American talks to convince the cautious prime minister, Lord Palmerston, and members of the cabinet and Parliament that he was both agreeable and inflexible. On 4 April he presented his credentials to Queen Victoria, noting that she was "not handsome" but that her expression of face and manner were engaging—and "very soon put her visitors at ease." A few weeks later he met the foreign secretary, Lord Clarendon, who greatly impressed him because of a likeness to John C. Calhoun. Dallas, thus, had begun to lay the groundwork for the continuation of negotiations on Central America by becoming acquainted with the proper Englishmen. He hoped to begin the negotiations over Central America soon after his arrival, but he did not know that a crisis beyond his control was developing that was jeopardizing his mission before it had even begun. His anxiety to commence these talks was quickly overshadowed by the activities of two men who were thousands of miles from London. The actions of British Minister John Crampton in Washington and filibusterer William Walker in Nicaragua placed new Central American negotiations in peril.[2]

Secretary of State William Marcy informed Dallas in late February that there were two important matters pending between the United States and Great Britain. The first concerned the interpretation of the Clayton-Bulwer Treaty of 1850; the second was the recruiting of Americans for the British army by British officers and agents. The treaty discussions had stagnated during Buchanan's tenure, but controversy over recruitment was about to explode. It had started during the Crimean War, when the United States had accused Minister Crampton and three British consuls (in New York, Philadelphia, and Cincinnati) of recruiting Americans to fight for Great Britain. At the time Washington had claimed that the four men were violating the Neutrality Act of 1818. Crampton had denied these charges, saying that he did not recruit but merely informed people of the advantages of enlisting. Although the alleged infractions had occurred from March to August 1855, Secretary of State Marcy had not asked for the recall of the officials until 28 December. After much delay Clarendon had rejected the request on 3 May 1856. As the Democratic Convention drew closer, Pierce and Marcy had resorted increasingly to the ever-popular sport of saber-rattling. Matters dragged on inconclusively until Dallas took office, at which point he wrote the secretary of state that he fully supported his efforts to remove Crampton. He also voiced the opinion that the United States should not yield one inch.[3]

Dallas waited anxiously to learn of Crampton's fate. Although he thought that the economic ties between the two countries would dissuade the British from precipitating a war, he expected them to engage in a series of retaliatory acts that might get out of hand and provoke one. The hotheaded minister prepared for the worst and proclaimed sanguinely, "when we are driven to that [i.e., war], we must throw the scabbard away, and tie the hilt to the hand." Moreover, he took delight in anticipating trouble and formulated plans for American naval squadrons to strike in the area if the situation exploded. He declared publicly in June that he would probably be dismissed by the British government and never return: a prediction that would take years for Americans to forget. Dallas said he would not be surprised if he were the last minister at St. James's and that "will certainly be fame if it be not honor." He informed Marcy that if the British retaliated with dismissal, the United States should never permit any diplomatic agent inside the dominions without receiving an ample apology.[4]

Marcy aided and abetted his pugnacious subordinate in twisting the lion's tail by dismissing Crampton and the consuls on 28 May. Although the secretary of state did not think that the British would demand the recall of Dallas, preparations were made for his withdrawal to the Continent as a precaution. Marcy worded his dispatch to the British government shrewdly, placing the blame for Crampton's activities on the minister rather than the Foreign Office. The secretary also accompanied the note with a second dispatch, which took a softer line on Central American issues. The tactic of slapping and soothing the British simultaneously kept them off balance. A momentary storm erupted in Parliament, but even a militant government organ like the London *Times* did not consider the dismissals a *casus belli*. American behavior was viewed as a political maneuver undertaken with an eye to the impending presidential election rather than a settled policy. Nonetheless, the *Times* advocated a hard line and the recall of Dallas. As it turned out, neither government was ready for a showdown. When Parliament met in mid-June to discuss the matter,

Prime Minister Palmerston urged restraint. His political opponents were critical but ineffective. The upshot was that Parliament ignored the agitation for the ouster of Dallas and supported the efforts of the cabinet to move the Central American talks off dead center. Even the *Times* backtracked and condemned Crampton for showing a lack of proper concern and dignity for his mission.[5]

Dallas was pleased, and perhaps a bit disappointed and amazed at the mildness and cordiality of Parliament's response. However, he expressed a feeling of relief at being permitted to stay in London and to reopen the Central American talks. His respite was temporary because he was obliged to cope with a second issue arising out of American recognition of William Walker's regime in Nicaragua. This provocative step had been taken about the time of the controversy over Crampton's activities.[6]

In effect, the administration condoned the activity of the adventurer who had forcibly taken over the government of Nicaragua in 1855. Although Marcy had denounced Walker and his methods, he had done little to halt the activity of filibusters launched from the United States. Foreign diplomats who hoped to reach an agreement on the problem were rebuffed or avoided by the secretary of state. The situation had been further inflamed by Walker's high-handed methods, which threatened British lives and property and placed taxes on foreigners, as well as jeopardizing their territorial and commercial position in Central America. So, the British government in the spring of 1856 agreed to supply 2,000 muskets to the Costa Ricans to aid them in ousting Walker. The Americans intercepted correspondence relating to this agreement and politicians promptly denounced Palmerston for meddling in Central American affairs in violation of the Clayton-Bulwer Treaty. The British, of course, recognized the administration's complicity in sustaining Walker and felt they were only protecting their interests in the area.[7]

Dallas was outraged by this maneuver, which he regarded as a transparent effort to establish unilateral control in the isthmus forbidden by the 1850 treaty. He cited the intervention in Costa Rica and the British search of an American packet carrying recruits to Walker as evidence of treachery. The situation grew in intensity as both nations increased their naval forces in the Gulf of Mexico. Pierce, who was an Anglophobe even before these incidents, made the most of the opportunity. Against Marcy's advice the president decided to recognize Walker's government and on 14 May received Padre Augustin Vijil, his representative. In taking such a step Pierce satisfied not only alleged indignity to the United States, but identified the

Democratic Party with what he thought would be a popular issue. Dallas approved of recognition because it would legitimize the Nicaraguan government and place the British in the role of meddlers in a conflict between two sovereign nations (Costa Rica and Nicaragua). He also had the satisfaction in mid-June of receiving a confession from Marcy that he had been slower than the American public to support Dallas and his policy.[8]

While the Americans, bristling over British aggression, united in a solid front, the British approached the situation more calmly. They learned concurrently about the recognition of Walker and the dismissal of Crampton. The British press, which had earlier blustered over relations with the United States, adopted a conciliatory tone. The *Times* explained recognition as another example of America's low political morality. The editors said that this, however, was not a cause for war and they promptly began to soften on the equally discomforting Crampton affair. The attitude of the press for peace was also maintained by the government. When Dallas presented Clarendon with a note from Marcy in mid-June that stated American acceptance of British good faith in the enlistment problem, the British were noticeably relieved. The ministry had aroused vocal parliamentary opposition over its recruiting policy and some of the British people felt that the entire policy had been erroneous. Despite recent American insults, the British (who had just settled their difficulties in the Crimea) were not hostile to the United States and were generally opposed to an open conflict. Some of Her Majesty's subjects now regarded British policy and the necessity of sovereignty in Central America as outdated. They were now willing to begin a gradual withdrawal from the area, while insuring the rights of the British citizens there. As the mood for mutual cooperation increased, the impact of the crises of 1856 became clearer. The diplomatic air between the two countries had been thoroughly cleared and the need for a change in British policy was now obvious. Out of near disaster the way had been paved for the renewal of talks on Central America upon a more friendly basis than had previously existed. After three hectic months Dallas could finally begin the true purpose of his mission.[9]

The clash of Anglo-American interest in Central America in the 1850s focused first on a decade-old struggle for this strategically sensitive zone, establishing a sphere of influence during the seventeenth century at Belize, which later came to be called British Honduras. Although the Americans propagated their Monroe Doctrine in the early nineteenth century, their interests in the region were negligible for several decades. But in 1846 the United States secured concessions from New Granada for a transit route through Panama. American interest was heightened by the Mexican War and the acquisition of California, twin developments that made an isthmian canal more desirable. The Polk administration therefore initiated the movement to obtain rights across a second route, the Isthmus of Tehuantepec, which would speed communications with the western coast of North America.[10]

Since the British were not deceived at the American aims, they swiftly took countermeasures. Moreover, they were in a good position to do so. Apart from their holdings in British Honduras, they had already pressed their influence southward along the eastern coast to the Bay Islands, a six-island chain off the coast of Honduras, and to the Mosquito Coast, between Cape Honduras and the San Juan River, which could be converted into a canal route. So, on 1 January 1848 the English manipulated influence into a protectorate by expelling the Nicaraguans from the port of San Juan (Greytown) and taking formal possession of it. Thus by 1850 the competition for canal sites was in full swing, with the Americans enjoying the advantage in Mexico and Panama and the British in full control of the Mosquito Coast.

Before Dallas appeared on the scene the rivals had reached a provisional settlement in the Clayton-Bulwer Treaty of 1850, which neutralized the area by prohibiting independent construction of a canal by either power. The Americans interpreted a vague additional provision that forbade colonization in the area to mean that the British were not obliged to withdraw from all of Central America, including the protectorate, and, of course, to refrain from establishing new colonies. As might have been expected, the British took a different view. They assumed that the treaty precluded American expansion and conferred on the British the same control over transit as the Americans.

The divergent interpretations assured trouble sooner or later, and the British precipitated it in March 1852 by "re-occupying" the Bay Islands, which the Americans regarded as Honduran territory. American politicians bewailed the transgression as a violation of both the Monroe Doctrine and the 1850 treaty. Although the British intended to keep what they had taken, they wanted peace badly enough to give the Americans a semblance of victory. So, with all of the graciousness that London could muster, she called for discussions over the interpretation of the Clayton-Bulwer agreement. The United States government was more conciliatory than the rabble-rousers in Congress; it wanted substantial concessions and got nowhere during 1854. In November of the following year Walker's filibuster had further upset the possibility of arbitration belatedly offered by Dallas and

Clarendon. Buchanan, backed by President Pierce, twice refused this offer and matters were still stalemated when Dallas arrived in London in March 1856. Meanwhile, congressmen had begun to agitate for abrogation of the Clayton-Bulwer Treaty: a solution that threatened to cost the United States more than she could possibly gain.[11] The first set of instructions to Dallas, on 29 February, was designed to keep negotiations alive without consenting to arbitration, which the administration felt would ultimately be unsympathetic to American goals. For once Dallas displayed more moderation than Secretary of State Marcy and urged settlement through a third party. In response, Marcy pointed out that the Senate was divided on the issue of arbitration and that a faction led by New York Senator William Seward favored abrogation of the treaty because of British violations. A number of politicos were adamant that under the treaty of 1850 the Mosquito Protectorate should be evacuated, the Bay Islands returned, and Belize limited. No territory should be held by the British that they did not possess in 1850. If arbitration were agreed to and the United States lost on these points, her position in Central America would be worse than prior to the treaty.[12]

While Dallas awaited the news of whether Pierce had agreed to arbitrate, William Brown, a member of Parliament, brought the minister a letter he had received from E. G. Squier, former American chargé d'affaires in Honduras. Squier, who had personal interests in peace in the isthmus because of heavy investments there, urged that Parliament make the Bay Islands solely a British-Honduran problem. The English could return the islands to the republic in a separate treaty. In addition, the king of the Mosquito Indians could be retired on a pension to Jamaica and the sovereignty of the land be turned over to Nicaragua. The Indians would still occupy it under British protection. San Juan would become a free port and Belize would be restricted to its 1850 borders. Marcy was immediately taken by this suggestion, which would remove a pressing Anglo-American problem without United States involvement.[13]

The problem of the Bay Islands quickly became the central issue in the contest between the two powers. On 1 April Dallas met with Sir Henry Bulwer to discuss interpretations of the 1850 treaty. The American minister inquired whether the islands were dependencies of Belize at the time of ratification. Sir Henry replied in the affirmative, and Dallas countered with the observation that they had not been formally colonized until 1852. The two men agreed the major issue was the protectorate and the islands were merely a point of honor. On 7 April Marcy informed Dallas that the president had decided to reject arbitration, and the pressure on the minister increased accordingly. The United States had always regarded the islands as a part of Honduras since that nation separated from Spain. Consequently, British occupation of them was a direct infringement of Honduran rights and a violation of the Treaty of 1850. The United States would not agree to arbitration that might result in the establishment of another Mosquito Protectorate. The administration would be interested, however, if the British would compromise and permit the islands to have a quasi-independent status similar to free cities within the Honduran Republic. All nations could then have free and equal commercial advantages in the area. Dallas was not opposed to such an alternative. He was pleased that Pierce had declined arbitration, because he finally became convinced that it "savors of concession." The minister advised a firm but calm policy of nonsurrender. He judged that if the United States remained strong, Palmerston would soon give way.[14]

The secretary of state sent Dallas his long-expected instructions on Central America on 24 May, accompanied by a letter informing him of Crampton's dismissal. The minister was to negotiate directly with Clarendon and to submit to arbitration—not the meaning of the Clayton-Bulwer Treaty—but only points of practical importance that could not be negotiated. Marcy agreed to allow a continuation of the British Mosquito Protectorate, as long as no land was claimed. Belize was to be restricted to its present borders and the Bay Islands would be returned to Honduras. Clarendon was impressed by American willingness to take a fresh look at the isthmian issues. The foreign secretary and Dallas agreed that new efforts should be commenced at once. As this conciliatory spirit abounded in early June as a result of Marcy's initiative, the dismissal of Crampton and retaliation against Dallas were brushed aside. The British Ministry was aware that its claim to the Bay Islands, especially as a colony, was tenuous at best and perhaps in violation of the Clayton-Bulwer Treaty. The islands—the major bone of contention in the proposed talks—were colonized to protect the rights and lives of British subjects living there. If guarantees could be made for their safety, Her Majesty's government was amenable to surrendering them to Honduras. In mid-June Dallas and Clarendon discussed the ground rules and issues to be considered in their direct negotiations. By 30 June the talks for a new Anglo-American Convention had begun.[15]

Throughout the summer of 1856 three-way negotiations were held in London. Clarendon and Dr. Juan Victor Herran, the Honduran minister, discussed the return of the Bay Islands and problems of trade and navigation. The foreign secretary and Dallas mulled over the British abandonment of the Mosquito Protectorate, restrictions on the size of Belize, and the status of the Bay Islands. The protectorate gave the diplomats little problem. The primary difficulty arose over the port of San Juan. In 1855 the United States had opposed free status for the town because it would detach the only important seaport from Nicaragua and dismember the state. By July 1856 the Americans had reversed themselves, thus eliminating the protectorate as an issue. San Juan (the river and the town) was to be part of Nicaragua, although it was to be a free city. A certain reservation would be demarcated as a district for the Mosquito Indians, who would govern themselves. If they wished, they could be incorporated into Nicaragua. Boundaries and other problems between that republic and Costa Rica affected by these adjustments would be made between these two nations under pressure from Great Britain and the United States.[16]

This left the Bay Islands and Belize as the major remaining issues. The settlement of the former was expedited by the completion of two Anglo-Honduran treaties in August. One dealt with commerce and amicable relations, but the second declared the islands as "free territory under the sovereignty of the Republic of Honduras." The islands would thus be generally autonomous—Dallas called it "empty sovereignty." This was obviously intended to protect the British subjects and their property. Dallas was somewhat skeptical of English generosity, but he recognized their goals. He raised no objection to the treaty, observing that if it was agreeable to the Hondurans this was sufficient. After the completion of these negotiations the talks between Dallas and Clarendon proceeded rapidly. It was agreed to restrict Belize to her 1850 borders and to underwrite the Anglo-Honduran Treaty, establishing the Bay Islands as free territory. On 29 August Dallas sent his handiwork to the United States for administration approval.[17]

The American minister was enthusiastic, satisfied, and proud to the point of arrogance over the Dallas-Clarendon Convention. Early in August he wrote to his friends about his approaching triumph. He recognized that he was politically defunct in the Democracy and had bowed out with his power at a low ebb in 1856, but the negotiations with Clarendon had elicited calm and goodwill between the two nations and restored his pride and self-esteem. Dallas believed that all he had been expected to do or to undertake had been accomplished. War—a favorite expression only months before—was no longer being discussed. Dallas stoically noted that "when it is a man's duty to make peace, he must close his heart to belligerent popularity." He was content to close his career with the reputation of having kept "two bull-dogs from tearing each other to pieces." The minister smugly asserted that the convention was right and honorable in every aspect, and he felt no anxiety over its fate. If the administration approved it, all well and good; if not, so be it. Despite his outward indifference to the outcome of the treaty, Dallas was deeply concerned about whether it would "receive the holy water and be admitted into the fold." He was certain that American approval of the convention would end the lingering British threat to Central America. Beneath the patriotic exterior, Dallas's correspondence throughout the period reveals the hope that the success of this pact would once again raise the Philadelphian in public esteem and perhaps lead to a presidential nomination.[18]

By the end of September Marcy had received the convention and presented it to Pierce for his approval. In the main he was satisfied, but he did propose some minor revisions, which he expected would encounter no objections from Lord Clarendon. The defects that the president observed—no doubt with Marcy's aid—concerned the boundary and the overly large area given to the Mosquito Indians, the lack of definite borders for the port of San Juan, and the validity of grants made to the Mosquito king. Dallas quickly submitted the reservations to the foreign secretary for discussion. Lord Clarendon was relieved at Marcy's promptness, because he was concerned about the British concessions in the Bay Islands and wanted to get the treaty ratified before they changed their minds. Dallas accepted Marcy's revisions but judged that they would be received with "difficulty, grumbling and procrastination." Such was the case, because the British politicians responded by questioning Dallas's power to negotiate. Lord Palmerston had assured Parliament in July that Dallas had full power as minister plenipotentiary to settle the Central American dispute. This was, of course, not true, since it was only in October (with the modifications) that Marcy granted him such authority. By this time the treaty had been completed. These additional powers enhanced Dallas's prestige with certain British diplomats, however, and permitted him to decide, rather than merely discuss, the final modifications. Dallas credited the granting of broad authority from the administration for aiding him in obtaining the desired American changes.[19]

On 17 October the treaty in its final form was dispatched to the United States. Dallas was more satisfied and confident than ever with his work. He believed that *all* differences that had previously existed between the two powers were now removed. The only potential source of danger that remained was the fanatic British repugnance for black slavery. If it were not for their dependence on southern cotton, Dallas feared that someday Great Britain might launch an emancipatory crusade against the United States. That was, of course, a future problem. For the present Dallas was nourished by praise from the European press, which dubbed him "the wily diplomat" and lauded the concessions he had smoothly wrung from the British. He smugly noted to Henry Gilpin, "That will do, won't it? And what is more, the whole of it is perfectly compatible with the honor and dignity of this great nation." But this self-satisfaction proved premature, for words of warning soon began to arrive from Washington. Marcy told Dallas that the convention would be accepted by the president and then submitted to the Senate, but he could not predict how it would fare in that chamber. Some senators, including their mutual friend James M. Mason, who was chairman of the Foreign Relations Committee, had indicated to the secretary that they might oppose the convention. Contrary to what Dallas believed, the conflict over Central America was far from finished.[20]

Dallas always reserved the time throughout 1856 to take notice of the developing picture on the presidential canvas. Secretary Marcy, a Pierce man, was his most reliable political correspondent. The minister, primarily because of the hostilities aroused by Kansas-Nebraska, disliked the president and looked for Douglas, Buchanan, and Senator R. M. T. Hunter of Virginia to be the contenders. Buchanan, who Dallas felt "betrayed extreme anxiety mingled with extreme confidence," was the front-runner and ultimately received the nomination in June. Dallas perpetually feared a dissolution of the Union resulting from the break-up of the Democracy and the unity of "Eastern and Anglican abolitionists [Republicans and Know-Nothings]." He viewed such an enemy alliance as so obvious that he could not comprehend their failure to execute it. The only salvation for the Democracy remained in Providence and a desperate hope that the American people still held the Constitution sacred.[21] Late in July the American Party selected former president Millard Fillmore as its candidate for the White House. Dallas rejoiced because he felt the stronger Fremont, a most respectable contender, could not win with his potential support split. Nevertheless, the minister realized that the election might be close, depending perhaps on the votes of California. He was eager for any election news, so that he could make preparations for prolonging or surrendering his mission. Pennsylvania was crucial for Dallas because if it did not back Buchanan, the London mission would undoubtedly go to a politician from another state. When the news of the triumph of the Democracy in the state elections in Penn-

sylvania was relayed to Dallas, he confidently predicted a solid Buchanan victory in November.[22]

Dallas awaited the election results with great anticipation and impa-
tience. When he received word of his party's success, he was relieved, but his fears for the Union did not abate. His mission in
London was finished, and already financially pressed he was anxious
to retire to the tranquillity of Walnut Street. He reasoned that whatever his fate, he had performed a great service to the republic "by
suddenly and unexpectedly changing the relations of two countries
from wrangling and war to kindness and peace." This would benefit
his children far more than if he had made several thousand dollars in
lawyer's fees. But anxieties about the future of the United States did
disturb his tranquillity. Throughout his political and diplomatic life he
had worked to preserve and benefit the Union, the Constitution, and
the Democracy. These were now in jeopardy because of a frightening,
fanatical sectionalism that divided the country and demanded supreme intervention to preserve it. Dallas pleaded for the kind of self-
sacrificing patriotism evidenced at the original Constitutional Convention. Although the minister had confidence in the political leadership
and abilities of President-elect Buchanan, he feared that neither the
Lancastrian (nor anyone else) would disengage himself long enough
from the present to strike out for the future.

> The two sections must not be permitted to drill their respective
> forces for four years and then confront each other for a defin-
> itive fight:—*that* would be to risk our existence as a nation upon
> an issue of uncertain result:—to such a pass matters should not
> be allowed to go:—the whole term of Mr. Buchanan would be
> wisely spent rendering sectionalism impossible at its expiration.

An aura of inevitability and pessimism pervaded Dallas's letters, as he
fell back upon the only arbiter for peace he knew—the Constitution.

Dallas's dejection over the fate of the Union, combined with his
satisfaction over his London accomplishments, prompted his desire to
retire to seclusion in Philadelphia. He felt he had sacrificed enough
for the United States in energy, and, characteristically, in finances to
warrant such a reward. He anxiously awaited word of the fate of the
treaty and the new presidential appointees, so he could ponder and
prepare for the future.[23]

Late in December the Dallas-Clarendon Convention was laid before
the Senate for approval. A Washington correspondent of the *New
York Times* lauded this implementation of the Clayton-Bulwer Treaty

and viewed it as an honorable British retreat and a substantial American victory in Central America. He doubted that there would be much difficulty with ratification. Secretary Marcy did not exude such confidence. Early in January he tallied the opposition, in and out of the Senate, to the treaty. The entire filibustering interest was against it, feeling that greater gains could be secured from the incoming administration. Senator John Slidell objected to the implied sovereignty of the Mosquito Indians, which was guaranteed by the United States and Great Britain. Some senators opposed this slight toehold, which might allow for later British intervention. There were also objections to the rough manner in which Nicaragua (still ruled by Walker) was handled in the negotiations.

Dallas allowed that there might be "trifling points" to which filibusters could object, but that it was basically a sound document. Those who desired rejection of the convention on such a slight matter should be required to devise a better plan. Dallas conjectured that in solving all the Central American difficulties, he might have upset the commercial, military, and political schemes of men in both nations. The minister was not surprised at opposition, realizing that the influence of interest groups, combined with the debility of the outgoing administration, did not strengthen the chance of approval. Both Dallas and Clarendon waited nervously throughout January. They corresponded frequently, analyzing the odds for success. During the past year the two diplomats had developed a deep personal liking and professional respect for each other, and this bound them closer as the tension heightened.[24]

While Dallas remained outwardly calm and reflected a cautious optimism to Clarendon, he spewed forth his growing bitterness to Marcy. Congress, the minister raged, was blind to taking advantage of a powerful opportunity. Those men too narrow to see the benefits the United States would garner by this convention should abdicate the role of statesmanship and become filibusters. The treaty should not be denounced merely because Walker was not favored, or even considered, by it. Dallas placed filibusters in the same category as abolitionists; both placed their own myopic goals above the best interests of the Union. The Philadelphian could not comprehend the logic of those Democrats who failed to realize that the convention dispelled British influence from the isthmus more surely, swiftly, and pacifically than Walker's brand of conquest.[25]

Dallas's fears of Democratic shortsightedness were not ill-founded. On 4 February the Senate defeated the treaty by returning it to committee on a 33 to 8 vote, where amendments would be added. Marcy remained alert to Senate dissatisfaction and pointed out the difficulties to Dallas. The secretary noted that major opposition was based on the argument that the convention was a clarification of the increasingly unpopular Clayton-Bulwer Pact. Another prime factor was the separate article dealing with the unseen Anglo-Honduran Treaty. Many southern senators objected to the term "free territory" and the prohibition of slavery in the Bay Islands. Marcy predicted this issue would be fatal to the Anglo-American agreement, unless it was saved by amendment. This sentiment was reiterated on 9 February, when the secretary labeled the opposition "formidable—too formidable to be overcome" without amendment. The antislavery provision was now undoubtedly the greatest hurdle. He cynically noted that the Buchanan men in the Senate were doing nothing to aid the passage of the convention.

Marcy's evaluation of the situation proved to be accurate. Committee Chairman Mason, ultimately a friend of the treaty, wrote to Dallas on 22 February explaining the major problem was the Bay Islands slave issue. He also declared that the president-elect was hostile to the treaty. This was confirmed by a communiqué from Buchanan to Clarendon which piously explained that the agreement would be rejected, partially because it was not in accord with George Washington's policy of noninterference and nonalliance. Buchanan felt the 1856 pact was the same as the Clayton-Bulwer Treaty, and the latter had never been popular in the United States. Nevertheless, Buchanan expressed the hope that Anglo-American relations would continue on their present friendly basis.[26]

Dallas and Clarendon were disappointed at this turn of events, but they hoped the amendments to the convention would be of such a minor nature that it could be saved. The American minister exuded a growing pessimism on the fate of their handiwork. On 2 March the Senate postponed by a vote of 25 to 20 its final decision until 5 March, the first day of the new administration. The bill reported out of the Senate contained two amendments. They struck out at the idea that the United States and Great Britain could agree to return to Honduras what was already hers, that is, the Bay Islands. Under the Dallas-Clarendon Convention the islands were a virtual British protectorate. The amendment required that the islands be unconditionally ceded to Honduras without any added provisions, so the possibility of a future British dominion would be eliminated. With the amendments sponsored by Jefferson Davis included, the Senate on 12 March ratified the convention by a narrow margin, 32 to 15, two votes more than the two-thirds required. Led by Senator Stephen Douglas, almost half of the twenty-eight Senate Democrats voted in the negative.[27]

The response of the British press was one of calm acceptance. The *Times* attacked the "southern fanatics" and the "jealous new administration," who had thrown roadblocks into the path of the treaty, but the editors expected (as did those of the *New York Times*) that the amendments were not sufficient to endanger the convention. Great Britain had done her best to alleviate the problems in Central America. What was troublesome was that American politicians had placed individual ambition before national welfare. Dallas was irate over the actions of the senators who had attacked his treaty. Their amendments were "a series of miserable little criticisms" unworthy of the dignity of the Senate and the seriousness of the occasion. He was appalled at the "paltry picking" of the filibustering senators who had delayed the passage of the bill for three months—until only one month remained before the expiration of the ratification deadline. A document satisfactory to the administrations and peoples of both countries had been pressed "into a dark hole and has been nibbled at by rats in search of food for faction."

Dallas expressed more restraint in his correspondence to the new secretary of state, Lewis Cass. He felt that the real substance of the convention remained basically unaffected by the amendments and that the British Ministry would approve the revisions, despite its rough handling by the Senate. On 7 April the minister dispatched the revised treaty to the Foreign Office for its examination. Dallas quickly perceived the soreness caused by the abrupt deletion of "free territory" from the Bay Islands provision. Since the recently completed Anglo-Honduran Treaty had not yet been ratified, it was debatable what effect this revision would have on the actions of Honduras, or on the British Parliament, which desired to maintain a limited degree of protection and autonomy for its subjects on the islands prior to Honduran approval of their agreement.[28]

Ultimately, the British could not accept the amended treaty. On 17 April Clarendon informed Dallas of a further change in the second separate article on the Bay Islands. The modification stated that the two powers should pledge themselves to guarantee the independence of the islands under Honduran sovereignty until the Anglo-Honduran Treaty was ratified. This would place the United States in the position of accepting a treaty on the basis of a nonratified one to which they were not a part.[29]

Dallas was thoroughly piqued at the proviso that tied his convention to the Honduran agreement. He could justify Clarendon's rejection of the proposed Senate amendments, but he could not abide this new wrench that was being thrown into the diplomatic machinery.

The British refusal provided a quiet death for the treaty since the agreed limited time on ratification expired in late April. Dallas, numbed with shock and depression, at first remained quiet about the failure of his work. He noted that the British refusal had caused no sensation in the local press and lamented that it was "only a single feather on its back that broke it down. The point of difference between the Senate and the Ministry was whittled to the smallest end of nothing. It is possible, after swallowing a camel, to gasp at a gnat." It took only one week for the impact of the disaster to affect the minister. Enraged, he attacked the Senate for the amendments that led to virtual British rejection: "They [the Senate] amend such instruments with all the freedom they amend ordinary bills, engrafting each his peculiar notion, and indulging claptrap and bunkum without stint. This is diplomacy run riot." Dallas bitterly complained about the senator (Jefferson Davis) who had offered the Bay Islands amendment. In only twenty words he alone had had the glory of killing the convention.[30]

The reaction of the British and American press to the failure of the convention varied greatly. The English editors wrote very little. When they did, it was an expression of disappointment that the slavery provision was permitted to defeat an otherwise sound treaty. Her Majesty's government, however, was obligated to protect the rights and property of its subjects in the islands. The Americans were much more vocal and opinionated in their explanations for the collapse of the settlement. Nationalistic papers, such as the *Baltimore Sun,* blamed the defeat on the recalcitrant English, who had refused to unconditionally cede the Bay Islands and had demanded American involvement in an entangling alliance. The more moderate and well-respected *New York Times* was representative of the papers that, while allowing for this patriotic motive, felt the issues of slavery and political jealousy were more significant. The *Times* pleaded with Buchanan to use his influence against southern expansionists and filibusters who had dealt the treaty its death blow.[31]

With the failure of the Dallas-Clarendon Convention it was left to the two governments to begin negotiations again on Central America. The United States returned to its plan of abrogating the Clayton-Bulwer Treaty, which received solid support from the president and the Senate. Both Congress and the administration suspected the British were trying to prohibit slavery and maintain a protective foothold on the isthmus. Thus, while the Americans were content to allow the matter to stagnate, the British took positive action. First, they moved for a new joint convention, which would include the French, to guarantee the protection and neutrality of a transit route through Panama. The United States of course refused any multilateral effort. The British then again suggested arbitration; and, once more, the Americans declined. Finally, the frustrated Foreign Office decided it would solve unilaterally the Central American problems. In November 1857 the ministry dispatched Sir William Ouseley to the isthmus to conclude treaties with the republics that would fulfill the goals of the defunct Dallas-Clarendon Convention. The Americans were fully apprised of Ouseley's mission and followed his progress closely. Unfortunately, Ouseley was too talented a diplomat for the good of either the United States or Great Britain. He negotiated treaties in 1858 and 1859 with Guatemala, Honduras, and Nicaragua that expanded and solidified the British position in Central America. The government of the United States was furious over this betrayal and the British, embarrassed by his actions, promptly recalled him. The Foreign Office recognized that the Buchanan administration was not only dangerously close to abrogating the Clayton-Bulwer agreement but was opening a drive for envelopment of the isthmus. In an effort to preserve the legal equality and maintain the possessions they had under the 1850 treaty, the British hoped to surrender quietly to the Americans, giving them no cause for radical action. Consequently, the British sent a new emissary to the republics, Charles Wyke, who in 1859 and 1860 negotiated agreements satisfactory to the Americans and consonant with their interpretation of the Clayton-Bulwer Treaty.[32]

Thus, even though the Dallas-Clarendon Convention had failed, it was highly significant. Commencing with this document, the two nations began to cooperate as never before in the Western Hemisphere. Although the treaty itself was not satisfactory, it laid the groundwork for future efforts. The United States had constantly tried to minimize or eliminate British influence on the isthmus. A simple renunciation of British claims in the region, avoiding any entangling alliances, was most satisfactory. Arbitration was out of the question because it might result in an unfavorable decision as well as violate the increasingly sacred principles of the Monroe Doctrine. The British, equally eager to end the quarrels and distrust, anxiously sifted through a variety of solutions. The tensions and bad feelings that persisted between 1850 and 1856 gave way to growing trust and cooperation. The convention of 1856 took the first step toward showing the United States that Great Britain did not desire to obstruct or hinder American plans for the area. The British gradually yielded hegemony to the Yankees and tacitly recognized the Monroe Doctrine. This lessened suspicions between the two powers, created greater trust and respect,

and helped to provide the close ties of the late nineteenth and twenti-
eth centuries.

Dallas observed the proceedings with weary resignation. He had
informed Cass in 1857 that he was ready for retirement, whether the
convention passed or failed. When it was defeated, he no doubt expected his recall at any moment. It never came. Buchanan shrewdly
realized that the sometimes calm but always courteous American minister was exceedingly popular with the British government, and especially with the nobility, and the president did not want to upset the
delicate balance in Anglo-American relations. More important perhaps, Dallas had powerful personal friends in Philadelphia and Washington, and the Lancastrian did not need his perennial rival meddling
in the affairs of the Democracy. Therefore, Buchanan decided to
retain the Philadelphian, but he reduced his powers to negotiate and
deliberately bypassed him in any vital diplomatic matters. Dallas,
aging but politically wise, knew (as did the British Ministry) that he
lacked the confidence of the administration. The president might have
preferred his resignation, but remaining at St. James's permitted Dallas to stay active diplomatically and socially and to continue—no
doubt to Dallas's amusement—the "game" they had begun in 1826.[33]

10

The Court of St. James's: The Slave Trade and Secession (1857–1861)

Throughout the remaining four years of his London mission, George M. Dallas was deliberately kept on the fringe of the decision-making process by the Buchanan administration. Secretary of State Cass (who succeeded Marcy in the spring of 1857) and the president attempted to negotiate with Her Majesty's government through or around, but never with, the guidance or influence of the American minister. A number of issues—some serious, some almost farcical—that required positive action arose between 1857 and 1861. Problems on the high seas, focusing on privateering and the right of search and seizure, dominated the period. But also to be considered was a dispute over the possession of San Juan Island in the Northwest and the gloomy secession crisis. Within his limited sphere and with the powers he possessed Dallas remained as active as possible in each of these situations. The story of his involvement is that of a man struggling to aid the Union and the Democracy and to create a place for himself in history.

The failure of the Dallas-Clarendon Convention did not seriously damage Dallas's credibility or popularity with the British government. He spoke at numerous parties and banquets during 1857 and was frequently a guest of nobility. On 24 June the minister received an honorary degree from Oxford University. Dallas's high social standing with the British aristocracy probably played a part in facilitating discussion of diplomatic problems with the ministry and Parliament.

Privateering had arisen as an issue at the Congress of Paris, which had convened in 1856 to settle the Crimean War. A declaration was presented in August to abolish privateers—privately owned ships commissioned by a belligerent nation to prey on enemy commerce. Great Britain, whose powerful navy and merchant fleet ruled the seas, was immediately interested. Dallas frowned upon such a resolution and told then secretary of state Marcy that he hoped the Europeans would not be so foolish as to attempt to force this "piece of cunning" on the Americans. The minister was undoubtedly shocked to learn that Marcy favored the abolition, under certain qualifications, and suggested an amendment that provided for the entire immunity of private property from capture.

Dallas complied with the ensuing instructions and submitted Marcy's proposal to the Paris Conference. In November he reported that the American proviso seemed to have strong support, especially from Prime Minister Palmerston and the British contingent. Dallas retraced his steps from the snide denunciations he had made in August and now referred to Marcy's idea as "sound and philanthropic" in its general principle. He emphasized, however, that the United States did not have adequate naval strength to enable her to abandon privateers. Dallas predicted the destruction of the American coastline and probable invasion in event of war if this measure was accepted.[1]

The Paris Conference recessed for the winter without taking any action on the matter, but Dallas feared that if it reconvened the outlawry would be enacted. In the interim, largely because of his own personal feelings, Dallas hesitated to open negotiations separately with the British on the question. Great Britain had not consulted the United States as to her sentiments and the minister thought it only proper to remain aloof from a strictly European matter. This was in no way in violation of his official instructions from the administration. He discussed the problem with the Prussian minister, however, who generally agreed with Marcy's position.

During the lull in the Paris talks the Marcy amendment became the subject of great debate in Great Britain. Elements of the British press attacked it as vague and insincere and suggested that the whole issue might better be postponed to a future day. Dallas still warned against it. He admitted that qualified abolition—exemption of private property on the high seas from capture by public armed ships—was superior to the naked proposal of eliminating all privateers; but any concession weakened the United States. Dallas felt the House of Commons would

accept Marcy's proposal and the British would then "gain everything." Their commerce would be secure and their fleets could prowl
the seas at will. The minister again wondered whether the secretary of
state knew what the consequences would be if the measure succeeded.
In a letter to Marcy in December he noted with resignation and obedience that the secretary had undoubtedly considered the results with his
usual wisdom and that the administration's policy must be made to
triumph.[2]

Dallas's opinions and qualms had no impact on Marcy. He continued in January to advocate the measure as being in the best interest of
the United States. Unfortunately for the secretary, the Paris Conference did not reconvene. Dallas asked whether he now wished to
present the proposal to each nation individually and, after having
obtained a majority, issue it as a virtual proclamation. Marcy rejected
this idea, however, and instructed Dallas not to initiate any official
negotiations on the subject, but to watch for positive signs from the
ministry and Parliament. The British cautiously avoided the topic and
Dallas suspected internal division within the government. The safety
of American and other merchantmen from attack by the Royal Navy
in the event of war was not looked upon with favor by the admiralty
or many members of Parliament. Such destruction could swiftly bring
an enemy to his knees.[3]

Dallas continued to see the issue in terms of British naval power
running rampant and commercial vessels plying the oceans unmo-
lested. The minister also objected to the larger issue of enforcement
of an international code on a sovereign nation. If the "combined
potentates of Europe" could impose their will on privateering, and in
effect render the Americans helpless on the seas, why could they not
at some future time abolish slavery? Dallas cautioned that the preven-
tion of such actions would not be helped by creating precedents or
voluntarily disarming the United States.

Ultimately Marcy's proposal met with failure. Negotiations were
instituted with the British in the waning weeks of the Pierce administration. Almost simultaneously, in the spring, the new president re-
tracted the offer and Parliament rejected it because the project was
not now "expedient in the judgment of Her Majesty's government."
Although the measure continued to receive strong support from Lord
Palmerston, it garnered equally powerful opposition from Lord John
Russell in the House of Commons. The proviso quickly died in the
ensuing stalemate. It was reported in 1859 that the Prussians were
seeking to revive it, but much to the relief of Dallas, who remained
adamant, nothing came of the effort. Thus the minister's first brush

with international law and problems on the high seas brought personal relief, but disappointment with the administration. They both would experience greater success in dealing with the old and bitter question of the right of visit and search of private vessels.[4]

The most serious problem Dallas encountered in the last three years of his mission was the crisis in 1858–59 over the right of search and seizure of American vessels. The issue itself had origins that were a half century old. In 1807 the United States and Great Britain had made the foreign slave trade illegal. American law later called it piracy. In Article 10 of the Treaty of Ghent of 1814 the two powers agreed to promote the abolition of the seaborne trade. The British eagerly pursued this goal and enacted treaties with numerous nations that granted the Royal Navy the right of search. The United States, however, was not one of these nations and consequently slavers rushed under the safety of her flag. By the 1850s the illicit trade had been carried almost exclusively under the American banner. In spite of this Her Majesty's navy throughout the period visited and searched suspected vessels without serious objection from the American government. Continuing American rejection of the right of visit and search caused the English to seek a theoretical basis on which they could justify their aggressive actions. They found it in a differentiation between the concepts of visit and search. The British did not claim any right to search American vessels, but they would allow an examination of a ship's papers to determine its nationality. The American government, while not openly rejecting this interpretation, saw no difference between visit and search and openly opposed the latter. In the Webster-Ashburton Treaty of 1842 the two countries pledged to maintain vessels totaling one hundred guns off the coast of Africa to eradicate the slave trade. In addition President John Tyler announced that the British had agreed to surrender the right of search. The British concurred with this statement, since they, unlike the Americans, separated visit and search. The United States still maintained that demonstration of the flag was conclusive proof of a ship's nationality.

The British responsibly abided by the pledges written into the Treaty of 1842 and provided far more than one hundred guns off Africa from 1843 to 1857, with the exception of the Crimean War period (1855–56). In contrast America, a second-rate naval power who jealously guarded its maritime independence, was notoriously lax in meeting its required quota. In only one year in fifteen (1853) did the total number of guns exceed one hundred, and by 1857 only three ships carrying a total of fifty guns were patrolling the coastal waters.

While the United States did nothing to suppress the slave trade and still conceded no right of search to the British, it did accept the fact that a British ship at its own risk might visit an American vessel. If the Royal Navy captain was in error and the ship was not a slaver, the owners could seek compensation for losses through Her Majesty's courts or the U.S. State Department. Some violations, which Dallas had protested, occurred in the early months of his mission, but the trouble did not really begin until 1857.[5]

With the conclusion of the Crimean War the Royal Navy turned its attention with renewed vigor to abolishing the slave trade. In May 1857 the American barque *Panchita* was captured and sent to New York as an alleged slaver by a captain in the Royal African Squadron. The owners promptly sued for damages and the incident, although typical of seizures since 1839, caused some irritation in the United States. Dallas immediately protested to Clarendon, declaring that the ship's cargo had nothing to do with its illegal seizure and the violation of a sovereign treaty right. Even proof of the *Panchita*'s activity in the trade could not justify this attack on the American flag. The foreign secretary eventually disavowed the seizure as an independent action on the initiative of the captain and in violation of the Treaty of 1842. He did not, however, reject the right of visitation, which Dallas in effect was protesting. In December the American minister was instructed to thank Clarendon for his disavowal of the *Panchita* incident and for censuring the officers responsible. The Americans hoped that this was the end of such matters and that measures had been taken by the admiralty to prevent any repetition. Those who believed this were quickly proven wrong.[6]

Although British violations of American sovereignty on the high seas had been comparatively infrequent since 1842, and the reaction to them in the United States had been mild because of British tact and the remoteness of the incidents, Dallas was wary of potential conflict on the issue. In January 1858 he urged Secretary of State Cass to withdraw from the binding slave-trade provision of the Webster-Ashburton Treaty. The minister believed that enforcement had been a failure; that British emancipation could be blocked; that there was an imperative need for black labor in the West Indies; that France had legally found a loophole that permitted her to conduct the trade; and that the venture was an entangling alliance. Since Dallas had no influence with the administration, he was undoubtedly not surprised that his plan was rejected. In April Cass pledged instead that the United States would firmly stand by the 1842 treaty. This more rigid posture probably reflected fear that more British boardings might occur. The new Derby-Malmesbury ministry, which had succeeded Palmerston and Clarendon in February, was delighted with this change in American attitude. Cass's desire, however, was not to placate the British. While he did not deny a qualified right of visit, it was intended that the British totally abandon the dangerous practice of visit and search and let the Americans deal with the violators under their flag.[7]

While the new American enforcement policy met with the approval of Her Majesty's government, no change in British enforcement was relayed immediately to the Royal Navy. Consequently, in April 1858, a series of seizures occurred in the Caribbean Sea that brought the two nations close to war. The actions, carried out under the initiative of the eager young captains themselves, were unprecedented in their intensity and completely aroused the American shipowners and government. As this explosive situation intensified, Dallas began a series of protests to the Foreign Office in May. He complained of the seizure of three American ships by British officers. Malmesbury, anxious to preserve good relations, admitted that two of them were entitled to compensation as a result of violations of the 1842 treaty, while the third was proven to be a Spanish slaver.[8]

This, unfortunately, was not the end of the crisis. On 18 May Cass informed Dallas of eleven more violations of American vessels in the Western Hemisphere. Congress was furious, and the secretary of state urged Dallas to determine if these actions were being sanctioned by the Foreign Office and to advise them of their responsibility to stop them. The American minister discussed the problem with Malmesbury and learned that he was as bewildered and concerned over the violations as the United States government. Nevertheless, Dallas advised him that the arrest, search, and seizure procedures must cease. The distressed foreign secretary informed Dallas he would promptly investigate the matter and attempt to ascertain the reasons for the increased activity of the Royal Navy. Malmesbury promised an inquiry, but he did not hint at the surrender of the British right of visit. Dallas realized that this investigation would not satisfy the Americans' sense of national outrage over the violations. Therefore, he decided to proceed to obtain firm commitments from the ministry that would guarantee American sovereignty.[9]

On 8 June Dallas had another interview with Malmesbury, in which the foreign secretary agreed in writing to what appeared to be a surrender of the British position on the right of visit. He admitted that British actions in the Caribbean were (if true) in violation of the 1842 treaty, and that the strict principles of international law regarding visit and search laid down in Cass's April memorandum were to be recognized. Although Her Majesty's government still desired a viable alternative method to determine the nationality of a ship without visit and search—and hoped that the United States might suggest one—the practice would be discontinued at once. The mode of verifying a flag would now be ascertained in treaty arrangements between separate nations. Dallas was elated at these concessions, noting that he "ought to mark this day with a white stone." He could not believe that Malmesbury had totally surrendered, unless he looked at the recorded minutes of their meeting. The Buchanan administration was completely satisfied by this agreement and Dallas basked in the glory of his success. He was convinced that his presentation of the excited state of American public opinion and his firm stand on unconditional British abandonment of the right of visit and search had won the day.[10]

In reality the ministry had made its concessions because of a combination of internal and external pressures, which had little to do with the protests of Dallas. Aside from the obvious motives of desiring to preserve peace and settle the Central American imbroglio, the commercial classes in Great Britain wanted to avoid a conflict. The idealistic advocates of the free trade Manchester School were in sympathy with American demands for freedom of the seas. The indiscriminate violations of the provisions of the Treaty of 1842 had agitated the law officers of the Crown, many M.P.s, the press, and the mercantile classes. The British had surrendered on the right of *visit and search* to the Americans. While this placated the United States, it had a disastrous effect on the slave trade, which could now theoretically operate without the hindrance of the Royal Navy. While the Americans relished their victory, Parliament discussed exactly what had been sacrificed. The Lords and Commons reflected caution and concern in their debate and much of their discussion focused upon the legal aspects of Cass's memorandum. Lord Aberdeen declared that the Malmesbury note was ludicrous, because he (Aberdeen) had surrendered the right of visit and search in 1841 in a memo to American Minister Andrew Stevenson. But Aberdeen maintained the right to determine the genuineness of any flag that was suspect. Lord Lyndhurst claimed that the British had lost nothing by Malmesbury's note, since no right had ever existed. What he did abandon—and quite wisely—was the assumption of a right. Cass and Dallas had protested the *right of visit* and this was explicitly renounced by the foreign secretary in 1858, whether or not it was assumed. Detentions would occur after June, but they were illegal and the British would be obliged to pay damages for violations. Any *casus belli,* however, had been removed and the American doctrine of freedom of the seas was strengthened.[11]

On 5 July Dallas participated in a gala Fourth of July dinner with American diplomats. He was toasted and flattered and easily persuaded to make a few remarks about his recent coup. His declaration that the British had surrendered on the issue of search and seizure had the 150 Americans cheering loudly. Two weeks later the minister received a highly complimentary dispatch from Cass on ending the controversy. Buchanan was also delighted with the course of events and congratulated Dallas. This expression of American satisfaction with the memorandum was communicated to Malmesbury, who reaffirmed the British concessions.[12]

Unfortunately the agreement between the governments on a point of law did not immediately end the violations on the high seas. For many months Dallas was plagued with complaints of actions of the Royal Navy in stopping American vessels. Malmesbury in turn urged the Buchanan administration to begin its promised (in April) implementation of the treaty, which would relieve the British of the total burden of halting the trade. Neither Buchanan, Cass, nor Dallas was anxious for the United States to take an active role and thus, as the Americans procrastinated, relations between Dallas and Malmesbury became increasingly strained. On 11 September the Philadelphian told the foreign secretary that he was thoroughly irritated over recent British violations, which numbered twenty-two. The minister presented rather weak claims in behalf of these vessels and the situation remained uneasy between the diplomats until the spring of 1859. By that time the Foreign Office, in denying the majority of the claims for compensation, showed that many of the ships visited either were slavers or were not entitled to American registry. This response, based on solid evidence, quieted Dallas, although he still muttered to Cass about Malmesbury's haughty and abrasive manner.[13]

After 1858 the issue over the right of visit was dead, but that of exhibition of the flag remained very much alive. The British, in sacrificing the right in the Malmesbury agreement, worked diligently with the Americans and the French in an effort to arrive at some convention on verification of flags. The French agreed in principle that force might be used to halt a suspected slaver, but that it could not be sunk. The more rigid British felt that a vessel could be fired on if necessary to force it to stop. The Americans dissented, adopting the French position and contending that every honest ship should display its flag to a man-of-war. Dallas disliked the United States position and argued that it was a surrender of liberty to compel a vessel to show its colors by any manner. In the spring of 1859 the three governments compromised. They agreed to instruct their merchantmen and navies that, although certain national flags (American) were immune from visit, a ship could be forced to show her colors. If a vessel was suspected of being a slaver, limited verification could be obtained by an inspection of her papers. Then, if the naval captain had erred in visting a vessel (i.e., the ship was a legitimate merchantman), a claim for indemnity could be filed against that nation. Also in May 1859 the United States moved finally to comply with her obligations off the African coast. A squadron was dispatched, but it did more to protect American ships from interference than to prohibit the slave trade. Although the British encouraged the United States and France to be more energetic and suggested conferences to create new strategies in 1859–60, including a maritime police force, they encountered cold responses. The burden would rest on the Royal Navy until the Treaty of 1862, when Secretary of State William Seward would commit the country to positive action.[14]

Thus between June 1858 and May 1859 the United States and England had solved the perennially controversial problem of visit and search. The two nations, beginning with the Dallas-Malmesbury Memorandum, not only arrived at a legal definition of visit and search, but after a year of negotiation they provided a viable and satisfactory alternative. Its failure was not the fault of the document but of American enforcement. Almost all points of conflict on the slave trade between the two nations had been settled. Certainly George M. Dallas deserves some of the credit for the successful outcome of the contest. Although he was never given any particular powers or instructions—except to act as a messenger in presenting the administration's position or registering claims for vessels—he played an active and significant part in finding a solution. Both Cass and Buchanan deliberately attempted to bypass Dallas in all negotiations. They never followed his suggestions, but the minister nonetheless obtained the Malmesbury concessions of June 1858 on his own initiative. After this moment of glory Dallas was again relegated to the role of a virtual bystander in discussions over flag verification. His private statements between 1859 and 1861 would have far more impact on American and British opinion than his diplomatic role.

The frustration and dissatisfaction of many Englishmen over American recalcitrance to do their part in eliminating the slave trade was in evidence long beyond the amicable accord of May 1859. The hostility of the Buchanan administration and the American minister toward the abolitionists and those who wished to destroy the slave trade was well known. After 1856 the British grew stronger in their sympathy for the antislavery Republican Party and sharper in their criticism of the Democrats. Dallas, a representative of a "doughface" administration and holder of his own personal views, was a likely target for radical barbs. When the minister received his honorary degree from Oxford in 1857, the students called him names and chastised him for representing a government that countenanced slavery. The *New York Times* considered such conduct embarrassing for Dallas and, in fact, "rude" and "indecent." The London press accepted it as "simply jolly."

While Dallas as American minister did not deserve such rough treatment, he personally represented everything the abolitionists opposed. The Union, the Democracy, and the Constitution were the three things most dear to him. The abolitionists were threatening all three and therefore had to be eliminated. Dallas considered blacks intellectually inferior and did not regard slavery as a moral evil, since it was sanctioned by the Constitution. It had a proven economic and social place in the South and thus should not be destroyed. The low opinion he held of the fanatics (as he called the abolitionists) was reflected in a letter in 1856 concerning the visit of Harriet Beecher Stowe to the Continent:

> Is she a citizen of the United States? Judging from the pertinacity with which she applies her talents to undermine the Constitution and degrade the character of her country, she is far worthier of repudiation and banishment than ever was Arnold or Burr. Genius does not always choose patriotism for a companion.

It had been rumored in the British press in 1859 that the legation discriminated against Negroes. They were supposedly accorded uncivil treatment and not recognized as citizens. Dallas was infuriated by this publicity and told his secretary, Benjamin Moran, that he would leave the country if any similar attacks were published. Moran scoffed at the threat and attributed it to Dallas's dreams of an 1860 presidential nomination. But there was no question that the minister was growing increasingly sensitive to attacks on the southern institution.[15]

The *coup de grace* was administered to Dallas by the aging abolitionist Lord Brougham at the International Statistical Congress in July 1860. A host of honored guests, including Prince Albert, was present at the public opening ceremonies in London. When the moment arrived for Brougham to address the gathering, he arose and, noting the American minister in the crowd, said, "I beg my friend Mr. Dallas to observe that there is in the assemblage before us a Negro and hope that fact will not offend his scruples." Dallas was stunned and remained in his chair in silence. Brougham was cheered loudly by the assembly. The reaction to the insult was instantaneous. Dallas fumed over whether it was a private indecency or if the British government should be held responsible. He also had second thoughts about whether he should have replied to Brougham or perhaps left the hall. The Philadelphian promptly wrote to Cass for instructions.

Two days later Brougham visited Dallas and attempted to explain that he meant no disrespect to the minister or his government. Dallas's honor would not be satisifed so easily, however. He demanded a public apology in front of the Statistical Congress. When Brougham came to see him on 20 July, Dallas refused to admit him. Other British nobles approached Dallas, apologizing and attempting to mollify him. When Brougham publicly apologized at the next session of the Congress, the message was delivered in a sarcastic manner that was worse than the original affront. Dallas, who was not present, was further alienated. Resolution of the matter was by then, however, out of his hands and a subject of debate in the Buchanan cabinet.[16]

The American government, the press, and much of the public was offended by Brougham's remark. The problem was what should be done about it. In mid-September Cass told Dallas that the administration would take no action in the incident. It was an offensive insult to the United States and her people, a large portion of whom (including Cass) considered the Negro inferior and unworthy of social and political equality. The British were merely continuing their agitation about what was solely an internal American issue. Cass said that the cabinet was divided over the correctness of Dallas's action, although the secretary personally believed that he should have left the room. Nevertheless, Cass agreed to Dallas's suggestion that a formal complaint should not be filed with the Foreign Office. The insult would be considered to have been committed unofficially by a private citizen and the matter would be closed. A few weeks later Dallas was invited by the Queen to visit Windsor Castle. No American minister had been so honored in over twenty-eight years. While ostensibly this was reciprocation for the generous treatment the Prince of Wales had received in the United States, the possibilities of deeper diplomatic implications after the Brougham affair were evident.[17]

Dallas encountered only one minor diplomatic conflict in the years immediately preceding the secession crisis. The Treaty of 1846, which provided for a dividing line of 49°, had not properly disposed of San

Juan Island, which was located between the American mainland and Vancouver Island. Both the United States and Great Britain claimed the island and had settlers on it. The British Hudson's Bay Company was raising sheep there, while about twenty-five American families were growing potatoes. San Juan had been discussed periodically since 1856, but no solution had been reached. Because of the size and population of the island, it did not become an important issue until the opposing sides on the island clashed in June 1859. An American farmer shot and killed a British-owned pig that was rooting out his potatoes. A vociferous debate ensued over claims and property violations. When American General William Harney, commander of the Military Department of Oregon, visited the island in July, he was presented with a petition of grievances by the settlers and requested to provide protection from Indian raids and the harassment of the Hudson's Bay officials. A few days later Harney sent General George Pickett with a small contingent of troops to guard "American rights."[18]

It was not until September that the activity on San Juan became public knowledge in Washington, D.C. Lord Lyons, the British minister, had received a protest from Governor Douglas of British Columbia, who was prepared to land British troops. The Buchanan administration quickly dispatched General Winfield Scott on 16 September to the area to preserve peace and arrange for negotiations and joint occupation. He arrived in mid-October and after a one-month stay his talks with Governor Douglas produced a temporary working arrangement that satisfied both parties.

Dallas and the British public did not learn of the San Juan difficulties until late in September and the minister was told nothing officially until 8 October. Dallas cynically noted in his diary that Cass's reluctance to keep him informed on the affair indicated that there was no intention to allow him to participate in the negotiations. He was undoubtedly surprised when he received the American position on 4 November and was instructed to present whatever arguments he could muster in support of that position.[19]

Dallas eagerly accepted the opportunity to take the diplomatic initiative. He viewed the entire San Juan problem as a "paper pellet." In itself the island was not particularly important, but it did create additional friction between the two powers. The minister wanted the issue settled quickly so that prolonged debate would not bring eventual war "for a patch of valueless earth somewhere on the moon." Although he felt that Harney had been indiscreet and unwise in occupying the island, Dallas firmly believed that it did belong to the United States by the Treaty of 1846. He interpreted the parallel to run through the Haro (not the Rosario) Straits. The minister studied the problem carefully and presented his argument to the foreign secretary, Lord John Russell, on 12 November. Although Dallas believed that both governments realized San Juan should belong to the United States, retention of the island had become a point of honor with the British. Their press was comparing it to the Isle of Wight and claiming its surrender would endanger British possessions in North America. Thus Dallas suggested the concession of a smaller island in the straits that would serve equally well for defense and would satisfy the British press and public. There was no immediate, official reaction to this proposal.

By March 1860 the Royal Marines had been landed on San Juan and joint occupancy was in effect. As discussions continued throughout the spring, Harney began to aggravate the situation by troop shifts to the island. He was recalled to Washington and given a one-year leave from the service. By the summer it became apparent in London that neither side would surrender the island. Consequently, the British initiated talks to bring about third-power arbitration. The issue was at this point when the secession crisis of December 1860 preempted discussions of all other topics.[20]

One of the reasons for the continued good relations between Dallas and Her Majesty's government was the fact that the Philadelphian was not a serious contender for the 1860 presidential nomination. As a result, he had no cause to arouse anti-British sentiment for his own political purposes at home. Although the Philadelphian did not consider himself in the running as a Democratic candidate, he had friends and enemies alike who were convinced otherwise. Dallas limited himself to the role of concerned observer and did no electioneering.

Dallas had admitted to several colleagues that the silence of the 1856 convention was the death knell of his political career. Some supporters were not willing to accept this and pictured Dallas in a role similar to that of Buchanan four years earlier. In September 1857 Judge George Woodward advised the minister to come home and make preparations for the campaign. Dallas's close friend Francis Markoe wrote him several times in 1859 and 1860 plotting strategy regarding the appropriate time for his return. Markoe's inquiry of 20 December about this subject prompted a strong rebuke from Dallas, who chastised him for assuming his candidacy. The minister also received correspondence concerning the nomination from several other backers, who declared that he would be considered in the event the convention was deadlocked.[21] Benjamin Moran also thought Dallas was a strong presidential aspirant. The assistant secretary hated the minister for his social snobbishness and his antipathy toward Buchanan. He considered Dallas's every move to have White House implications. Moran believed that the Philadelphian's frequent indignation and mention of recall were attempts to improve his chances for the presidency by martyrdom.[22]

While those close to him talked about the White House, Dallas never gave any indication, one way or another, of his position. He undoubtedly would not have refused the Democracy's nomination had it been proffered, but he remained consistent in his philosophy that the office should seek the man. As the United States was thrown deeper into sectional spasms over Bleeding Kansas and the Dred Scott decision, which the Republicans exploited, Dallas's concern grew for the Union and his party. He attempted to remain optimistic in 1858–59 about the political scene. The reversals the Democracy had suffered in the state elections and the House of Representatives in the North would stimulate the party to greater unity and secure the triumph in 1860. Similar threats had confronted the Democrats six or seven times before, and victory was always the result. Dallas could not believe that the party would remain sectionally divided and it certainly could not merge with the Republicans. Many of the rebels (Douglas, Walker, and Forney) might remain aloof until they were sure Buchanan would not be renominated, but they would eventually have to return to the fold. Dallas allowed that there might be dissent before the selection at Charleston, but afterward opposition was not only wrong but absurd. He was confident that the Democracy would win in 1860 no matter who was nominated, and he could see no reason for a permanent split in the ranks. Dallas, always the loyal Democrat, optimistically noted to Louis Coryell:

> I'll accept cheerfully any one of them [the candidates]: preferring to be sure a Southerner, but never discontented with the best possible result. When we can't do the best, let us at least do the best we can. Be the candidate whom he may, nail the flag, and never despair of the Republic.

Dallas received the southern nominee he desired in John Breckinridge of Kentucky. But, unfortunately, the divided Democracy also presented a northern candidate, Stephen Douglas of Illinois. The Constitutional Union Party nominated a southerner, John Bell of Tennessee, to make it a four-way race. In the ensuing split Republican Abraham Lincoln won with less than 40 percent of the popular vote. Dallas waited anxiously for news of the impact of the election on the South.

Sectionalism had splintered his party; he feared it would sunder the Union.[23]

Dallas tried to maintain cautious optimism. His initial reaction to the news of Lincoln's victory and the talk of southern secession was that it would produce widespread financial panic throughout the country. The Republican Party was trying to appease the South, but its stance on "irrepressible conflict" and an alliance with the abolitionists made the South's position difficult, since southerners could logically assume that destruction of their rights and property would soon occur. Dallas noted that fortunately the South was led by "violent, effercesing [*sic*] and unsuccessful ranters," such as William L. Yancey, Robert Barnwell Rhett, and Robert Toombs. These men were second-rate politicians and if no better leaders appeared the Union might yet be preserved.

The compromise proposals advocated by Buchanan in his annual message on 4 December were severely criticized by the minister. The idea of restoring the old Missouri Compromise line was unconstitutional and impractical. Dallas felt the main problem was that the conflict between the national Fugitive Slave Law and state personal-liberty laws had not been resolved. A House committee should amend the Fugitive Slave Law so that it would be satisfactory to both sections and would permit neither one to win the victory.[24]

Dallas's naive optimism that such a revision of the slave laws would heal the breach in the Union was shattered when South Carolina seceded on 20 December. The minister grew more pessimistic as the Buchanan cabinet began to collapse late in the month. All cabinet members from the South resigned, as did crusty old Secretary of State Cass. Dallas lamented the defection of good men like Secretary of the Treasury Howell Cobb. He also regretted Cobb's action, since "a good cause is really only injured by violence, and best promoted by calm and steady action." Dallas realized gloomily that the departure from Washington of the leading southerners would enable the abolitionist extremists to push their doctrines through Congress. He lamented, "My country, my country, whither in the intoxication of your liberty are you plunging!"[25]

By 3 January 1861 Dallas had lost all hope in the government. He told Moran that he firmly believed the Union had been destroyed. The minister was exceedingly depressed and stopped attending all social events. His secretary noticed that Dallas was mentally and physically declining, probably because of the tension and anxieties over the condition of the Union. Moran noted that he was "rapidly failing" and that his memory was defective. "In fact," Moran said, "he is really breaking up.'' This analysis is no doubt extreme in explaining Dallas's mental state. The minister gave no indications of a mental collapse in his letters or in his diary. He was, however, a deeply shaken, bitter, disillusioned man who wanted only to escape from events that he could neither understand nor control. He thought his party, the Constitution, and the Union had been shattered. There was nothing left for him now but to hide from the debacle in some interior part of the country. He found no satisfaction in representing a divided nation and hoped that he could return to Pennsylvania as soon as possible. In a letter to his daughter Susan he wrote:

> Perhaps men in public life may gradually get accustomed to the state of things, but just now under the influence of the sudden and terrible national fall from careening exultation to wretched disruption and shame, the burden is hard to bear.

Before the minister could retire to the quiet life he desired so much, he was obliged to deal with one final problem in London—preventing recognition of the new Confederate government.[26]

On 16 March 1861 President Jefferson Davis appointed William L. Yancey, Pierre A. Rost, and A. Dudley Mann as commissioners to Great Britain to negotiate for British recognition of the Confederacy. Although these men did not arrive in London until mid-April, the United States government was cognizant of the mission and urged Dallas to act before their arrival. On 4 April the minister received a letter from Secretary of State William Seward instructing him to prevent as far as possible British recognition of the seceded states. Dallas promptly arranged an interview with Lord John Russell, but the foreign secretary would not commit himself on any policy for his government.

A few days after the three commissioners arrived in London Russell invited Dallas to his house. At this meeting on 2 May he told the American that the emissaries were in the city and he was willing to see them unofficially. He also pointed out that Great Britain and France had agreed to pursue a joint policy on recognition, whatever the policy might be. The idea of free trade, cheap cotton, and millions of British customers in the South undoubtedly played some part in Russell's reception of the Confederates on 4 May. Three days later the announcement of British neutrality was made in Parliament. The British, with their own self-interest primarily in mind, were cautiously contemplating their actions before agreeing to official recognition of a divided United States.[27]

Dallas was conscious of the precarious state of relations between the United States and Great Britain vis-à-vis the Confederacy in April 1861. He had, however, neither the will nor the knowledge of Lincoln's policy to assert the northern position. Therefore, Dallas was obedient but not aggressive in executing Seward's instructions. For example, he declined to begin discussions on the subjects of a blockade and privateers. He tried earnestly to prevent recognition by encouraging a "wait-and-see" policy for the Europeans. Any action on their part, he declared, would widen the American breach while there was still hope that it might be sealed.

Dallas was personally hindered in his negotiations by a natural sympathy for the South and her institutions. He had many old friends and supporters there—one of whom, envoy A. Dudley Mann, visited him immediately after his arrival in London—and was reluctant to alienate them by what might be interpreted as a defense of an abolitionist Republican position. He was not, however, a secessionist (as Moran had labeled him). He carried out his instructions carefully until 16 May, the day on which he thankfully turned the legation over to Charles Francis Adams.[28]

Until the final few months of his tenure Dallas's mission had been a qualified success. Between 1856 and 1861 the two powers had settled a number of vexing questions. Among the more important were the solutions of the Clayton-Bulwer differences and the abandonment of the rights of visit and search. Only the San Juan Island dispute, a minor question, remained to be negotiated. Then the Civil War disrupted the harmony and profitable commerce that had been growing since 1815. Dallas departed from England in May with an air of weariness and relief. The physical and financial burden the mission had placed on Dallas seemed irredeemable. The damp, chilly weather bothered his teeth and he contracted frequent colds. The climate confined the family to the house, destroying appetite, sleep, and, most important, morale. Although George was initially enraptured with the numerous parties and concerts, he sought to modify his involvement in the tiring, endless, and financially taxing London social scene, particularly after the completion of the Clarendon Convention. The forceful pressures of his wife and daughters, however, compelled his attendence. Sophy reveled in her flirtation with European nobility, who represented a welcome relief from her borderline socioeconomic position in Philadelphia. His daughters relished the attention paid them by young aristocrats and the constant round of fetes. Even Philip broadened his horizons with a long visit to Ireland with two compatriots. A cross-channel jaunt to France and clothes-buying spree in Paris in 1858 undoubtedly raised Sophy's and daughter Charlotte's spirits (Charlotte had come to visit with her husband, Charles Morrell), but they depleted Dallas's bank account. Certainly before 1861 George longed for Walnut Street and the love of his grandchildren. He maintained a steady correspondence with his married daughters, especially Catherine, who lived in Philadelphia. Her husband, "Fitz," had been entrusted with the care and maintenance of Dallas's property and modest investments. When the wealthy Dixon purchased a rural estate, "Farley," outside the city in 1858, Dallas wistfully advised, "Keep your minds steadily occupied by farming or reading and your hearts always on the children, and I will vouch for your finding country life far more noble, independent and happy than a residence in any city on earth."

The weary diplomat had enjoyed his service in London far more than that in St. Petersburg. He had thrived on the political, social, and intellectual stimulation he received in Great Britain. Nevertheless, while Dallas admired England, he never liked it. He combined in a love-hate relationship a respect for the prowess of her navy and the expanse of her empire; an admiration of her leaders, society, and culture. Yet he jealously disliked her righteous arrogance, disdained her monarchical form of government, and attacked the brutality of her colonial wars. Dallas, however, made a very real contribution to Anglo-American harmony through his actions and mere presence. But the Civil War did much to erase the good will he had helped create. The Philadelphian, now old and tired, hoped to find on Walnut Street escape and solace from his crumbling world.[29]

Conclusions

George M. Dallas returned to Philadelphia in June 1861, where he encouraged a throng gathered in front of his house to support "the Union, the whole Union, the Union forever." The weary politician and diplomat spent the summer contemplating the fate of the nation and pondering whether he could do anything to help avert the disaster of open conflict. By mid-July he understood both that the situation was desperate and that he could do nothing about it. As a eulogist later observed, "he looked on, lamenting, perhaps, with Richelieu, that he could not wield the sword of earlier days, but content to look on, even as the statues of dead men gaze upon us from their cold niches, and they see the world pass them by." Dallas wrote sadly to Francis Markoe that he had battled for over forty years for the Constitution and the rights of the South, but the "mushroom men at Montgomery" threw away any gains by their reckless and foolish actions. Much as he detested abolitionists, Dallas felt that they were less responsible for secession than the southern fire-eaters. He felt the bitterness of a man who had worked for the South and then had been betrayed by it. Nevertheless, he said for the present that he would be silent. If the political tide changed in either the North or South and the extremists were displaced, he would eagerly cry out for peace and reunion. Dallas doubted, however, that this would soon occur: "I have placed myself exactly where I stood in 1833—against Calhoun and his ideas of nullification and secession and there I shall stand to the last, be the men in power big or little, black or white, honest or jacks."[1] His reluctance to take sides was typical of the older generation, which cherished the dreams of being national in sentiment and local in its political loyalties. The rapid polarization of opinion in the 1850s had shattered the dream and left Dallas, and countless Americans like him, without what they regarded as viable alternatives. They were expected to choose and felt their choices meaningless.

Dallas's reluctance to commit himself publicly on the crisis of the Union was dispelled by the armed clashes of July and August 1861. On 17 September a nonpartisan rally was held in Philadelphia to celebrate the anniversary of the signing of the Constitution. Benjamin Rush, a friend of the Dallas family, persuaded the former vice-president to make the keynote speech. In this address Dallas fully sustained the war and attacked the folly of secession. He appealed to the people to unite in their efforts and to prosecute it with success. The disaster of Bull Run had broken Dallas's silence. Sidney George Fisher noted in his diary on 16 September, "Who wants to hear an old hack politician, whom everybody despises, twaddle about the Constitution which he cannot understand and has all his life disregarded." Two days later Fisher praised Dallas for his patriotic efforts, labeled him a leading Democrat, and called him a gracious gentleman. After this address Dallas was asked to speak by supporters of the Union and later in the war by antiadministration Democrats. He refused, however, to participate actively in politics in any manner and contented himself with quietly casting his vote for McClellan and Pendleton in 1864.[2]

The seclusion of his Walnut Street residence and a modest law practice were intended to sustain and occupy the aging Philadelphian in his last years. But much to his surprise, diversion presented itself in the form of Benjamin Moran, Dallas's former assistant secretary in London. Moran had remained in England, where he was an agent and trustee of the Atlantic and Great Western Railroad and, consequently, a friend of James McHenry, the European who was the moving force behind the enterprise. McHenry was an entrepreneur who dabbled in investments of all kinds, including the Pennsylvania holdings of the Duke de Rianzares, the husband of Queen Mother Christina of Spain. The duke had invested well over $2 million into properties in the Commonwealth, including a waterworks, a gasworks at Germantown, and an iron foundry at Farrandsville. In his opinion these properties were being mismanaged by attorneys John and Christopher Fallon of Philadelphia and the duke was eager to transfer the control of his affairs to McHenry, who could appoint a local administrator of his own choosing. On the advice of Moran, Dallas was suggested for the task.

In May 1862 Moran began a correspondence with Dallas regarding the duke's affairs. After being assured of autonomy in handling the estate and being promised a $2,500-a-year retainer, the Philadelphian finally accepted. Unfortunately for everyone, John Fallon was not easily persuaded that the contract he had with the duke was now invalid and a lengthy court battle ensued, resulting finally in compromise and a reaffirmation of Dallas's position. Perhaps the fiscal crisis of the war years took its toll of the Dallas-managed properties, because by January 1863 he valued the total holdings at a little over $800,000. Problems mounted as the water at the waterworks became poisoned and court action followed, while the ironworks remained unprofitable. But the Philadelphian, reminding himself perhaps of the security of the fee, continued to devote much of his time to the duke's affairs.

Dallas's perseverance paid off in an additional position, which proved to be a sinecure. In December 1862 McHenry and Moran discussed the need for a new president of the Atlantic and Great Western Railroad. The two men, who had established a large investment center in Liverpool, were keenly aware of their dependence on European funds. With the advent of the Civil War, foreign influence in the railroad grew even stronger and it became necessary to consolidate under new management. The Atlantic and Great Western Railroad needed a leader whom the British investors admired and trusted. Again, Dallas was suggested by Moran as the ideal choice and McHenry quickly agreed. The Philadelphian was to be only a token president of the combined Ohio–New York–Pennsylvania operation; the important decisions would be made by McHenry and the three branch presidents under Dallas. George would be liberally rewarded for the use of his good name in London. In January 1863 he accepted the lucrative $10,000-a-year post. Moran deemed the agreement "mutually beneficial" and it undoubtedly enabled Dallas to spend the rest of his life in financial comfort. He abandoned his regular practice and the Philadelphia Directory elevated him from "attorney-at-law" to "gentleman."

There is a distinct possibility that the aging and financially strapped former vice-president was chosen for these tasks because McHenry, Moran (who felt nothing but animosity for Dallas personally), and their agents in the United States saw Dallas would be malleable and would turn a blind eye to questionable stock purchases or transactions involving both the railroad and the duke's ample holdings. Whether he did so is difficult to ascertain. Certainly by February 1864 Dallas was suspicious of some unusual ties between the railroad representatives and several of the duke's (i.e., McHenry's) agents in the United States. If he did become suspicious, Dallas never broached the subject with Moran or McHenry and he continued to perform his often routine tasks dutifully.[3]

On 30 December 1864 Dallas traveled into the city to shop and take care of several business matters. His health was very good and notes appear in his memoranda book until 29 December. Then, suddenly, and apparently of a heart attack, Dallas died quietly at his home on New Year's Eve. At his widely publicized funeral, Secretary of State William Seward and the chief justice of Pennsylvania, George Woodward, served as pallbearers. The coffin was taken to St. Peter's Episcopal Churchyard, where Dallas was interred near naval hero Stephen Decatur, artist Charles Willson Peale, and, ironically, banker Nicholas Biddle. As expected, Dallas received generous praise from Democratic newspapers in obituaries that emphasized his integrity, ability, and charm. His critics were more restrained. Sidney George Fisher said Dallas was a man of ordinary ability who, through strenuous exertion, a fluent tongue, and high social position, had managed to attain political recognition. Fisher was resentful of what he regarded as a demogogic and partisan public posture at odds with Dallas's private inclination to caution and self-restraint. Benjamin Moran conceded that Dallas was a gentleman and ascribed their bad relations in London to the influence of the Dallas family. In any case Dallas had accomplished much in his forty years of service to the state and federal governments.[4]

Dallas's death left his family in a stable, but not prosperous, financial situation. His estate was appraised at $45,000 in 1865, but after debts were paid and modest annuities deducted for Sophy and his son Philip, only $18,000 remained. This was comprised mostly of city and state bonds and Tioga Railroad stock.

Thus George M. Dallas died as he had lived: without the financial independence to match his social position. It was undoubtedly hoped that Philip would assume the financial burdens of the family, but his death in 1866 eliminated that possibility. Sophy died in 1869 and was buried near her husband and son in St. Peter's Churchyard. Fortunately, several of the daughters had married well, especially Catherine Dallas Dixon. Their independent wealth helped to sustain the remaining unmarried sisters, Julia (d. 1897) and Sophia (d. 1899) in comfortable Philadelphia surroundings. Because Philip never married there are no direct descendants of George Mifflin Dallas alive today bearing the Dallas name. It has been carried, however, through the Dixons, who interestingly enough have intermarried with the Biddle family to produce numerous twentieth-century leaders of Quaker City society and business.

Unlike some of his contemporaries, Dallas has been neglected rather than maligned by historians. Virginia Beck has sympathetically studied his political career in a brief master's thesis and Bruce Ambacher in a 1970 dissertation at Temple University examines Dallas's relations with the Family Party. The two major scholarly works that consider Dallas in detail are Philip Klein's *Pennyslvania Politics* and Charles Snyder's *The Jacksonian Heritage*. Klein presents the best evaluation of Dallas's presenatorial career. He views him correctly as a prominent young politician who sought control of the state and desired to place Calhoun in the White House. While Klein is not particularly critical of any of Dallas's actions, the sympathy and admiration that are evident for Buchanan are certainly absent for Dallas. Snyder's effort is the most balanced evaluation of Dallas in the 1840s. He sees the vice-president as an influential politician around whom the anti-Buchanan forces could rally. The Philadelphian was hindered in his bid for the presidency by his limited following and the lack of zest for political combat.

Other studies consider Dallas peripherally; for example, Klein's *James Buchanan,* Charles Sellers's *James K. Polk,* and James Shenton's *Robert John Walker*. None of these biographies is especially kind to Dallas. The early sympathy Klein evidenced for Old Buck in *Pennsylvania Politics* is more pronounced in his second work. As Buchanan rises in Klein's estimation, Dallas steadily falls. Sellers rightly portrays Polk as caught in the middle of the Dallas-Buchanan feud. The Philadelphian emerges as a somewhat inept and egotistical individual whom the president was able to maneuver deftly. Shenton pictures Dallas as kindly, old, likeable Uncle George. Walker's actions and influence, rather than Dallas's, determined the political destiny of the Philadelphian in the 1840s.

Much more research has been done on the diplomatic phases of Dallas's career, especially the London mission. Sister Theresa Donovan's two articles are the only works that deal directly with Dallas. She is generally sympathetic and complimentary. Her articles illustrate the problems Dallas confronted in London and Washington, but they deliberately do not examine in depth the negotiations or solutions to these difficulties. This has been done for the Dallas-Clarendon Convention by Mary Williams in her general study of Anglo-American isthmian relations; by Robert Scribner in his dissertation on William Marcy; and by Richard Van Alstyne in his dissertation and numerous articles. Each of these justly emphasizes the skill of Marcy in 1856, but they also credit Dallas with patience and hard work in completing the practical negotiations. The scholars respect his diplomatic ability and the good relations he maintained with the British government through a series of crises. Emmett Harshbarger and Hugh Soulsby in their works on the slave trade express similar feelings toward Dallas as a capable minister, although they consider British policy much more important than any American action in settling the visit-and-search question. The only historian who is harshly critical of Dallas's diplomacy is Beckles Willson in *America's Ambassadors to England*. Willson sees Dallas as an arrogant, haughty buffoon who was more concerned with emphasizing his republicanism and criticizing British society than in fulfilling his duties as American minister.

Dallas began and closed his public career as a consistent supporter of the Union, the Constitution, and the Democracy. As both politician and diplomat his actions were generally guided by what he judged best for the three and, of course, for himself. A complex blend of realist and idealist, he weighed the pros and cons of an argument carefully before committing himself. If his deeds occasionally met with the disapproval of a greater authority, for example, President Jackson in the bank war, the Philadelphian stoically prepared himself for the consequences. The rewards he received for loyalty to his party, in an era in which such devotion was almost a religious experience, did not totally satisfy Dallas. He coveted the power, but mostly he desired the position of great men. He feigned reluctance for the limelight and determination to have it was an exercise in self-delusion and resulted in deep bitterness and frustration with a Democracy blind to his full potential and Union-preserving ideas.

Dallas was a capable politician. While not in the same category with Martin Van Buren or Thomas Hart Benton, the Philadelphian was a dedicated, faithful Democrat (some may call him a political hack) who was perpetually worthy of consideration and consultation by his party. From the administration of James Monroe to that of James Buchanan, Dallas or his lieutenants controlled the Democracy of the Quaker City. In an era of third parties and close elections, a town the size of Philadelphia was important, and could be crucial, to a national candidate. Although he did not extend any influence beyond Philadelphia after Jackson's presidency, Dallas's maintenance of a local machine and his constant opposition to Buchanan made him the logical choice around whom Old Buck's enemies could gather. Dallas's connections with the Lancastrian's rivals and his own powerful friends and relations in Washington, such as William Wilkins and Robert John Walker, enabled him to hold greater positions of influence and power than his own energies merited.

As a candidate Dallas was one of the less attractive figures in the antebellum period. He was understandably unpopular with the masses. His proud and aristocratic manner and prominent social background, which aided him in his diplomatic missions, cursed his career in national politics. Although some of his ideas on such subjects as the tariff, the national bank, Manifest Destiny, and slavery in the territories were accepted by many Americans, he failed to communicate them effectively to the people. He lacked both the charisma and the motivation for high public office. Dallas's driving force—as he pointed out in an 1856 letter to a friend—was an all-pervasive desire for historical fame. Only once (the vice-presidency) was he selected by a vote of the people to serve in government at any level. This is not to imply that Dallas would have refused the presidency if the Democracy had nominated him. He did everything possible to make himself available (except in 1848) without campaigning. Until the Civil War he harbored slim hopes that his party would call him to be the savior of the country. Without an active state organization and after a long career in politics, during which he alienated many elements of the Democracy, he was never a solid contender for the White House.

As a diplomat the Philadelphian presents a somewhat different picture. In this role he was generally smooth and effective, and he executed his assigned tasks thoroughly and with a high degree of competency. His popularity in St. Petersburg and London aided in his duties. Frequently domestic opposition was a major obstacle to success.

Dallas, as a nineteenth-century American, is a study in patriotism and Jacksonian nationalism. His support for the Union and the Constitution never wavered during his entire political career. As a "strict constructionist," he advocated change through constitutional amendment, not compromise. While he strongly upheld states' rights as guaranteed by the Constitution, he violently opposed nullification and secession. Dallas believed in Manifest Destiny and a strong Union, which would someday dominate North America.

Finally, Dallas was deeply materialistic. His background and rearing imbued him with a fondness for the better things in life, but he used many of them—opera, theater, the arts—as an expression of a life-style, void of influence on his personal outlook. He disliked self-sacrifice. As a devoted family man, he delighted in providing his wife and children with all the advantages a proper Philadelphia family should have. He resigned posts and refused others because the remuneration was too small. Periodically he relented and entered public office because of his desire for fame and because of a feeling of *noblesse oblige*. Such stints were of limited duration, however, and he consistently returned to his more lucrative legal practice. Dallas's materialism—to which he admitted many times—partially explains his ambivalence and hesitancy in pursuing public office.

By 1860 Dallas and his ideas and methods were out of touch with political reality. He turned to traditional remedies to preserve the Union, but in the heated partisan climate of the decade before the Civil War, few people listened. By then the giants of Dallas's generation had died. Jackson, Clay, Webster, Benton, and Calhoun were gone. Those who were left—Marcy, Cass, Buchanan, Taney, Van Buren—were, like Dallas, old, tired anachronisms. The leadership of the Democratic and Republican parties passed to a new generation before the war. George Mifflin Dallas was representative of a transitional generation of American politicians who helped the United States bridge the gap between the brash young nation that challenged Great Britain in 1812 and the worldly giant that emerged in an age of economic revolution a half century later.

Notes

Chapter 1

1. Walters, *Alexander James Dallas;* Beck, "The Political Career of George M. Dallas," pp. 3–8.

2. Walters, *Alexander James Dallas,* pp. 112–13. The eldest son, Alexander James, had already entered the navy as a career man, and the youngest, Trevanion Barlow, was still a child. The three daughters were Sophia, who married Richard Bache in 1805, Maria, wed to Alexander Campbell of Norfolk, Virginia, in 1813, and Matilda, who would marry Judge William Wilkins of Pittsburgh in 1818. Two sons, Charles and Robert, had died in boyhood.

3. *Dallas address to his Class at Princeton, 1810.* George M. Dallas Manuscripts, Library Company Collection, Historical Society of Pennsylvania, Philadelphia [hereafter referred to as Dallas MSS (LCC), HSP].

4. Alexander J. Dallas, *A History of the Family Dallas,* 2:136–37.

5. Undated (1816?), Case 5, Dallas MSS, Temple University; Walters, *A.J. Dallas,* p. 235; Beck, "Dallas," pp. 11–14; Dallas, *Dallas Family,* 2:136–48, 83–99.

6. Mrs. Dallas to Dallas, 24 March 1816, Dallas MSS, HSP.

7. Eulogy of Charles J. Biddle on Dallas, reprinted in *Daily Age* (Philadelphia), 13 February 1865, Dallas MSS, HSP.

8. For Dallas's legal career, see the records of the Philadelphia Court of Common Pleas, 1817–29. Dallas was *not* kept on retainer by the bank as a sinecure. He worked steadily on numerous cases throughout the period, as witnessed by the many letters between Dallas and Thomas Wilson and William McIlwaine, cashiers of the Second Bank of the United States in the Etting MSS, B.U.S., HSP. For an interesting collection of Dallas poetry, see Temple University Libraries, MSS 2764: Dallas Papers, Box 5 (hereafter cited as Dallas MSS, Temple University).

9. Only three of Dallas's seven children would marry. Charlotte wed Cuban merchant Charles Henry Morrell, Catherine married wealthy Bostonian FitzEugene Dixon, and Elizabeth was betrothed to Richmond doctor David H. Tucker.

10. Dallas, *Dallas Family,* 2:148.

11. Klein, *Pennsylvania Politics,* pp. 47–48; see Phillips, "Democrats of the Old School in the Era of Good Feelings," *Pennsylvania Magazine of History and Biography* 95 (1971):363–82.

12. Klein, *Pennsylvania Politics,* pp. 90, 96–97, 129. Ingham was a congressman and Bucks County manufacturer; Wilkins a judge and Pittsburgh banker.

13. *Pamphlet to Democratic Electors in 1856,* Dallas MSS, HSP. Bache's sister was married to Thomas Sergeant. Kehl, *Ill Feelings in the Era of Good Feelings,* pp. 200–201.

14. Klein, *Pennsylvania Politics,* pp. 101–2, 129; *Pamphlet on Dallas Speech at*

Pittsburg, 1847, Dallas MSS (LCC), HSP. In 1824 the *Aurora* was merged with the *Franklin Gazette,* then under the editorship of Family member John Norwall.

15. Typically, Buchanan refused to commit himself to Calhoun. He was nominally a Federalist and thus stayed on the fence, ready to jump to any side without embarrassment. Charles F. Adams, ed., *The Memoirs of John Quincy Adams,* vol. 6, p. 42. Dallas to unknown, 10 July 1822, Dallas MSS (LCC), HSP; Klein, *Buchanan,* pp. 44–48; Klein, *Pennsylvania Politics,* p. 130. It was freely acknowledged that the masses supported Andrew Jackson, but few politicians at this early date thought he would be nominated. William Crawford of Georgia and Henry Clay of Kentucky were both sectionally and nationally prominent political figures who hoped to succeed Monroe in 1824.

16. Klein, *Pennsylvania Politics,* pp. 132–35; Dallas to Mrs. Dallas, 11 February 1823, Dallas MSS, HSP.

17. Meigs, *The Life of John Caldwell Calhoun,* pp. 296–97; Wiltse, *John C. Calhoun, Nationalist, 1782–1828,* pp. 282–83; Klein, *Pennsylvania Politics,* pp. 135–40. Bryan and his followers were furious over the "sellout." It was rumored in Federal newspapers that he was considering revealing the backroom bargains made by the Family. When he did so, a distressed Dallas was moved to write letters to Bryan's men pleading for party loyalty. [Dallas to George B. Porter (Lancaster), 8 August 1823, University of Michigan Historical Collections, Ann Arbor.] This exposure and division did not hurt Shulze, who won the election handily, 89,000 to 64,000, over Independent-Republican Andrew Gregg. The acid anti-Catholic campaign literature that came from Philadelphia and was endorsed by Dallas is an interesting sidelight to the election. [Philadelphia Democratic Committee letter, 16 June 1823, HSP Collections: Townsend-LeMaistre Collection (under Barnard).]

18. Calhoun to M. Sterling, 5 January 1824; Calhoun to J. G. Swift, 25 January 1824, Hay, ed., "John C. Calhoun and the Presidential Campaign of 1824 (some unpublished Calhoun letters, II)," *American Historical Review* 40 (January 1935): 288–89.

19. Dallas to William Darlington, 27 January 1824, HSP Collections: Canarroe Papers, 4:33; Klein, *Pennsylvania Politics,* pp. 161–62; Klein, *Buchanan,* p. 48; Meigs, *Calhoun,* pp. 304–7; Wiltse, *Calhoun,* pp. 282–83; *Niles' Register,* 23 February 1824.

20. John C. Calhoun to Virgil Maxcy, 27 February 1824, quoted in Meigs, *The Life of John Caldwell Calhoun,* p. 308; Klein, *Pennsylvania Politics,* p. 163. Rumors circulated after the Pennsylvania convention that an arrangement had been made between Calhoun and Jackson to the effect that the general would relinquish the White House after four years. Calhoun supporters, who were furious at Dallas and the Family for their political about-face, viewed such rumors skeptically as an attempt to cover up the desertion of their champion. [Hay, "Calhoun Letters," notes to Numbers 19, 16 April 1824, and 21, 10 November 1824; Klein, *Pennsylvania Politics,* pp. 157–58; Adams, ed., *Memoirs of John Quincy Adams,* vol. 6, 18 and 29 January 1824; vol. 6, 31 January, 4 February 1824; 31 January 1825.

Chapter 2

1. The 1824 election statistics in Pennsylvania were Jackson, 36,100; Adams, 5,441; Crawford, 4,206; Clay, 1,690 (Klein, *Pennsylvania Politics,* pp. 101–2). Most recent

historiography (for example, the work of Richard P. McCormick) has indicated that the election of 1824 was fought over personalities rather than issues. A possible exception to this, written many years ago, is Herman Halperin, "Pro-Jackson Sentiment in Pennsylvania, 1820–1828," *Pennsylvania Magazine of History and Biography* 50 (1926): 193–240, which declares that the real issue in 1824 was the *method* of selecting a president. In the Turnerian tradition Halperin portrays the western agrarians and the working class staging a political revolution behind Jackson to kill "King Caucus." The election is seen as a battle for political power in which "the people" are victorious. A more recent interpretation is by Paul C. Nagel, "The Election of 1824: A Reconsideration Based on Newspaper Opinion," *Journal of Southern History* 26 (August 1960): 315–29. Nagel persuasively argues that there were definite issues in the campaign and election, including slavery, sectionalism, the tariff, internal improvements, and centralization of governmental power. He deals mostly with New England and the South, however, making scant reference to the Keystone State. Pennsylvania does not fit Nagel's pattern because it is both pro-American System and pro-Jackson. State politicians were certainly concerned about issues, but they felt that Jackson, Calhoun, or Clay (depending upon the faction) held the proper views. All the factions were concerned primarily with defeating Crawford and the New York–Virginia alliance. In the absence of an organized party system, the issues alone certainly were not enough to turn out the popular vote in 1824. The total vote was only one-third that of 1828.

2. Dallas to Ingham, 1, 6, 16 February 1825, Dallas MSS, HSP.

3. Dallas to Ingham, 16 February 1825, ibid.

4. "Memoirs of a Senator from Pennsylvania, Jonathan Roberts, 1771–1854," *Pennsylvania Magazine of History and Biography* 62 (July 1938): 409; Klein, *Buchanan*, pp. 21, 54–55; Klein, *Pennsylvania Politics*, pp. 101–2.

5. Dallas to Ingham, 11 August 1827, Dallas MSS, HSP; Adams, ed., *Memoirs of John Quincy Adams*, vol. 7, 7 May 1828; Klein, *Pennsylvania Politics*, pp. 204–8; Remini, *The Election of Andrew Jackson*, pp. 143–44. In the Philadelphia defeat in 1827 John Sergeant, the administration candidate for Congress, soundly trounced Judge Joseph Hemphill, who had the solid backing of the Family. This occurred despite a Jacksonian surge across the remainder of the Commonwealth.

6. Klein, *Buchanan*, pp. 57–59, 67–79. The scandal noted in Klein involved Jackson's indictment of Amalgamator leader James Buchanan in 1827 for being a party to the recent Clay-Adams "corrupt bargain." Old Hickory accused Buchanan of being an agent for Clay. This argument is refuted by Richard R. Stenberg, "Jackson, Buchanan, and the 'Corrupt Bargain' Calumny," *Pennsylvania Magazine of History and Biography* 68 (1934): 61–85. Stenberg claims that this charge was deliberately evoked by Jackson for political reasons and had no basis in fact. Charles M. Snyder, *The Jacksonian Heritage: Pennsylvania Politics, 1833–1848*, p. 24.

7. The Amalgamators did not have a candidate in 1829. They had hoped to have Governor Shulze on the ticket after his convention defeat, but he vacillated and finally decided not to run. They then had to be content with undermining Wolf (while paying him lip service) in any way possible, including support of the Anti-Masonic candidate, to keep Wolf's vote total small. (Klein, *Pennsylvania Politics*, pp. 277, 288.) The Anti-Masonic Party emerged as a potent political force in Pennsylvania in the summer of 1829. It rallied to its side the Adams men, now left without a party, and added those who had become increasingly alienated from Jackson because of his vetoes. The Anti-Masons were a powerful force in the southern, southeastern, and western parts of the Commonwealth for over a decade. They finally elected Ritner governor in 1835, when the Democrats split, but maladministration ruined the party and hastened a complete

coalition with the Whigs by 1840. For detailed studies of Pennsylvania Anti-Masonry, consult Charles McCarthy, *The Antimasonic Party: A Study of Political Antimasonry in the United States, 1827–1840* (American Historical Association *Annual Report for 1902,* I) (Washington, D.C.: Government Printing Office, 1903), pp. 367–574. Also note C. M. Andrews, "Anti-Masonic Movement in Western Pennsylvania," *Western Pennsylvania Historical Magazine,* December 1935.

8. Dallas to Ingham, 7 March, 1, 2, 9 April 1829, Dallas MSS, HSP; Klein, *Pennsylvania Politics,* pp. 258–59; Beck, "Dallas," pp. 19–20.

9. Dallas to Ingham, 14 November 1829, Dallas MSS, HSP; Klein, *Pennsylvania Politics,* p. 302.

10. The original bank charter provided for the appointment of *five,* not *four,* directors by the president. Dallas to Ingham, 21 September, 15 October 1829, Dallas MSS, HSP.

11. Dallas to Ingham, 24 October, 9 November, 2, 9 December 1829, 7, 12, 19 January 1830, ibid.

12. Dallas to Ingham, 30 December 1829, undated (1830?), ibid.

13. Dallas to Ingham, 1 April 1829, 17 November, 26 December 1830, ibid. By December 1830 Dallas, the Philadelphia aristocrat, was attacking a proposed constitutional amendment that would limit a president's tenure to one four-year term. He denounced it because the provisions would reduce the power and prestige of the Executive and aid "none but the rich, and are they the proper rulers for this country?" (Ibid.)

The patronage problem was an especially difficult one with the various factions in Pennsylvania at this time. Jackson did not remove as many people as his supporters might have desired or expected. This may be illustrated by using the example of the postmasters. In Pennsylvania only thirty-five were removed by Jackson (in a state that strongly voted for him in 1824) in contrast to New York, where four times that number were ousted (in a state that was equally opposed to him in 1824). Carl Russell Fish, *The Civil Service and the Patronage* (New York: Longmans, Green, 1904), p. 126. Sidney H. Aronson, *Status and Kinship in the Higher Civil Service* (Cambridge, Mass.: Harvard University Press, 1964) shows that while Jackson spoke in egalitarian terms regarding the holding of public office, his own appointments reflected the kind of dependence on a professional and college-educated elite that characterized Adams and Jefferson. Thus the "mobs" of the Keystone State frontier or city Democrats who followed Jackson were not likely to receive appointments on the basis of loyalty alone.

14. Dallas to Ingham, 17, 4 November 1830; T. I. Heston to Dallas, 10 December 1830, Dallas MSS, HSP.

15. Dallas to Ingham, 28 October, 4 November 1830, 11 January 1831, ibid.

16. Dallas to Ingham, 29 March, 5 April 1831, Dallas MSS, HSP. McLean, appointed to the Supreme Court by Jackson in 1829, was a perennial presidential aspirant. In 1831 he declined the nomination of the Anti-Masonic Convention for the office. The Ohio legislature in 1836 selected him as their candidate and he accepted, but of course he had little chance for victory against Van Buren. There is little doubt that Dallas refused to run both because he felt McLean could not win and because he felt it was too early to make a decision, rather than the factors of inexperience or the office itself. A little over a year later he was anxious to be Pennsylvania's favorite-son selection for vice-president.

17. Dallas to Ingham, 8 May 1831, ibid.

18. Klein, *Pennsylvania Politics,* pp. 335–36; Klein, *Buchanan,* p. 73. The balloting as reported in *Poulson's American Daily Advertiser,* 16 December 1831:

	1	2	3	4	5	6	7	8	9	10	11
Geo. M. Dallas	34	35	35	37	37	38	44	54	62	62	67
Joseph Hemphill	27	27	26	26	25	24	27	31	38	38	30
Richard Rush	33	33	33	33	33	33	32	32	31	30	30
J. R. Burden	18	18	19	19	21	21	13	4			
H. A. Muhlenberg	17	17	17	15	13	13	13	9			
Scattering	3	2	2	2	2	2	2	1	1	1	1

19. It should be noted that Jackson was also a Mason.

20. *Pennsylvania Telegraph,* 11 January 1832; Beck, "Dallas," pp. 22–25.

Chapter 3

1. Dallas (Washington) to Mrs. Dallas (Philadelphia), 25 December 1831; 5 January 1832, Dallas MSS, HSP.

2. Snyder, *Jacksonian Heritage,* p. 24; Klein, *Pennsylvania Politics,* p. 343; Biddle (Philadelphia) to Dallas, 31 December 1831, Nicholas Biddle MSS, Biddle Family Papers, Library of Congress. The vote in the State Senate on the rechartering was unanimous. In the House it was 75 to 11.

3. Thomas Cadwalader (Washington) to Biddle, 20, 23, 25, 26 December 1831; McGrane, ed., *The Correspondence of Nicholas Biddle,* pp. 147–52; Biddle to McDuffie (Washington), 6 January 1832, Biddle MSS, Biddle Family Papers; Biddle to Dallas, 6 January 1832, ibid.; Wilburn, *Biddle's Bank: The Crucial Years,* p. 33. Wilkins had been president of the Bank of Pittsburgh, Monongahela Bridge Company, and the Greensburg and Pittsburgh Turnpike Company. See Slick, "The Life of William Wilkins."

4. Dallas to Mrs. Dallas, 6, 7 January 1832, Dallas MSS, HSP; Dallas to Henry Gilpin (Philadelphia), January 1832, ibid.

5. *Niles' Register,* 14 January 1832; *National Intelligencer,* 10 January 1832; Govan, *Nicholas Biddle,* pp. 173–74. Van Buren in his autobiography reflected that Dallas was "doubtless a sincere friend of the President, wanted his success, but felt obliged to his state." It seems unlikely that the Little Magician reported such sentiments to Jackson in 1832. See Fitzpatrick, ed., *The Autobiography of Martin Van Buren,* p. 622.

6. Dallas to Biddle, 9 January 1832, Nicholas Biddle MSS, Library of Congress; Biddle to Dallas, 11 January 1832, Biddle MSS, Biddle Family Papers, LC. Horace Binney (1780–1875), a Philadelphia-born lawyer and politician, was a bank director and served one term in Congress (1833–34) as a Whig; but he is best known for his fine multivolume work on Pennsylvania Supreme Court decisions. Biddle to Binney (Washington), 25 January 1832, Biddle MSS, Biddle Family Papers, LC; Dallas to H. Gilpin, 15, 28 January 1832, Dallas MSS, HSP.

7. Binney to Biddle, 23 January 1832, Biddle MSS, LC; U.S., *Register of Debates in Congress,* 22d Cong., 1st sess., 1832, 8, pt. 1, 20 January 1832, p. 150; Dallas to Mrs. Dallas, 25 January, Dallas MSS, HSP. Another exchange between Benton and Dallas occurred on 8 February over the legality of bank drafts.

8. Govan, *Biddle,* p. 181; Biddle to Binney, 6 February 1832, Nicholas Biddle MSS,

Biddle Family Papers, LC; Biddle to Charles J. Ingersoll (Washington), 6 February 1832, ibid.

9. Dallas to Gilpin, 5 February 1832, Dallas MSS, HSP.

10. Ingersoll to Biddle, 6, 9, 12, 15 February 1832, Biddle MSS, LC. Biddle to Ingersoll, 13 February 1832, Nicholas Biddle MSS, Biddle Family Papers, LC.

11. Biddle to Ingersoll, 20 February 1832, Nicholas Biddle MSS, Biddle Family Papers, LC; Biddle to Dallas, 10 March 1832, ibid.; Ingersoll to Biddle, 23 February 1832, Biddle MSS, LC; Ingersoll to Biddle, 7 March 1832, ibid. Biddle continued to remind Dallas of his opportunities and obligations, however, almost to the day the bill was reported out of committee.

12. Ingersoll to Biddle, 11 March 1832, Biddle MSS, LC; Dallas to Mrs. Dallas, 22 March 1832, Dallas MSS, HSP.

13. *Niles' Register,* 17 March 1832. This contains the full context of the Committee Report, including the modifications. Dallas to Mrs. Dallas, 2, 10, 12 April 1832, Dallas MSS, HSP; Dallas to Gilpin, 9 April 1832, ibid.

14. *Debates in Congress,* 22d Cong., 1st sess., 8, pt. 1, 23 May 1832, pp. 943–50; 2 June 1832, pp. 1014–16; 11 June 1832, p. 1073; Dallas to Mrs. Dallas, 28 May 1832, 6 June 1832, Dallas MSS, HSP. Immediately after the bank vote was taken Dallas revealed that he had been a stockholder in the institution until January 1832. At that time he sold his shares to avoid possible conflict-of-interest charges.

15. *Debates in Congress,* 22d Cong., 1st sess., 8, pt. 3, 3 July 1832, p. 3852. Adam King of York County voted no. Dallas to Gilpin, 10 July 1832, Dallas MSS, HSP; Dallas to Mrs. Dallas, 11 July 1832, ibid.; *Debates in Congress,* 22d Congress, 1st sess., pt. 1, 14 July 1832, p. 1296.

16. Dallas to Gilpin, 13 July 1832, Dallas MSS, HSP; Wilburn, *Biddle's Bank,* p. 15; Biddle to Richard Rush, 20 September 1831, Nicholas Biddle MSS, Biddle Family Papers, LC. This letter indicates that Biddle was strongly anti-Mason, in contrast to Dallas, a dedicated Mason. Dallas to George Wolf, 2 March 1834, HSP Collections: Wolf Papers. Dallas indicated at this time that he favored a large state bank. See Eiselen, *The Rise of Pennsylvania Protectionism,* p. 196. Biddle had been a Family Party candidate for Congress in 1818 and 1820, but was soundly defeated both times in Federalist Philadelphia. Phillips, "Democrats of the Old School," p. 374.

17. *Harrisburg Chronicle,* 9, 16, 30 July 1832; *Pennsylvania Reporter,* 20, 27 July 1832; *Pittsburgh Gazette,* 20 July 1832.

18. Bartlett, "Chief Phases of Pennsylvania Politics in the Jacksonian Era," p. 96; *Pennsylvania Reporter,* 22 June 1832; *Debates in Congress,* 22d Cong., 1st sess., pt. 1, 22 June 1832, p. 1123; 3 July 1832, p. 1174, ibid.; pt. 3, 4 June 1832, pp. 3256–57; 3 July 1832, p. 3853.

19. *Pennsylvania Intelligencer,* 14 December 1831; 18 January 1832; *Niles' Register,* 7 January 1832; Dallas to Ingham, 29 May 1830; 30 June 1831, Dallas MSS, HSP; Cadwalader to Biddle, 26 December 1831, McGrane, ed., *Biddle Correspondence,* p. 152; Eiselen, *Pennsylvania Protectionism,* pp. 195–96.

20. Dallas to Mrs. Dallas, 12 January, 8 February 1832, Dallas MSS, HSP; Slick, "Wilkins," pp. 49–50; *Debates in Congress,* 22d Cong., 1st sess., 8, pt. 1, 16 January 1832, p. 107.

21. *Debates in Congress,* 22d Cong., 1st sess., pt. 1, 27–28 February 1832, pp. 462–86. *Niles' Register,* March 1832.

22. Dallas to Gilpin, 8, 24 April 1832, Dallas MSS, HSP; Dallas to Mrs. Dallas, 25 June 1832, ibid.

23. Dallas to Mrs. Dallas, 27 June 1832, Dallas MSS, HSP; *Pennsylvania Reporter,*

29 June 1832. Pennsylvania believed it had the solid support of the president in the tariff fight. The press frequently quoted his messages as evidence of the similarity of views. Yet what Jackson considered "sound tariff principles" is still open to debate. *Debates in Congress,* 22d Cong., 1st sess., pt. 1, 9 July 1832, p. 1219; 12 July 1832, pp. 1284–85; ibid., pt. 3, 28 June 1832, pp. 3830–31; Dallas to Gilpin, 13 July 1832, Dallas MSS, HSP; Eiselen, *Pennsylvania Protectionism,* pp. 111–12; Slick, "Wilkins," pp. 50–51.

24. Stanwood, *American Tariff Controversies in the Nineteenth Century,* 1:402; *Debates in Congress,* 22d Cong., 2d sess., 9, pt. 1, 21 February 1833, pp. 698–99; 1 March 1833, pp. 793–95; "Dallas Remarks on Clay's Reduction Bill—1833," Dallas MSS, HSP; *Pennyslvania Intelligencer,* 14 March 1833 (National Republican); *Pennsylvania Reporter,* 19 February, 5 March 1833 (Democratic); *Pennsylvania Telegraph,* 2 March 1833 (Anti-Masonic); Eiselen, *Pennsylvania Protectionism,* p. 122; Wilkins took no active part in these debates, but several times had indicated that he would compromise on the still-high 1832 rates. When the final vote was taken, however, he registered his "nay" with Dallas. See Slick, "Wilkins," p. 57.

25. "Dallas Remarks on Clay's Reduction Bill—1833," Dallas MSS, HSP; *Debates in Congress,* 22d Cong., 2d sess., 9, pt. 1, 1 March 1833, pp. 793–95; Dallas to Ingham, 30 December 1829; 15 March, 3, 17 April 1830, Dallas MSS, HSP.

26. Dallas to Ingham, 16 August 1830; 29 May 1831, Dallas MSS, HSP. Dallas had first warned the nation about the horrors of disunion and those who espoused nullification in his Senate speech of 27 February 1832. Eiselen, *Pennsylvania Protectionism,* p. 116; Dallas to Jackson, 6 December 1832; Bassett, ed., *Correspondence of Andrew Jackson* 4:496; Dallas to Mrs. Dallas, 1, 8, 10 December 1832, Dallas MSS, HSP.

27. *Debates in Congress,* 22d Cong., 2d sess., 9, pt. 1, 8 February 1833, pp. 414–20. Dallas lost many friends over nullification. In addition to Calhoun Samuel Ingham identified himself solidly with the doctrine and its author. Dallas to George Wolf, 24 April 1834, Dallas MSS, HSP; Slick, "Wilkins," p. 56.

28. Buchanan (Lancaster) to Jackson, 10 September 1831, Buchanan MSS, HSP; Dallas to Gilpin, 28 January 1832, Dallas MSS, HSP; Dallas from unknown, 31 December (1831?), ibid.; N. R. Butts to T. Rogers (Philadelphia), 21 January 1832, HSP Collections: Dreer Collection; Dallas to Gilpin, 31 January 1832, HSP Collections: Gilpin Papers, Box 2; Dallas to Gilpin, 8 March 1832, Dallas MSS, HSP; *Harrisburg Chronicle,* 8, 15 March 1832; *National Intelligencer,* 10 March 1832; *Niles' Register,* 10 March, 26 May 1832; Beck, "Dallas," pp. 27–28.

29. Crippen, *Simon Cameron: Ante-Bellum Years,* p. 20; J. A. Hamilton to Van Buren, 12 February 1832, Van Buren MSS, Library of Congress; Dallas to Mrs. Dallas, 26 January 1832, Dallas MSS, HSP; Klein, *Buchanan,* pp. 96–97.

30. Election returns for president:

	Jackson	Adams	Clay	Crawford
1824	36,000	5,400	1,700	4,200
1828	101,650	50,800		
1832	91,000	66,700	(anti-Jackson electors)	

Election returns for governor:

	Wolf	Ritner
1829	78,000	52,000
1832	91,000	88,000

These voting figures have been rounded off in some instances. Klein, *Pennsylvania Politics,* pp. 340–50, 407–10; Dallas to Gilpin, 10 July 1832, Dallas MSS, HSP.

31. Dallas admired the president throughout his career. In December 1832 he told Gilpin, "He [Jackson] is a much abler man than I thought him: one of those naturally great minds which seem ordinary, except when the fitting emergency arises." Dallas to Gilpin, 1 December 1832, Dallas MSS, HSP.

32. All of Dallas's "Whiggish" votes from January to June 1832 are recorded in *Niles' Register,* 22 June 1844. Dallas to Mrs. Dallas, 9 January, 5 February, 29 March, 12 April, 29 May, 5 June 1832, Dallas MSS, HSP. Mrs. Dallas to Dallas, 12, 15, 16, 17 January 1833, ibid. Dallas to Mrs. Dallas, 12, 25 January, 1 February 1832; 27 January 1833, ibid. Mrs. Dallas to Dallas, 30 January, 1 February 1833; 5, 10, 14 December 1832; 3 February, 24, 28 January 1833, ibid.

33. Dallas to Mrs. Dallas, 6 December 1832, Dallas MSS, HSP; Dallas to Judge E. Lewis, 26 October 1833, ibid.; Bartlett, "Jacksonian Politics," p. 79; Klein, *Buchanan,* pp. 98–102.

Chapter 4

1. Dallas to George Wolf, 26 October, 27 February, 29 August 1834, HSP Collections: Wolf Correspondence. Although Dallas was not popular in Washington, the administration respected his power in Pennsylvania. Therefore, he was consulted and cajoled to keep his loyalty.

2. Dallas to Wolf, 3 December 1834, ibid.; Jackson to Van Buren, 23 September 1833, Bassett, ed., *Jackson Correspondence* 5:207.

3. Dallas to Wolf, 6 February 1832, HSP Collections: Wolf Correspondence; Wolf to Dallas, 13 February 1832, ibid.; Dallas to Wolf, 24 March, 21 September, 6, 21 December 1834; 24 January 1835, ibid. Dallas's other major duty as attorney general was to advise the governor and the courts on due process of the law. See Beck, "Dallas," pp. 47–49.

4. Snyder, *Jacksonian Heritage,* pp. 53–54, 59; Klein, *Buchanan,* p. 108; Dallas to W. C. Rives (Washington), 15 March 1836, W. C. Rives MSS, Library of Congress; Dallas to Wolf, 7 November 1834, 27 March, 17 September, 14 October, 8, 16 November 1835, HSP Collections: Wolf Correspondence; Dallas to Col. John Thompson, 28 February 1835, ibid.; Wolf to Robert Vaux (Philadelphia), 17 December 1835, ibid.

5. Dallas to Wolf, 9 December 1835, ibid.; Snyder, *Jacksonian Heritage,* pp. 72–73; Dallas to Mrs. Dallas, 18, 20, 21 January 1836, Dallas MSS, HSP; Dallas to Gilpin, 18, 22 January 1836, ibid. Dallas hated Harrisburg and the state government. He told Mrs. Dallas, "I am heart sick at finding everything so servile, corrupt and vulgar. God knows I would not be Governor one year, if obliged to bring my children and you into such a place as this." Dallas to Mrs. Dallas, 21 January 1836, ibid. He confided to Gilpin, "what corruption and brutal vulgarity are domineering here—it outherods Herod." Men, consumed by gambling and drinking, sold political favors to the highest bidder. Dallas to Gilpin, 21 January 1836, ibid.

6. Dallas to Wolf, 27 February, 2 March 1834, HSP Collections: Wolf Correspondence.

7. Snyder, *Jacksonian Heritage,* pp. 84–85; Dallas to East Smithfield Committee, 6 July 1836, Dallas MSS, HSP.

8. Gilpin to Van Buren, 14 September 1836, Van Buren MSS, LC. Gilpin hoped to capitalize on the Dallas letter and run its author for Congress in 1836. For some unknown reason the plan did not develop. Ingersoll to Van Buren, 14 October 1836, ibid.

9. *Remarks in the Senate on the Admission of Michigan,* 3 January 1837, Moore, ed., *The Works of James Buchanan,* 3:146–47; Dallas to Buchanan, 12 January 1837, Buchanan MSS, HSP; Buchanan to Dallas, 14 January 1837, ibid.; Klein, *Buchanan,* pp. 111–12. Klein states that the exchange of letters marked the point at which Buchanan, for the first time in his life, became the acknowledged leader of the State Democrats and fountainhead of federal patronage for Pennsylvania. This may not have been true as late as August 1837. At that time Buchanan wrote Van Buren complaining that all of the patronage of the customs house, the mint, etc. was going to the city and county of Philadelphia ("Dallas, Gilpin, Chew and Rush I would recall to your memory") and urged that men of the interior be selected. Buchanan to Van Buren, 29 August 1837, Van Buren MSS, LC.

10. Snyder, *Jacksonian Heritage,* pp. 84–85. The Democrats remained divided on the bank issue in the constitutional convention between the radicals, who wanted to repeal the charter by legislative action, and the conservatives, who favored constitutional amendment. The deadlock resulted in no decisive action, but the Panic of 1837 did the job for the party. The bank collapsed in 1841. Klein, *Buchanan,* pp. 109–10; entries for 5, 8, 9, 11 November 1836; 9 January 1837, Nicholas B. Wainwright, ed., *The Diary of Sidney George Fisher,* pp. 10–12, 17, 18; Buchanan to Van Buren, 18 November 1836, Van Buren MSS, LC; Dallas to Daniel Broadhead, 19 November 1836, Dallas MSS, HSP; Dallas to Gilpin, 15 February 1836, ibid. Results of presidential elections were as follows:

	Jackson	Anti-Jackson
1832	90,983	66,716

	Van Buren	Harrison
1836	91,475	87,111

Klein, *Pennsylvania Politics,* p. 411; Snyder, *Jacksonian Heritage,* p. 222.

11. Crippen, *Cameron,* pp. 30–31; Klein, *Buchanan,* p. 113; Van Buren to Dallas, 16 February 1837, Van Buren MSS, LC. Dallas opposed the appointment of Muhlenberg as secretary of the navy. He felt it would result in the "distraction and destruction of Pennsylvania," and he would not recommend to the Democratic leaders that he accept it. Dallas to Gilpin, 12 March 1837, HSP Collections: Gilpin Collection, Box 2.

12. Entry for 21 October 1839, Nevins, ed., *The Diary of Philip Hone,* 1:428.

13. Dallas to Gilpin, 12 March 1837, HSP Collections: Gilpin Collection, Box 2; *Niles' Register,* 22 April 1837; Dallas, *History of the Dallas Family,* pp. 101–34, 151–81. Mrs. Dallas to Mrs. Nicklin (her mother), 1 July 1837, Dallas MSS (LCC), HSP; Dallas to Mrs. Nicklin, 15 August 1837, Dallas MSS, HSP; entries for 29 July, 6 August 1837, Dallas, ed., *George M. Dallas Diary,* pp. 7, 10. The only other issue beside the Pacific Northwest that Dallas dealt with in his service in Russia was the production and growth of Russian tobacco and the duties placed on it by the United States. U.S., 26th Cong., 1st sess., House Doc. No. 229.

14. Thomas, *Russo-American Relations,* pp. 92–99.

15. Dallas to Forsyth, 27 June 1837, Dallas to Nesselrode, 27 August 1837, 25th Cong., 3d sess., Sen. Doc. No. 1, pp. 50–53; Thomas, *Russo-American Relations*, p. 99.

16. Dallas to Forsyth, 27 June, 16 August 1837, 25th Cong., 3d sess., Sen. Doc. No. 1, pp. 50–52.

17. Dallas to Nesselrode, 27 August 1837, Dallas to Forsyth, 8 September 1837, ibid., pp. 52–53; Thomas, *Russo-American Relations*, p. 101.

18. Dallas to Forsyth, 25 December 1837, Dallas to Nesselrode, 28 December 1837, Dallas to Forsyth, 14 January 1828, 25th Cong., 3d sess., Sen. Doc. No. 1, pp. 54–55.

19. Nesselrode to Dallas, 23 February 1838, ibid., p. 58. Thomas, *Russo-American Relations*, pp. 101–2.

20. Dallas to Nesselrode, 5 through 17 March 1838, 25th Cong., 3d sess., Sen. Doc. No. 1, pp. 60–65; Thomas, *Russo-American Relations*, pp. 103–4.

21. Nesselrode to Dallas, 9/21 March 1838, 25th Cong., 3d sess., Sen. Doc. No. 1, p. 69; Thomas, *Russo-American Relations*, pp. 104–5.

22. Dallas to Nesselrode, 14/16 March 1838, Dallas to Forsyth, 16 April 1838, 25th Cong., 3d sess., Sen. Doc. No. 1, pp. 71, 65; Thomas, *Russo-American Relations*, p. 105.

23. Dallas to Forsyth, 13 May 1838, 25th Cong., 3d sess., Sen. Doc. No. 1, pp. 71–75; Thomas, *Russo-American Relations*, pp. 105–7.

24. Entries for 10 October, 18 November 1837, *Dallas Diary*, pp. 18–19, 29–30.

25. Dallas to Maria Wilkins (Pittsburgh), 23 December 1838, Dallas MSS, (LCC), HSP; *Niles' Register*, 4 November 1837.

26. Dallas to Maria Wilkins, 10 December 1837, 10 June 1838, Dallas MSS, (LCC), HSP; entries for 7 January 1858, 30 December 1837, *Dallas Diary*, pp. 224–25, 44–46.

27. Mrs. Dallas to Mrs. Nicklin, 3 November 1838 (1837?), 21 January 1838 (1839?), Dallas MSS (LCC), HSP; Dallas to Gilpin, 2 May 1838, ibid.; entries for 1 November 1837, December 1837–April 1838, 28 December 1838, 7 June 1839, *Dallas Diary*, pp. 24–28, 33–89, 153–54, 192–93. Dallas did have an opportunity to return home but rejected it. In June 1838 Mahlon Dickinson retired from the Department of the Navy, and Dallas had the chance to take his post as secretary. After much thought he decided, "being now across the Atlantic, I had better remain tranquil sometime longer." He could not see how his serving in the cabinet would be useful to his country or his friends and that the post might more advantageously be filled by an eastern or western man. Entry for 25 March 1838, ibid., p. 82.

28. Dallas to Gilpin, 2 May 1838, Dallas MSS (LCC), HSP; Mrs. Dallas to Mrs. Nicklin,, 21 January (1839?), ibid.; Dallas to Maria Wilkins, December 1837, ibid.; Dallas to James Burnham (London), 14 September 1837, Dallas MSS, HSP.

29. Dallas to Mrs. Nicklin (1837), Dallas MSS (LCC), HSP; Dallas to Mrs. Nicklin, 3, 10 October 1838, ibid.; Philip to Mrs. Nicklin, 5 November 1837, ibid.; Mrs. Dallas to Mrs. Nicklin, 13 September 1837, ibid.; Dallas to Alexander (his cousin), 10 December 1837, ibid.

30. Dallas to Mrs. Nicklin, 3 December, 28 August 1838, ibid. Dallas's mother died of apoplexy at the age of seventy-six during the first year he was gone. This was a severe blow to the family, which had always been very close. Dallas to Mrs. Nicklin, 15 May 1839, ibid.; Dallas to Gilpin, 28 March 1839, HSP Collections: Gilpin Collection, Box 2.

31. Entry for 7 June 1839, *Dallas Diary*, pp. 192–93; Dallas to Mrs. Nicklin, 8 July 1839, Dallas MSS (LCC), HSP.

32. Dallas to Maria Wilkins, October (?) 1837, ibid.; entries for 23–24 July 1839, *Dallas Diary*, pp. 207–14; T. B. Dallas to George M. Dallas, Dallas MSS, HSP; *Niles' Register*, 10 August 1839.

Chapter 5

1. Dallas to Van Buren, 31 December 1839, Van Buren MSS, LC; Dallas to Gilpin, 27 December 1839, Dallas MSS, HSP.

2. David R. Porter had defeated Anti-Mason Joseph Ritner in the 1838 gubernatorial race. Snyder, *Jacksonian Heritage,* pp. 144–45; Klein, *Buchanan,* pp. 129, 131; Dallas to Gilpin, 27 December 1839, Dallas MSS, HSP; Dallas to Gilpin, 3 January 1840, HSP Collections: Gilpin Collections, Box 2; Buchanan to David R. Porter, 8 January 1840, Buchanan MSS, HSP. Dallas to Van Buren, 3 January 1840, Dallas MSS, Rosenbach. Josiah Randall to Dallas, 11 January 1840, Dallas MSS, HSP. Defense of Commodore Elliott, 11 May–20 June, 1840, ibid. Dallas to William Rawle, 17, 18, 21 June 1841, ibid.

3. The Dallas-Buchanan struggle carried over to the vice-presidential contest in 1840. Buchanan pushed W. R. King of Alabama and Dallas urged Secretary of State John Forsyth. Buchanan hoped to use King as a steppingstone for his own presidential ambitions in 1844, while Forsyth was the center of an anti-Buchanan movement. The plans of neither side prevailed, since incumbent Richard M. Johnson was renominated. Klein, *Buchanan,* pp. 131, 135, 137; Snyder, *Jacksonian Heritage,* p. 146; Dallas to Gilpin, 23 February, 17 March 1840, HSP Collections: Gilpin Collection, Box 2; Dallas to Van Buren, 26 February 1841, Van Buren MSS, LC.

4. Dallas to Gilpin, 5 December 1839, Dallas MSS, HSP; entry for 15 October 1837, *Dallas Diary,* pp. 23–24; Klein indicates that Dallas's faction was the "pro-Bank Party" [p. 135] and that it was decidedly weakened by the bank's demise in 1841. This not only removed the clique's source of funds but also a major issue that had been used constantly to create dissension. This may be true, but Dallas *personally* did not claim to be probank. Dallas was frequently asked to speak at Democratic antibank rallies [Invitation from Allegheny County Democrats, 22 December 1843, Dallas MSS, HSP] and responded to numerous inquiries about his position by referring to his advocation of the repeal of the 1836 charter by constitutional amendment. Dallas to William McDonald (New York), 24 December 1842, Dallas MSS, HSP.

5. Klein, *Buchanan,* pp. 139, 154–55; Snyder, *Jacksonian Heritage,* pp. 174–75; Dallas to Philadelphia Democratic Committee, Dallas MSS, HSP; Gilpin to Van Buren, 23 November 1842, Van Buren MSS, LC.

6. Sellers, *James K. Polk: Continentalist, 1843–1846,* pp. 29, 54–55, 78–79; Dallas to Richard Rush, 5 December 1843, Rush MSS, Princeton University. The drive for Commodore Stewart was ridiculous, but many Pennsylvanians, including Buchanan, took it seriously for a time (Klein, *Buchanan,* p. 139). *Washington Globe,* 3 June 1844; *National Intelligencer,* 14 June 1844; *Niles' Register,* 15 June 1844; Sellers, *Polk,* p. 54; Dallas to Walker, 5 February 1844, Walker MSS, LC; entry for June (?) 1844, *Fisher Diary,* p. 170; Dallas to Pittsburgh Committee, January (1845?), Dallas MSS, HSP. Dallas pressed the admission of Texas as far and fast as he could as presiding officer of the Senate in 1845. His efforts were remembered by those Texans who named Dallas County after him. Dallas to Mrs. Dallas, 16 December 1845, ibid. Shenton, *Robert John Walker,* pp. 2, 9–10.

7. Sellers, *Polk,* p. 79; Snyder, *Jacksonian Heritage,* p. 177; Klein, *Buchanan,* pp. 159–60. Polk was not a dark horse within the party, since he had been considered a leading contender for the vice-presidential spot in 1844. His elevation to the first position on the ticket, however, was the result of luck and some brilliant political management.

8. Shenton, *Walker,* p. 48; Sellers, *Polk,* p. 99; Lambert, *Presidential Politics in the United States 1841–1844,* pp. 155, 163–64; *Niles' Register,* 1 June 1844. This issue

contains the proceedings of the entire Democratic Convention. Fairfield to his wife, 29, 30 May, 2 June 1844, Staples, ed., *The Letters of John Fairfield,* pp. 339–41.

9. This is the account of Dallas's receiving word of his nomination as recorded in Benjamin Perley Poore's *Perley's Reminiscences.* Staples, ed., *Fairfield Letters,* p. 374. Fairfield, however, perhaps out of fear of his wife's reaction, denied being in Philadelphia that night, saying he was snugly in bed in Washington dreaming of his wife, children, and home. Fairfield to his wife, 9 June 1844, ibid., pp. 341–42; Walker (Philadelphia) to Polk, 31 May 1844, Polk MSS, LC; Shenton, *Walker,* p. 48.

10. Cave Johnson (Washington) to Polk, 31 May 1844, Polk MSS, LC; Gideon Pillow (Philadelphia) to Polk, 2 June 1844, ibid.; G. Crockett (Washington) to Polk, 3 June 1844, ibid.

11. Fairfield to Polk, 2 June 1844, ibid.; Calhoun to F. Wharton (Philadelphia), 14 July 1844. Jameson, ed., *Correspondence of John C. Calhoun,* p. 601. Dallas still thought highly of Calhoun in 1844. Wharton reported to the South Carolinian, "He [Dallas] went on to say that there was one man who was the great man of this country, and that was Mr. Calhoun." Wharton to Calhoun, 31 May 1844, ibid., p. 962.

12. A. Eyck to Van Buren, 4 June 1844, Van Buren MSS, LC; Van Buren to George Melville (Philadelphia), 3 June 1844, ibid.; Van Buren to J. F. H. Claiborne (Mississippi), 21 June 1844, ibid.; Robert Letcher to Buchanan, 7 July 1844, Buchanan MSS, HSP; William King (Paris) to Buchanan, 14 November 1844, ibid.; Forney to Buchanan, 11 June 1844, ibid.

13. Entry for June? 1844, *Fisher Diary,* pp. 169–70; *National Intelligencer,* 3 June 1844; *New York Tribune,* 1, 12 June 1844; *Philadelphia North American,* 1 June 1844. On 1 June the "Old Warrior," a radical campaign publication of the *Pennsylvania Telegraph,* attacked Dallas as a "Jacobin Aristocrat" for his state bank letter of 1836, and for the fact that he prided himself on being a descendant of Lord Byron. See *Pennsylvania Telegraph,* 5 June 1844.

14. Dallas to Muhlenberg, 5 June 1844, Dallas MSS, HSP; Dallas to Van Buren, 6 June 1844, ibid.; Dallas to Thomas Ritchie, 21 June 1844, ibid.; Dallas to Polk, 26 June 1844, Polk MSS, LC.

15. Typical of the personal abuse heaped on Clay by the Democratic press was an article that attacked his moral character, his dueling, gambling, profanity, and, of course, the "corrupt bargain." *Harrisburg Democratic Union,* 14 August 1844; *Washington Globe,* 1 November 1844. Dallas's stand on the bank question disturbed portions of the Democratic press also. *Niles' Register,* 15 June 1844; *New York Tribune,* 15 June 1844.

16. *Harrisburg Democratic Union,* 30 October, 14 August 1844; *Pittsburgh Daily Morning Post,* 10, 11 June 1844; John Wentworth (Washington) to Dallas, 4 June 1844, Dallas MSS (LCC), HSP; Dallas to Wentworth, 8 June 1844, ibid. In this letter Dallas also took a stand against the distribution of public lands (as the Democratic platform called for), which was a popular measure in Pennsylvania, and one which he had supported in 1832. H. O. Foster (Washington) to Dallas, 31 May 1844, ibid.; Dallas to Foster, 4 June 1844, ibid.; "A Staunch Democrat" (Buffalo) to Dallas, 7 June 1844, ibid.

17. Annexation was popular in Pennsylvania with both the press and the party. There was little dissension over the issue and most Democratic congressmen and legislators gave it their support. This was not the case in New York and New England, however, where the Democracy was divided. Snyder, *Jacksonian Heritage,* pp. 176, 182. Henry Clay continued to vary his stance on Texas throughout the campaign, so the Whig press never really knew what position to take.

18. Merk, "Presidential Fevers," p. 4.

19. Muhlenberg to Dallas, 3 June 1844, Dallas MSS, HSP; Dallas to Ritchie, 21 June 1844, ibid.; Donelson (Philadelphia) to Polk, 31 May 1844, Polk MSS, LC; J. Miller (Harrisburg) to Polk, 31 May 1844, ibid.; Isaac McKinley (Harrisburg) to Polk, 3 June 1844, ibid. Polk also received numerous letters from New York urging a tariff as much for revenue as for protection.

20. Sellers, *Polk,* pp. 119–21; Shenton, *Walker,* pp. 52–53; Lambert, "Election of 1844," pp. 192–93; Dallas to Polk, 26 June 1844, Polk MSS, LC; Dallas to Polk, 6 July 1844, ibid. In this same letter to Polk Dallas expressed his strong disagreement with the Tennessean's decision to stand for one term only; Dallas felt it would undercut the president's power. However, the Philadelphian did agree with Polk that neither of them should travel around the country during the campaign, that the party would benefit most by their tranquillity.

21. *Pennsylvania Telegraph,* 5 June, 31 July, 7 August 1844; *National Intelligencer,* 11 June 1844 (quoting from a Uniontown, Pa., paper); *New York Tribune,* 29 June, 11 July 1844.

22. *Harrisburg Democratic Union,* 24 July, 31 July, 7, 14 August, 25 September, 16, 30 October 1844; *Pittsburgh Morning Post,* 5, 6 June 1844.

23. Benjamin Howard (Maryland) to Dallas, 30 June 1844, Dallas MSS, HSP; Dallas to Polk, 10 July, 3 September 1844, Polk MSS, LC; Gilpin to Van Buren, 1, 15 October 1844, Van Buren MSS, LC.

24. Dallas to Polk, 26 July, 7 August 1844, Polk MSS, LC.

25. Dallas to John Willis, 27 August 1840, Dallas MSS (LCC), HSP; *Pennsylvania Freeman,* 20 June 1844; Dallas poetry, Dallas MSS, Temple University; Dallas to Polk, 8, 16 October 1844, Polk MSS, LC. Polk used the Dallas letter of 8 October as a desperate measure to stir Tennessee voters against Clay and abolitionism. This blatantly sectional tactic failed to help him and Polk lost his home state in the November election.

26. Dallas to Polk, 7, 11 August, 3 September, 8, 9, 10, 11, 16 October 1844, Polk MSS, LC.

27. Dallas to Polk, 1, 6 November 1844, ibid.; Polk to Dallas, 8, 9 November 1844, Dallas MSS, Temple University. *Niles' Register,* 15 February 1845; Snyder, *Jacksonian Heritage,* pp. 222, 225. In the election of 1844 Polk had 167,245 votes to Clay's 160,863 in Pennsylvania. This was a similar total and margin of victory to the gubernatorial race a month earlier. The voting totals in the presidential race in Pennsylvania showed an increase over 1840 of approximately 25,000 votes for each party. The great increase in voter participation occurred in the Van Buren–Harrison election. *Washington Globe,* 4 November 1844.

28. *National Intelligencer,* 4, 5 November 1844; entry for 29 December 1844, *Fisher Diary,* pp. 177–78; *Harrisburg Democratic Union,* 6 November 1844; *Philadelphia North American,* 25 October, 4, 5 November 1844.

Chapter 6

1. Dallas to Polk, 17 November, 15 December 1844, Polk MSS, LC; Dallas to Polk, 12 December 1844, Dallas MSS, HSP.

2. Forney, *Anecdotes of Public Men,* 1:63–64; Sellers, *Polk,* pp. 193–95; Dallas to Walker, 6 November 1844, Walker MSS, LC; Dallas to Walker, 7, 11 February 1845, Dallas MSS, HSP.

3. Dallas to Mrs. Dallas, 14, 16, 18 February 1845, Dallas MSS, HSP. Dallas was particularly impressed with Sarah Polk. Her easy, unaffected, and lively manner caused Dallas to comment, "I go for the new lady all hollow. She is certainly mistress of herself and I suspect of somebody else also." Sellers, *Polk,* pp. 191–94; Shenton, *Walker,* pp. 58–59; Henry Simpson to Dallas, 25 February 1845, Dallas MSS, HSP; Dallas to Polk, 15 December 1844, 9 January 1845, Polk MSS, LC; Dallas to Walker, 27 December 1844, Walker MSS, LC; Walker to Dallas, 24 January 1845, Dallas MSS, HSP; Dallas to Mrs. Dallas, 15, 20, 21, 22, 23 February 1845, ibid.

4. Shenton, *Walker,* pp. 59–60, 62–64; Sellers, *Polk,* p. 194. Klein, *Buchanan,* p. 166; Dallas to Mrs. Dallas, 26 February 1845, Dallas MSS, HSP; Benjamin Rush (Philadelphia) to Dallas, 7 March 1845, Rush MSS, Princeton; Jackson to Polk, 2 May 1845, Bassett, ed., *Andrew Jackson Correspondence,* 6:405.

5. Shenton, *Walker,* pp. 58–60, 62–64; Klein, *Buchanan,* p. 166; McCoy, *Polk and the Presidency,* p. 62. The Van Buren men were angered at Buchanan, who had done nothing to prevent the passage of the two-thirds rule at the Baltimore convention. This action denied their champion the presidential nomination. At the same time many Van Buren men were opposed to Walker, who was an avowed annexationist and expansionist. Graebner, "James K. Polk: A Study in Federal Patronage," pp. 627–28.

6. *National Intelligencer,* 5 March 1845; Sellers, *Polk,* pp. 209, 193–95; Graebner, "Polk and Patronage," pp. 617–18; Seth Salisbury (Pennsylvania) to Dallas, 28 February 1845, Dallas MSS, HSP; Henry Simpson to Dallas, 25 February 1845, ibid,; Buchanan to F. Shunk, 18 December 1844, Buchanan MSS, HSP; Dallas to Mrs. Dallas, 12 March 1845, Dallas MSS, HSP.

7. Klein, *Buchanan,* pp. 167–69; Snyder, *Jacksonian Heritage,* p. 191; John McCahen (Pennsylvania) to Dallas, 13 March 1845, Dallas MSS, HSP; Democratic Committee to Dallas, 18 March 1845, Dallas MSS (LCC), HSP; Dallas to committee, 24 March 1845, ibid.; *Niles' Register,* 28 June 1845; Crippen, *Cameron,* p. 62; John K. Kane to Dallas, 15 March 1845, Dallas MSS, HSP.

8. Sellers, *Polk,* pp. 293–97; Dallas to Polk, 29 April 1845, Polk MSS, LC. In this letter Dallas also urged Henry Welsh's appointment as naval officer. During these struggles for patronage power the meetings of the respective factions in Pennsylvania were often disrupted by the opposition.

9. Polk to Dallas, 23 August 1845, Polk MSS, LC; Dallas to Polk, 3 September 1845, ibid.; Sellers, *Polk,* pp. 293–297. Dallas to Walker, 7, 11 February 1845, Walker MSS, LC; Sellers, *Polk,* pp. 293–97; entry for 4 March 1846, Quaife, ed., *The Diary of James K. Polk,* 1:264. Polk and Dallas were both aware of the situation involving Horn, and the president noted "If Mr. Horn is rejected, [I intend] to disappoint those who cause the rejection." Polk later appointed a political independent to the collectorship. Forney to Buchanan, 7 June 1845, Buchanan MSS, HSP.

10. Unknown to Dallas, 1845, Dallas MSS, HSP; Dallas to Polk, 27 March 1845, Polk MSS, LC; Simpson to Van Buren, 18 March 1845, Van Buren MSS, LC.

11. Forney to Buchanan, 10, 21, 28 June 1845, Buchanan MSS, HSP; Dallas to Coryell, 5 November 1847, HSP Collections: Lewis S. Coryell Papers; Graebner, "Polk and Patronage," pp. 627–28; John S. Barbour to Calhoun, 21 May 1845, Jameson, ed., *Calhoun Correspondence,* p. 1037; Sellers, *Polk,* p. 299.

12. Merk, "Presidential Fevers," pp. 13–14; Dallas to Philip Dallas (his son), 1 December 1845, Dallas MSS, HSP; Sellers, *Polk,* pp. 322–23; Dallas to Rush, 1 Decem-

ber 1845, Rush MSS, Princeton. Polk was an avowed Oregon man, but no one was exactly sure what his position was, although many men thought they knew. Benton was still angered at the southern Democrats for their failure to support Van Buren at the 1844 Convention. He was hostile to the administration because Polk had dismissed Blair and established his own organ, the *Washington Union,* under the Ritchie family, and because the president had not appointed a Van Buren man to the cabinet. Calhoun was unhappy also because of the lack of cabinet appointments for his faction, as well as the fact that he opposed the addition of more potential "free" territory to the Union— which would result from the occupation of Oregon.

13. Dallas to Rush, 4 December 1845, ibid.; Dallas to Mrs. Dallas, 4, 9 December 1845, Dallas MSS, HSP. Dallas assured Mrs. Dallas that his defeat was not personal but the result of a factional dispute between Benton and the administration. See Merk, "Presidential Fevers," p. 14. Merk says that "southern Democrats" were the ones who rebelled and joined the Whigs to defeat Dallas. See Sellers, *Polk,* p. 350.

14. Dallas to Rush, 25 April 1846, Rush MSS, Princeton; Sellers, *Polk,* p. 356.

15. Klein, *Buchanan,* pp. 167–69; Sellers, *Polk,* pp. 351–53; Randall to Dallas, 17 December 1845, Dallas MSS (LCC), HSP; Dallas to Mrs. Dallas, 23 January 1846, ibid.; Dallas to John Fox (Pennsylvania), 27 January 1846, ibid.; Dallas to Phillips (Pennsylvania), 2 March 1846, HSP Collections: Dreer Collection, Presidents.

16. Dallas to Rush, 4 December 1845, Rush MSS, Princeton; Dallas to Mrs. Dallas, 4 December 1845, Dallas MSS, HSP; Forney to Buchanan, 27 February 1846, Buchanan MSS, HSP.

17. Dallas to Mrs. Dallas, 4 December 1845, 7, 8 June 1846, Dallas MSS, HSP.

18. Sellers, *Polk,* pp. 329–30; Shenton, *Walker,* p. 74; entry for 28 November 1845, Quaife, ed., *Polk Diary,* 1:106; Dallas to Mrs. Dallas, 2 December 1845, Dallas MSS, HSP; Dallas to Rush, 4 December 1845, Rush MSS, Princeton.

19. The tariff was named after James J. McKay, a Democratic representative from North Carolina and chairman of the Ways and Means Committee. Many people more accurately referred to it as the Walker Tariff. Klein, *Buchanan,* pp. 172–73; *National Intelligencer,* 23 October 1845; 2 July 1846. Quotations are from the *Harrisburg Union.*

20. Crippen, *Cameron,* pp. 70–72; Stanwood, *Tariff,* 1:80; Shenton, *Walker,* p. 83; Snyder, *Jacksonian Heritage,* p. 195; Dallas to Phillips, 3, 7 July 1846, HSP Collections: Dreer Collection, Presidents; Rush to Dallas, 27 November 1844, Dallas MSS (LCC), HSP.

21. Forney to Buchanan, 9 July 1846, Buchanan MSS, HSP; Dallas to Mrs. Dallas, 13, 15, 17, 23 July 1846, Dallas MSS, HSP.

22. *Washington Union,* 27 July 1846; Shenton, *Walker,* p. 83; Crippen, *Cameron,* pp. 72–73; Dallas to Mrs. Dallas, 23 July 1846, Dallas MSS, HSP; entry for 24 July 1846, Quaife, ed., *Polk Diary,* 2:46; Dallas to Phillips, 28 July 1846, HSP Collections: Dreer Collection, Presidents. Daniel Sturgeon, a protectionist Democrat, was the other senator from Pennsylvania.

23. Forney commented to Buchanan on 27 July, "Dallas is in a fix. God help him." Forney to Buchanan, 27 July 1846, Buchanan MSS, HSP; John Fairfield to his wife, 22, 26, 28 July 1846, Staples, ed., *Fairfield Letters,* pp. 412–13; Crippen, *Cameron,* pp. 73–75, 263n; Sellers, *Polk,* 461–62; Eiselen, *Pennsylvania Protectionism,* pp. 194–98; *Niles' Register,* 15 August 1846; *Washington Union,* 29 July 1846. Buchanan demonstrated his usual evasiveness on the tariff. He hoped to use it to his political advantage by supporting and opposing it in the proper regions of the country. Shenton, *Walker,* pp. 84–85, 100–101. Cameron arose a short time before the vote on the third reading was taken and made a plea to Dallas as a Pennsylvanian "to save his state and its great

interests'' by voting against the bill. Konkle, *E. Lewis,* pp. 99–100. Dallas's analysis of nonsectional voting on the tariff was generally correct. The split was on a party basis. See the state votes in the *Philadelphia North American,* 30 July 1846.

24. Dallas to Phillips, 28 July 1846, HSP Collections: Dreer Collection, Presidents; Dallas to Mrs. Dallas, 28, 30 July 1846, Dallas MSS, HSP; Shenton, *Walker,* pp. 84–85; McCoy, *Polk Presidency,* p. 147; Stanwood, *Tariff,* 1:80–81. A few weeks later Dallas wrote to a friend in Pennsylvania, ''I entertain no apprehension whatever as to the result of the commotion springing out of the casting vote in Pennsylvania. . . . The will of the majority of the people and . . . Congress are not to be corrupted, cowered, and thwarted by combinations of money power.'' No matter how well disposed one was, Dallas said, to promote and protect domestic industry, it cannot be done constitutionally if against the ascertained sense of the nation: ''We cannot fly in the face of the great majority merely to please the manufacturers who constitute not 1/50 of the vast concern of domestic industry.'' Dallas to Reah Frazer, 22 August 1846, HSP Collections: Gratz Collection.

25. Sellers, *Polk,* pp. 467–68. Only in Pennsylvania was the tariff met with such hatred. The South and West were generally joyful over its passage, while most of the Northeast was sullen and fearful. Crippen, *Cameron,* p. 75; Eiselen, *Pennsylvania Protectionism,* p. 198; *Washington Union,* 31 July, 1 August 1846; entry for 30 July 1846, *Hone Diary,* 2:769.

26. Dallas MSS, Box 1, Clippings: *Philadelphia North American,* 29, 30 July, 1 August, 1 August; *Pennsylvania Freeman,* 30 July 1846. Quotes from the *Spirit of the Times* and the *North American. Harrisburg Pennsylvania Telegraph,* 5 August, 2 September 1846; *Pittsburgh Daily Gazette,* 3, 5 August 1846; *New York Tribune,* 4 August 1846; *Niles' Register,* 4 August 1846.

27. *Philadelphia North American,* 18 September 1846; *Pennsylvania Telegraph,* 5 August 1846. Quotes from the *Baltimore Clipper,* 2 September 1846.

28. *Harrisburg Democratic Union,* 5 August, 9 September 1846; *Pittsburgh Daily Morning Post,* 1, 5 August 1846; *Washington Union,* 28, 29, 31 July, 1 August 1846; *Washington Union,* 31 July, 4 August 1846 quoting *New York Globe; Washington Union,* 4 August 1846, quoting *New York Morning News; Washington Union,* 4 August 1846, quoting *Savannah Georgian.*

29. *Philadelphia Public Ledger,* 3, 6 August 1846; *Washington Union,* 28 July, 4 August 1846; Stanwood, *Tariff,* 1:386, 2:35, 71; Taussig, *A Tariff History of the United States,* pp. 130–31.

30. *Pennsylvania Telegraph,* 2 September 1846; *Niles' Register,* 5 September 1846. Dallas realized the lasting effects his casting vote and the tariff would have on the Pennsylvania Democracy. Even though he might have desired a return to the higher rates, he was proud of the measure and of Walker's success in executing it. Shenton, *Walker,* pp. 95–96; Merk, ''Manifest Destiny,'' p. 185; Dallas to Walker, 17 October 1846, Walker MSS, LC; Dallas to Mrs. Dallas 13 April 1847, Dallas MSS, HSP.

Chapter 7

1. Dallas to Rush, 26 January 1846, Rush MSS, Princeton; Dallas to Mann, 7 September 1855, Dallas MSS, HSP; entry for 6 July 1848, Quaife, ed., *Polk Diary,* 4:5.

2. Dallas to Phillips, 2 March 1846, HSP Collections: Dreer Collection, Presidents. Dallas had also expressed fears about a war with England in 1839–40 over the Northeast boundary between Maine and Canada.

3. Dallas to Mrs. Dallas, 23 March, 15 June 1846, Dallas MSS, HSP; Dallas to Rush, 20 March 1846, 25 April 1846, Rush MSS, Princeton; Rush to Dallas, 29 April 1846, Dallas MSS (LCC), HSP. Rush was originally a 60° man and was in complete agreement with Dallas's scheme. Sellers, *Polk,* pp. 394–97.

4. Dallas to Mrs. Dallas, 10, 12 April, 11, 12, 13 May 1846, Dallas MSS, HSP. For a complete study of the ineffectiveness of the opposition to the war consult John Schroeder's fine synthesis *Mr. Polk's War: American Opposition and Dissent, 1846–1848* (Madison: University of Wisconsin Press, 1973).

5. Dallas to R. Rush, 19 February 1846, Rush MSS, Princeton; Dallas to Mrs. Dallas, 19, 20 May 1846, Dallas MSS, HSP; Dallas to Walker, 6 July 1847, Walker MSS, LC; Dallas to ?, undated (1847?), Dallas MSS, HSP.

6. Dallas Tehuantepec letter, Dallas MSS (LCC), HSP; Merk, *Manifest Destiny,* pp. 134–35; Dallas to Mrs. Dallas, 1 February 1849, Dallas MSS, HSP. This scheme aroused continued interest throughout the 1850s. Although the Treaty of Guadalupe-Hidalgo of 1848 failed to contain the desired provision, it was ceded by the Gadsden Treaty in 1853.

7. Fuller, *The Movement for the Acquisition of All Mexico, 1846–1848,* pp. 105–27; *Philadelphia Public Ledger,* 27 September 1847; quotation from *Niles' Register,* 19 February 1848; *Washington Union,* 12 February 1848.

8. Fuller, *Acquisition of Mexico,* pp. 135–37; Dallas to Mann, 7 September 1855, Dallas MSS, HSP. Dallas made frequent reference in his correspondence to the superiority of the Anglo-Saxon race over the "millions of Mexico." Dallas did not restrict his racism to Latins and blacks. In praising the Treaty of Guadalupe-Hidalgo he noted the creation of an empire on the Pacific that would truly open trade with "the rich Orientals. . . . 300 million bug-eating, rat relishing Chinese can be fed American flour and wheat, just as we fed the Irish." Dallas to Chew, 10 October 1848, from the Philadelphia *Public Ledger,* 15 June 1849.

9. W. Stapp (Frankfort, Ky.) to Dallas, 22 November 1847, Dallas MSS (LCC), HSP; Dallas to Stapp, 2 December 1847, ibid.; "A Young Friend" (Indiana) to Dallas, 31 August 1845, ibid.; John Marshall (Mississippi) to Dallas, 30 October 1847, Dallas MSS, HSP; J. R. Tucker (Virginia) to Dallas, 22 February 1848, ibid. This interesting letter incorporates both praise for the vice-president as a candidate and fear over the possibility of absorbing millions of "colored Mexicans" into the United States if annexation was completed. N. Rowley (Philadelphia) to Dallas, 23 June, 1845, ibid.; Unknown (Washington) to Dallas, 11 October 1845, ibid.; Joseph Severns (Philadelphia) to Dallas, 16 September 1845, Dallas MSS, (LCC), HSP; Dallas to Severns, 17 September 1845, ibid.; Simpson to Dallas, 14 December 1845, ibid.; Forney to Buchanan, 14, 16, 24 December 1845, Buchanan MSS, HSP.

10. Snyder, *Jacksonian Heritage,* pp. 205–7; Dallas to Polk, 3 September 1845, Polk MSS, LC.

11. Forney to Buchanan, 8 November 1846; 30 March 1847, Buchanan MSS, HSP; Snyder, *Jacksonian Heritage,* pp. 208–9. Dallas was also captivated by the Taylor image. He wrote Mrs. Dallas in April, "If such a noble fellow as Taylor cannot command universal and heartfelt celebration, there is no patriotism left. I care not one cent what his party predelections may be." Dallas to Mrs. Dallas, 13 April 1847, Dallas MSS, HSP. Before the United States achieved victories in Mexico Dallas had exclaimed, "General Taylor is henceforth a splendid constellation." Dallas to Mrs. Dallas, 26 May 1846, ibid.

12. Dallas speech at Pittsburgh, 17 September 1847, Dallas MSS (LCC), HSP; *Washington Union,* 24 September 1847; Morrison, *Democratic Politics and Sectionalism,* pp. 87–88. Dallas to Lewis, 16 October 1847, Konkle, *E. Lewis,* pp. 146–48; Snyder, *Jacksonian Heritage,* p. 202.

13. *Pittsburgh Daily Gazette,* 20, 21, 22 September 1847; *Pittsburgh Daily Morning Post,* 21, 23, 27, 29 September 1847. *Washington Union,* 24 September 1847; Van Dyke to Buchanan, 2 December 1847, Buchanan MSS, HSP. Two or three hundred thousand copies of Dallas's Pittsburgh speech were published in pamphlet form for state distribution.

After Martin Van Buren publicly endorsed the proviso in late 1847 Dallas indicated he would support him at the 1848 Convention. The vice-president advised strongly, however, against any open announcement of the New Yorker's candidacy in 1847. Van Buren and Cass provided an alternative to Buchanan for Dallas and he was probably laying the groundwork for later support—which never came—in his letter. Dallas to Van Buren, 2 November 1847, Van Buren MSS, LC; Shenton, *Walker,* pp. 109–10.

14. Snyder, *Jacksonian Heritage,* pp. 210–11. Dallas had under his control in Philadelphia the courts, customs houses, inspectors, clerks, watchmen, and ward and precinct committeemen. See entry for 1 November 1847, Quaife, ed., *Polk Diary,* 3:208. Polk was obviously displeased with Buchanan's presidential ambitions and made his feelings public by staying with the Dallases when he visited Philadelphia late in 1847. See Klein, *Buchanan,* p. 201.

15. Forney to Buchanan, 30 September, 17 November 1847, Buchanan MSS, HSP; Plitt to Buchanan, 27 November 1847, ibid.; Chew to Dallas, 1 December 1847, Dallas MSS, HSP; Philadelphia Committee to Dallas, 1 January 1848, Dallas MSS (LCC), HSP; Snyder, *Jacksonian Heritage,* pp. 212–13.

16. Snyder, *Jacksonian Heritage,* p. 213; Klein, *Buchanan,* pp. 199–201; Plitt to Buchanan, 2, 3, 6 January, 4 March 1848, Buchanan MSS, LC; Crippen, *Cameron,* pp. 102–3; Morrison, *Politics and Sectionalism,* pp. 100–101. E. W. Hutter was quite correct when he told Buchanan, "It is now as clear as the sun at noon-day, that out of Philadelphia Dallas has scarce the shadow of a party." Hutter to Buchanan, 5 March 1848, Buchanan MSS, HSP.

17. Hutter to Buchanan, 6 March 1848, ibid.; Albert Ramsey to Buchanan, 13 March 1848, ibid.; Buchanan to Forney, 1 March 1848, ibid.; Buchanan to A. Plumer, 2 March 1848, ibid.; J. I. Abert to Coryell, 12 April 1848, HSP Collections: Lewis Coryell Papers.

18. J. A. Campbell (Mobile) to Calhoun, 20 December 1847, Jameson, ed., *Calhoun Correspondence,* p. 1153; H. Gourdin (Charleston) to Calhoun, 4 February 1848, ibid., p. 1160; Hopkins Holsey (Georgia) to H. Cobb, 31 December 1847, Phillips, *The Correspondence of Robert Toombs, Alexander H. Stephens, and Howell Cobb,* pp. 91–94; Morrison, *Politics and Sectionalism,* pp. 108, 113–14, 124.

19. James W. Taylor (Cincinnati) to John Van Buren, 18 April 1848, Van Buren MSS, LC; G. Ag. Worth (New York) to Marcy, May 1848, Marcy MSS, LC; Forney to Buchanan, 11 May 1848, Buchanan MSS, HSP. Dallas received two votes in the New Jersey state convention. C. C. Wagener to Buchanan, 22 May 1848, ibid.; J. Foltz to Buchanan, 24 May 1848, ibid.; Crippen, *Cameron,* pp. 102–3. Throughout the convention the Pennsylvania delegates maintained their loyalty to Buchanan. They cast their twenty-six votes for the secretary of state on every ballot. Dallas to Walker, 3 June, 21 July 1848, Walker MSS, LC; Dallas to Cass, 21 October 1848, Cass MSS, University of Michigan Library. Dallas was almost killed in April 1848, when a man jumped from a

window in a Washington building and landed on the canopy of his coach, narrowly missing the vice-president's head. Dallas to son Philip, 8 April 1848, Dallas MSS, HSP.

20. Dallas to Phillips, 16 December 1848, HSP Collections: Dreer Collection, Presidents; Dallas to Mrs. Dallas, 16 December 1848, 23 January 1849, Dallas MSS, HSP; entry for 13 December 1848; 9, 16 January 1849, Dallas Diary MSS, HSP. This diary had been edited and published by Roy F. Nichols. See his "The Library: The Mystery of the Dallas Papers (Part II)," pp. 475–517. The proviso was "struck out" by a 32 to 17 vote in the Senate. Entry for 12 February 1849, Dallas Diary MSS, HSP; Shenton, *Walker,* pp. 109–10.

21. Dallas to Phillips, 16 December 1848, HSP Collections: Dreer Collection, Presidents; entry for 10 December 1848; 2 March 1849, Dallas Diary MSS, HSP. Dallas to daughter Sophy, 17 January 1849, Dallas MSS, Temple University.

22. Dallas to Mrs. Dallas, 10 December 1848; 12 January, 6 February 1849, Dallas MSS, HSP; entries for 14 January, 6 February 1849, Dallas Diary MSS, HSP.

23. Dallas to Mrs. Dallas, 15 July, 7 December 1848, 29, 30 January 1849, Dallas MSS, HSP.

24. Dallas to Mrs. Dallas, 11 March 1845; 9 April, 21, 28, 31 May, 18 June 1846, Dallas MSS, HSP. Dallas to Mrs. Dallas, 7 April 1846; 28 March, 2, 5, 15, 21 April 1847, ibid. Dallas to newspaper (undated; 1846?), ibid. Shenton, *Walker,* pp. 121–22. Dallas to Cadwalader, 24 January, 21 February 1849, Cadwalader Collection, HSP. Cadwalader to Butler, 13 March 1849, ibid. Wainwright, "Butler vs. Butler: A Divorce Case Incident." pp. 101–7. Dallas to Phillips, 23 June 1846, Dallas MSS, HSP. Mrs. Dallas to Dallas, 28 March 1847, ibid. Dallas to Phillips, 10 December 1845, Dallas MSS, Temple University.

25. The only regret Dallas had upon leaving the Senate was that Martin Van Buren might be elected a senator from New York and he would not be there to witness his actions. If the Little Magician went to Washington, Dallas lamented, the Senate would include Cass, Calhoun, Clay, Webster, Benton, and Van Buren. "Why was this reunion postponed until after my time?" Entries for 28 January, 2 March 1849, Dallas Diary MSS, HSP; *Washington Union,* 6 March 1849.

Chapter 8

1. Dallas to Foote, 16 May 1850, Dallas MSS, HSP. Dallas expressed his feelings about compromise in a letter to Judge Ellis Lewis in 1847, "Compromise, in one aspect is encroachment, in another it is base and unfaithful surrender, in no aspect is it constitutional." Dallas to Lewis, 20 November 1847, Dallas MSS (LCC), HSP; Dallas to Reading Committee, June 1850, ibid.; Dallas to Union meeting in Philadelphia, 21 November 1850, ibid.; Dallas to Georgia Committee, 19 November 1850, ibid.; Dallas to Mrs. Dallas, 26 December 1849; 14 January, 28 June 1851; 23 January, 3, 4, 5, 8 February 1852; 8 December 1854, Dallas MSS, HSP. Dallas address at Lafayette College, 4 July 1835, ibid.

2. Dallas to Guy M. Bryan (Texas), 25 July 1851, ibid. Dallas suggested the amendment procedure because "the Act for the extradition of fugitives is a pretext for protracted and persevering war upon the guarantees of the Constitution." *New York Times,* 11, 13 October 1851.

3. Dallas to Union meeting in Philadelphia, 21 November 1850, Dallas MSS (LCC), HSP. Dallas only found fault with the execution of the Fugitive Slave Law. He considered the other four provisions of the Compromise to be irreversible. Dallas to Pennsylvania Committee, 14 November 1850, ibid. Dallas Review of Book on Quakerism, 1853, ibid. R. Moses (Georgia) to Dallas, 27 November 1850, ibid.; Dallas to Mrs. Dallas, 5 February 1852, Dallas MSS, HSP; *New York Times,* 31 May 1852. Box 1, Clippings, Dallas MSS, HSP; *New York Times,* 23, 29 December 1851.

4. Curti, "Young America," pp. 34–55; Dallas to Mrs. Dallas, 27 January 1852; Dallas MSS, HSP; Dallas to Cass, 1 May 1852; Dallas MSS, (LCC), HSP; Dallas to James M. Mason (Virginia), 1 June 1852, Dallas MSS, HSP; Nichols, *The Democratic Machine,* pp. 63, 77. Thomas Ritchie had urged a ticket of Dallas and Andrew Stevenson of Virginia for 1852 in his Richmond *Enquirer.* Dallas to Mrs. Dallas, 5 February 1852, Dallas MSS, HSP.

5. Nichols, *Franklin Pierce,* p. 210; *New York Times,* 8 June 1852; Dallas to Pierce, 11 June, 4 July 1852, Pierce MSS, LC.

6. Nichols, *Pierce,* p. 228; Dallas to Elizabeth Tucker, 11 January 1853, Dallas MSS, Temple University.

7. Nichols, *Pierce,* p. 341; Henry Learned, "William L. Marcy," in Bemis, ed., *The American Secretaries of State and Their Diplomacy,* 4:199; Dallas to Reah Frazer, 24 April 1854, HSP Collections: Dreer Collection.

8. Dallas to Rush, 1 January 1855, Rush MSS, Princeton; Dallas to Mann, 7 September 1855, Dallas MSS, HSP.

9. J. F. House to Dallas, 31 March 1854, Dallas MSS, (LCC), HSP; Dallas to Mann, 7 September 1855, Dallas MSS, HSP; Forney to Buchanan, 13, 23 July 1855, Buchanan MSS, HSP; *New York Times,* 3 November 1855; Scharf and Westcott, *History of Philadelphia,* 1:219.

10. Dallas to Rush, 6 November 1855, Rush MSS, Princeton.

11. Joel Jones to Coryell, 24, 26 May 1856, HSP Collections: Coryell Papers. Dallas to Buchanan, 26 December 1856, Dallas, ed., *George M. Dallas,* no. 44, pp. 73–74. (Hereafter referred to as the *Dallas Letters.)* For an extended discussion of the campaign see Ambacher, "Dallas, Cuba and the Election of 1856," pp. 318–32. A fine recent study of Pennsylvania politics and the roles of Buchanan and Dallas in the Democracy in the 1850s is John F. Coleman's *The Disruption of the Pennsylvania Democracy, 1848–1860* (Harrisburg: The Pennsylvania Historical and Museum Commission, 1975).

Chapter 9

1. Mason to Dallas, 24 January 1856; Dallas to Pierce, 26, 29 January 1856, Dallas MSS (LCC), HSP; Marcy to Buchanan, 28 January 1856, Marcy MSS, LC. Dallas got the nod for the mission over New Yorker Horatio Seymour. Buchanan to Marcy, 15 February 1856, ibid.; Dallas to Marcy, 13 March 1856, ibid.; *London Times,* 14 February 1856. The *Times* welcomed the new minister, "George Mapplin Dallas, L.L.D." *New York Times,* 5 April 1856; Klein, *Buchanan,* p. 247.

2. Dallas to Markoe, 8 April 1856, Dallas MSS, HSP; *New York Times,* 21, 30 April

1856; Dallas to Marcy, 4 April 1856, Marcy MSS, LC; Dallas to Dixon, 29 April 1856, HSP Collections: Society Miscellaneous Collection.

3. Marcy to Dallas, 29 February, 28 April 1856, Marcy MSS, LC; R. Van Alstyne, "John F. Crampton, Conspirator or Dupe?," *American Historical Review* 41 (April 1936):492–502. The author claims that Crampton was neither a conspirator or a dupe, but merely a loyal British subject following the orders of his Foreign Office, while trying to remain inside American law. Spencer, *The Victor and the Spoils: A Life of William L. Marcy,* pp. 369, 372–73. Note also H. B. Learned, "William L. Marcy," in Bemis, ed., *American Secretaries of State and Their Diplomacy,* 6:237–62.

4. Dallas to Marcy, 20 March, 20 April 1856, Marcy MSS, LC: Dallas to J. P. H., 16 May 1856, *Dallas Letters,* 1, no. 15, pp. 39–40; Dallas to Marcy, 6 June 1856, ibid., 1, no. 22, pp. 45–47; Dallas to Mason, 31 May 1856, ibid., 1, no. 19, p. 43; Dallas to Mr. D., 6 June 1856, ibid., 1, no. 21, p. 45. Dallas noted revealingly, "My longing for historical fame would certainly be satiated if it were to turn out that I am to be the last of our ministers at this court."

5. Marcy to Dallas, 23 May 1856, Dallas MSS (LCC), HSP; Marcy to Dallas, 27 May 1856, Marcy MSS, LC; Marcy to Dallas, 30 May 1856, Dallas MSS, HSP; Nichols, *Pierce,* pp. 461–63; Marcy to Dallas, 10 June 1856, Dallas MSS, Huntington Library; *London Times,* 3, 12, 16, 18 June 1856. Van Alstyne, "British Diplomacy and the Clayton-Bulwer Treaty, 1850–1860," pp. 179–83; *New York Times,* 4 July 1856. Crampton was later knighted by the queen for his services while in the United States.

6. Dallas to Marcy, 17 June 1856, *Dallas Letters,* 1, no. 27, pp. 50–51. Dallas was kept constantly informed on the affairs of Parliament by M.P. William Brown. Dallas to Dixon, 29 April 1856, HSP Collections: Society Miscellaneous Collection.

7. Williams, *Anglo-American Isthmian Diplomacy 1815–1915,* pp. 210–11. Scroggs, *Filibusters and Financiers,* is old, but it is still the best study of the Walker venture. Scribner, "The Diplomacy of William L. Marcy," p. 291.

8. Williams, *Isthmian Diplomacy,* pp. 211–13; Van Alstyne, "British Diplomacy," pp. 170–71; Nichols, *Pierce,* pp. 461–63; Spencer, *Marcy,* pp. 372–73; Marcy to Dallas, 13 May 1856, Dallas MSS, Huntington Library; Dallas to Marcy, 16 May 1856, Marcy MSS, LC; Dallas to Marcy, 23, 27 May 1856, Manning, ed., *Diplomatic Correspondence of the United States,* p. 646. Dallas had acted as legal counselor for another filibuster, H. L. Kinney, in May 1855 in Philadelphia. Scroggs, *Filibusters,* p. 103; Dallas to Marcy, 16 June 1856, Marcy MSS, LC; Dallas to John P. Heiss, 17 November 1856, "Walker-Heiss Papers," *Tennessee Historical Magazine,* December 1915, pp. 340–41.

9. Williams, *Isthmian Diplomacy,* pp. 214–16; Marcy to Dallas, 16 June 1856, Marcy MSS, LC; Van Alstyne, "British-American Diplomatic Relations," pp. 184–88. Walker was not ousted until May 1857 and thus was in power during the period in which the Anglo-American negotiations were executed. *New York Times,* 12 July 1856; Dallas to Marcy, 3 July 1856, Marcy MSS, LC; Marcy to Dallas, 13 July 1856, Dallas MSS, Huntington Library; Donovan, "President Pierce's Ministers at the Court of St. James," pp. 468–69.

10. Nichols, "The Missing Diaries of George M. Dallas," pp. 295–97; Levett, "Negotiations for Release from the Inter-Oceanic Obligations of the Clayton-Bulwer Treaty," pp. 32, 39, 44–45.

11. Levett, "Clayton-Bulwer Treaty," pp. 44–45, 48–53, 55–56; Van Alstyne, "British-American Relations," pp. 1–8, 14, 19–20. Marcy to Dallas, 29 February 1856, Marcy MSS, LC. The British had previously settled in the Bay Islands and they did not regard their colonization as a violation of the treaty.

12. Marcy to Dallas, 29 February, 14 March 1856, Marcy MSS, LC; Dallas to Marcy, 29 February 1856, ibid. Spencer, *Marcy*, p. 370.

13. Scribner, "Diplomacy of Marcy," p. 298; Dallas to Marcy, 28 March 1856, Marcy MSS, LC; E. G. Squier to William Brown, 23 March 1856, Manning, ed., *Diplomatic Correspondence*, 7:641.

14. Dallas to Marcy, 1, 6 April 1856, Marcy MSS, LC; Marcy to Dallas, 7 April 1856, ibid. Dallas urged postponement of a final presidential decision on arbitration on 6 April in a dispatch to Marcy. He wanted more time to "inform" Parliament in greater depth of the American position. Pierce had already made his choice, however, and the news reached Dallas in late April.

15. Marcy to Dallas, 24 May 1856, Manning, ed., *Diplomatic Correspondence*, 7: 132–38; Spencer, *Marcy*, pp. 373–74. Marcy to Dallas, 27 May 1856, Marcy MSS, LC; Williams, *Isthmian Diplomacy*, pp. 216–24; Scribner, *Marcy*, pp. 299–300. Marcy demanded as a *sine qua non* for talks that Nicaragua would maintain a strong position in accepting or rejecting provisions regarding her sovereignty, although the less required of her the better. Dallas firmly supported the American position on the Bay Islands. Dallas to E. G. Squier, 1 June 1856, *Dallas Letters*, 1, no. 20, pp. 43–44.

16. Scribner, "Diplomacy of Marcy," pp. 299–300; Williams, *Isthmian Diplomacy*, pp. 224–26; Marcy to Crampton, 9 May 1855, Manning, ed., *Diplomatic Correspondence*, 7:112–14; Dallas to Clarendon, 7 July 1856, ibid., p. 666; Draft on Protectorate, Dallas to Clarendon, 9 July 1856, Dallas MSS (LCC), HSP; Dallas to Marcy, 4, 29 July, 8 August 1856, *Dallas Letters*, 1, no. 32, 42, 43, pp. 57–58, 69–73.

17. Williams, *Isthmian Diplomacy*, pp. 226–27; Scribner, "Diplomacy of Marcy," p. 301; Russell, *Improvement of Communications with the Pacific Coast as an Issue in American Politics, 1783–1864*, pp. 216–17; Dallas to Marcy, 29 August 1856, Manning, ed., *Diplomatic Correspondence*, 7:683–86; Dallas to Marcy, 26 August 1856, Marcy MSS, LC; Dallas to Marcy, 22 August 1856, *Dallas Letters*, 1, no. 46, pp. 76–77.

18. Dallas to Col. Page, 12 August 1856, ibid., 1, no. 44, pp. 73–74; Dallas to Gilpin, 19 August 1856, ibid., 1, no. 47, pp. 77–78; Dallas to Markoe, 29 August 1856, Dallas MSS (LCC), HSP; Dallas to Marcy, 2 September 1856, Marcy MSS, LC.

19. Marcy to Dallas, 22 September 1856, ibid.; Dallas to Marcy, 10, 12 October 1856, ibid.; Scribner, "Diplomacy of Marcy," pp. 301–2. Dallas to Marcy, 4, 8, 15 July 1856, Marcy MSS, LC; *New York Times*, 16 July 1856.

20. Dallas to Marcy, 17 October 1856, Manning, ed., *Diplomatic Correspondence*, 7:688–92; Nichols, *Pierce*, pp. 492–93; Dallas to J. F. H. Claiborne (Mississippi), George M. Dallas MSS, LC; Dallas to Gilpin, 17 October 1856, HSP Collections: Society Autograph Collection; Marcy to Dallas, 7 November 1856, Marcy MSS, LC.

21. Marcy to Dallas, 7 April, 13 May 1856, Dallas MSS, Huntington Library; Dallas to Markoe, 8 April 1856, Dallas MSS, HSP; Dallas to Col. Page, 12 August 1856, *Dallas Letters*, 1, no. 44, pp. 73–74. Dallas noted to Marcy in July that certain prominent Know-Nothings were writing letters to influential Englishmen attempting to disrupt his negotiations and discredit the Democracy. Dallas to Marcy, 25 July 1856, ibid., 1, no. 40, pp. 66–67; Dallas to Judge Joel Jones, 25 July 1856, ibid., 1, no. 41, pp. 67–68.

22. Dallas to Marcy, 29 July, 24, 28 October 1856, ibid., 1, no. 42, 60, 62, pp. 69–70, 95, 96–97; Dallas to Rev. Binney, 31 October 1856, ibid., 1, no. 63, pp. 97–98.

23. Dallas to T. J. Miles, 25 November 1856, ibid., 1, no. 73, pp. 108–9; Dallas to Dixon, 7 November 1856, HSP Collection: Society Miscellaneous Collection.

24. *New York Times*, 26 December 1856; Marcy to Dallas, 4 January 1857, Marcy MSS, LC; Dallas to Mr. Hutchinson, 12 January 1857, *Dallas Letters*, 1, no. 86, pp. 128–29; Dallas to Judge King, 13 January 1857, ibid., 1, no. 88, pp. 130–31; Dallas to

Marcy, 23 January 1857, ibid., 1, no. 91, pp. 134–35; Dallas to Clarendon, 24 January 1857, ibid., 1, no. 92, pp. 135–36; Clarendon to Dallas, 23 January 1856, Dallas MSS, Huntington Library.

25. Dallas to Marcy, 20 January 1857, Marcy MSS, LC; Dallas to Gilpin, 30 January 1857, *Dallas Letters*, 1, no. 93, pp. 136–37.

26. *New York Times*, 5 February 1857; *London Times*, 23 February 1857. Marcy to Dallas, 6, 9, 23 February 1857, Dallas MSS, Huntington Library. Many senators felt that Dallas had been deceived and had not known about the antislavery provision in the Anglo-Honduran Treaty. He had known, but he felt it was not an American concern. Mason to Dallas, 22 February 1857, Dallas MSS, HSP. Mason also noted the hindering effect of an outgoing administration in pushing the Convention through unamended. J. Thomas (Washington) to Dallas, 23 February 1857, Dallas MSS (LCC), HSP; Buchanan to Clarendon, 23 February 1857, Moore, ed., *Buchanan Papers*, 10:102–3; Buchanan to Cass, 24 October 1857, ibid.

27. Clarendon to Dallas, 16 February 1857, Dallas MSS, Huntington Library; Dallas to Clarendon, 15, 23 February, 3 March 1857, *Dallas Letters*, 1, no. 97, 98, 99, pp. 142–43; *London Times*, 3 March 1857, *New York Times*, 13 March 1857; Holt, *Treaties Defeated by the Senate*, pp. 91–92. Holt shows that the division in the Senate was not along political or constitutional lines but was determined by other personal and nationalistic factors. H. Learned, "William L. Marcy," in Bemis, ed., *American Secretaries of State and Their Diplomacy*, 6:233–35.

28. *New York Times*, 13 March 1857; *London Times*, 31 March 1857; Dallas to Markoe, 3 April 1857, *Dallas Letters*, 1, no. 106, pp. 151–53; Dallas to Cass, 7, 10 April 1857, ibid., 1, no. 107, 110, pp. 153, 155–56. Buchanan, contrary to his best judgment, had signed the treaty on 19 March and it was quickly dispatched to England. Dallas erroneously told Clarendon that the president favored the treaty. Dallas to Clarendon, 7 April 1857, ibid., no. 108, p. 154.

29. Clarendon to Dallas, 17 April 1857, Dallas MSS (LCC), HSP; Levett, "Clayton-Bulwer Treaty," pp. 68–69. Van Alstyne in "British-American Relations" calls the English rejection of the amended treaty a blunder, which prolonged the settlement of the issue another three years. The Bay Islands remained a problem until an Anglo-Honduran treaty of 28 November restored them to the Republic. Dallas to Cass, 17 April 1857, *Dallas Letters*, 1, no. 111, pp. 156–58; Dallas to Cass, 16 April 1857, Manning, ed., *Diplomatic Correspondence*, 7:697. Simply, the British position on 17 April was that they would not ratify the convention with the United States, unless Honduras approved the treaty, which prohibited slavery in the Bay Islands. Once Honduras agreed, Great Britain would sign the Convention with the United States, omitting the slavery provision. The Hondurans ultimately declined to ratify their treaty.

30. Dallas to Mr. Kennedy, 21 April 1857, *Dallas Letters*, 1, no. 112, pp. 158–59; Dallas to Cass, 24 April 1857, ibid., 1, no. 113, pp. 159–60; Dallas to Col. Murray, 28 April 1857, ibid., 1, no. 114, pp. 160–61; Dallas to Cass, 25 April 1857, Cass MSS, University of Michigan Library.

31. *London Times*, 25, 26 May 1857; *New York Times*, 4, 6, 12 May, 12, 16 June 1857.

32. Van Alstyne, "British-American Relations," pp. 192–94, 201–3; Levett, "Clayton-Bulwer Treaty," pp. 68–69, 76, 85–90; Scribner, "Diplomacy of Marcy," pp. 302–4; *London Times*, 29 November 1858; Learned, "William L. Marcy," in Bemis, ed., *American Secretaries of State and Their Diplomacy*, 6:366–68; Cass to Dallas, 28 April 1858, Dallas MSS, HSP; Cass to Dallas, 12 August 1859, Manning, ed., *Diplomatic Correspondence*, 7:216.

33. Van Alstyne, "British-American Relations," pp. 206, 216; Dallas to Cass, 1857, Dallas MSS (LCC), HSP; Donovan, "Difficulties of a Diplomat: George M. Dallas in London," pp. 423, 427, 439.

Chapter 10

1. Dallas to Marcy, 22 August, 27 November 1856, Marcy MSS, LC; Dallas to Cass, 25 November 1859, *Dallas Letters,* 2, no. 302, pp. 169–70.

2. Dallas to Marcy, 12 December 1856, Marcy MSS, LC; Dallas to Marcy, 1 December 1856, *Dallas Letters,* 1, no. 77, pp. 112–13; Dallas to Mason, 8 December 1856, ibid., 1, no. 80, pp. 115–16.

3. Marcy to Dallas, 4 January 1856, Marcy MSS, LC; Dallas to Marcy, 6, 20 January 1857, ibid.

4. Dallas to Mr. O'Sullivan, 12 January 1857, *Dallas Letters,* 1, no. 87, p. 130; Dallas to Cass, 28 April 1857, 25 November 1859, ibid., 1, no. 115, pp. 161–62, 2, no. 302, pp. 169–70.

5. Harshbarger, "The African Slave Trade in Anglo-American Diplomacy," p. 252; Soulsby, *The Right of Search and the Slave Trade in Anglo-American Relations, 1814–1862,* p. 142; Marcy to Dallas, 7 March 1856, Marcy MSS, LC.

6. U. S., 35th Cong., 1st sess., Senate Executive Document 61. This contains the correspondence dealing with the seizure and claims of the *Panchita.* U. S., Department of State, Dallas to Clarendon, 16 September, 9 December 1857. Despatches from U.S. ministers to Great Britain (14 March 1856–20 May 1859), National Archives, Washington, D.C. (Hereafter cited as State Department, Despatches, Great Britain.)

7. Dallas to Cass, 8 January 1858, Cass MSS, University of Michigan Library. Entry for 27 February 1858, *Dallas Diary,* pp. 247–49; Van Alstyne, "British-American Relations," pp. 227–28.

8. Harshbarger, "Slave Trade," pp. 266–68; Soulsby, *Right of Search,* pp. 158–59; Van Alstyne, "British-American Relations," pp. 228–30; Dallas to Malmesbury, 10 May 1858, Dallas MSS (LCC), HSP; Dallas to Cass, 11 May 1858, State Department, Despatches, Great Britain, National Archives; U.S., Department of State, Cass to Dallas, 12 May 1858, State Department, Instructions, Great Britain (February 1856–12 August 1861).

9. Cass to Dallas, 18 May 1858, State Department, Instructions, Great Britain, National Archives; entries for 29 May, 6 June 1858, *Dallas Diary,* pp. 275–76; Dallas to Cass, 1 June 1858, State Department, Despatches, Great Britain; Malmesbury to Dallas, 1 June 1858, ibid.; Van Alstyne, "British-American Relations," pp. 231–34; Dallas to Malmesbury, 5 June 1858, Dallas MSS (LCC), HSP; Harshbarger, "Slave Trade," pp. 270–75.

10. Entry for 8 June 1858, *Dallas Diary,* pp. 276–77; Dallas to Cass, 11 June 1858, *Dallas Letters,* 2, no. 203, pp. 28–29; Dallas to Cass, 8 June 1858, State Department, Despatches, Great Britain; Soulsby, *Right of Search,* pp. 163–64; Harshbarger, "Slave Trade," pp. 274–76, 282. Van Alstyne, "British-American Relations," pp. 235–37; *London Times,* 8, 15, 16 June, 5 July 1858. Also consult U.S., 36th Cong., 2d sess., House Executive Documents 2 and 7 for a record of problems of search and seizure in 1858–60, including Cass-Dallas correspondence.

11. Soulsby, *Right of Search*, pp. 164–65; *New York Times,* 29 June 1858; L. Einstein, "Lewis Cass," in Bemis, ed., *American Secretaries of State and Their Diplomacy,* 6:316–23; Harshbarger, "Slave Trade," pp. 290–97. Van Alstyne, "British-American Relations," pp. 239–45. The author contends that the British did *not* abandon the right of visit and search, because they applied the memorandum only to American vessels and because they continued the practice itself. *New York Times,* August 1858.

12. Entries for 6, 17, 19, 20 July, 27 September 1858, Wallace and Gillespie, eds., *The Journal of Benjamin Moran,* 1:364–66, 377–78, 435. (Hereafter cited as *Moran Diary.*) Moran was assistant secretary of legation to Dallas. *New York Times,* 21 July 1858; Cass to Dallas, 1 July 1858, State Department, Instructions, Great Britain; Dallas to Cass, 23 July 1858, State Department, Despatches, Great Britain.

13. Entries for 17, 18 June, 18 October 1858, *Dallas Diary,* pp. 278–79, 296–97; Dallas to Malmesbury, 11 September 1858, State Department, Despatches, Great Britain; Soulsby, *Right of Search,* pp. 166–67; Harshbarger, "Slave Trade," pp. 284–90; Dallas to Cass, 25 March 1859, State Department, Despatches, Great Britain.

14. Soulsby, *Right of Search,* pp. 170–73; Harshbarger, "Slave Trade," pp. 298–303; Dallas to Cass, 27 October 1858, State Department, Despatches, Great Britain; Dallas to Mr. Miller, 24 May 1859, *Dallas Letters,* 2, no. 272, pp. 124–25; Van Alstyne, "British Right of Search," pp. 44–46. By June 1859, when the Derby-Malmesbury ministry fell, the foreign secretary and Dallas were on excellent terms. The American minister truly regretted his fall from power. Entries for 7 March, 18 June 1859, *Dallas Diary,* pp. 316–17, 345–47; Dallas to Malmesbury, 19 June 1859, Dallas MSS (LCC), HSP.

15. Entry for 24 July 1860, *Dallas Diary,* pp. 410–11; entry for 10 December 1859, *Moran Diary,* 1:613–14; *New York Times,* 11 July 1857; Dallas quotation in Dallas to Marcy, 7 November 1856, Marcy MSS, LC; Donovan, "Difficulties of a Diplomat," pp. 428–29.

16. Entries for 16, 18, 20, 24 July 1860, *Dallas Diary,* pp. 407–11; Donovan, "Difficulties of a Diplomat," pp. 429–31; entry for 13 August 1860, *Fisher Diary,* pp. 358–59; entry for 17 July 1860, *Moran Diary,* 1:695. The Negro in question was American black nationalist and separatist Dr. Martin Robison Delaney, who had just returned from a tour of Africa.

17. Markoe to Dallas, 20 August 1860, Dallas MSS, HSP; Cass to Dallas, 11 September 1860, Dallas MSS (LCC), HSP; entry for 17 November 1860, *Dallas Diary,* pp. 415–16; Dallas to Markoe, 23 November 1860, *Dallas Letters,* 2, no. 340, p. 222.

18. Long, "The Sun Juan Island Boundary Controversy," pp. 200–210.

19. Ibid., pp. 217, 233; *London Times,* 19, 20 September, 17 November, 23 December 1859; entry for 9 October 1859, *Dallas Diary,* pp. 363–64.

20. Long, "San Juan," pp. 245–46, 261, 288; *London Times,* 17 November 1859; entries for 29 October, 5, 12 November 1859, *Dallas Diary,* pp. 366–70; Van Alstyne, "British–American Relations," pp. 268–69. The island was finally arbitrated by Kaiser Wilhelm I in 1872, as provided for by the Treaty of Washington of 1871, and declared to be an American possession. Dallas to Cass, 23, 30 September, 28 October, 25 November, 28 December 1859, *Dallas Letters,* 2, nos. 294, 295, 298, 302, 307, pp. 156–59, 163, 169–71, 177; Dallas to Lord Napier, 19 October 1859, ibid., 2, no. 297, pp. 162–63.

21. Donovan, "Difficulties of a Diplomat," pp. 424–25; Dallas to Mrs. Dallas, 4 September 1857, Dallas MSS, HSP; Markoe to Dallas, 20 December 1859, 3, 7 February, 18, 23 June 1860, ibid.; Coryell to Dallas, 12 February 1860, ibid.; C. Albert to Dallas, 10 April 1860, ibid.

22. Entries for 5 February 1858; 7 September 1857, *Moran Diary,* 1:235, 128–29. Moran was Buchanan's secretary of legation when the Lancastrian was in London, and he became a strong political follower afterward.

23. Dallas to Dixon, 4 November 1858; 15 June 1860, HSP Collections: Society Miscellaneous Collection; Dallas to Beverly Tucker (Virginia), 7 November 1858, HSP Collections: E. C. Gardiner Collection; Dallas to unknown, 10 August 1859, HSP Collections: Dreer Collection, American Statesmen; Dallas to Gilpin, 29 August 1859, HSP Collections: Gilpin Papers; Dallas to Coryell, 21 April 1859, *Dallas Letters,* 2, no. 260, pp. 107–8; Markoe to Dallas, 24 July 1860, Dallas MSS, HSP. Markoe told Dallas that if Breckinridge succeeded, the Philadelphian could probably remain in London or would become secretary of state.

24. Entries for 3, 19 December 1860, *Dallas Diary,* pp. 420–21, 423. Buchanan's Address, 1860, Moore, ed., *Buchanan Papers,* 11:26–27. This deals with relations with England and notes that San Juan was the only outstanding problem between the two powers.

25. Entries for 23, 25, 29 December 1860, *Dallas Diary,* pp. 423–25. Cass's resignation and the mention of Governor D. Dickinson of New York as his successor caused Dallas to comment, "so we go from one unfit to another more so."

26. Entries for 3 January 1861; 22 November, 3 December 1860, *Moran Diary,* 1:763, 747, 750; Dallas to Susan Dallas, 22 February 1861, Dallas MSS, HSP. Although he wanted to retire to the country, Dallas said he would forgo this ("despite his white hair, toothless gums and flaccid purse") because Mrs. Dallas preferred the bustle of the city and Walnut Street. Dallas to Markoe, 1 March 1861, *Dallas Letters,* 2, no. 342, p. 223. Dallas's hopes for reunion were rekindled by the ill-fated Virginia Peace Convention. The minister wrote, "Amen! Anything to save a great constitutional country from the self-immolating stroke of panic."

27. Harris, "America and England in 1861," pp. 4–5; entries for 3, 4, 8, 9 April 1861, *Moran Diary,* 1:795–97.

28. Entries for 18 April, 6, 10, 11 May 1861, *Moran Diary,* 1:799, 806–8. Dallas did help to arrange for the sale of arms to Virginia in May 1860. Virginia Commissioners to Dallas, 29 May 1860, Dallas MSS, HSP; Harris, "1861," pp. 15–18. Seward complained of Dallas's lack of aggressiveness in presenting the northern position to Russell. Entry for 13/20 May 1861, Charles F. Adams Diary MSS, Adams Papers, Massachusetts Historical Society.

29. Dallas to Markoe, 12 March 1861, *Dallas Letters,* 2; entry for 28 April 1861, *Dallas Diary,* pp. 442–43; Dallas to Dixon, 17 February, 5 June, 10 July, 2 October 1857, Dallas MSS, HSP.

Conclusions

1. Dallas to Francis Markoe, 8 July 1861, Dallas MSS (LCC). B. R. Wood, United States minister to Denmark, wrote to Charles Sumner in August 1861, reporting the rumor that Dallas had told people in England that there would be a peaceable dissolution of the Union. Harris, "1861," p. 22n, *Daily Age* (Philadelphia), 13 February 1865.

2. Dallas Philadelphia Address, 1861, Dallas MSS, HSP; entries for 16–18 Septem-

ber 1861, *Fisher Diary;* Donovan, "Difficulties of a Diplomat," p. 432; Dusinberre, *Civil War Issues in Philadelphia, 1856–1865,* p. 234.

3. Entries for 1 March, 2 September 1858, *Moran Diary,* 1:256, 420; entry for 5 January 1863, ibid., 2:1103; Dallas Notebook, 4, 19, 22 December 1862; 5, 9 January 1863, Dallas MSS (LCC), HSP; Felton, "The History of the Atlantic and Great Western Railroad." Statement of Dallas estate, 1865, Dallas MSS (LCC), HSP. Moran to Dallas, 24 May, 4 December 1862, Dallas MSS, HSP; Dallas to Moran, 5 June, 22 December 1862, ibid.; Dallas to McHenry, 24 August, 11 October, 17 November 1862; 2 January 1863, ibid.

4. *New York Tribune,* 2 January 1865; *Hartford Courant,* 2 January 1865; Westcott and Scharf, *History of Philadelphia,* 2:821; entries for 5 April 1865; 22 February 1868, *Fisher Diary,* pp. 490, 537; entries for 17, 18 January 1865, *Moran Diary,* 2:1367.

List of Sources

Primary Sources

Manuscripts

Adams Family Papers. Massachusetts Historical Society, University of Nebraska, Lincoln. (microfilm)

Biddle Family Papers (Nicholas Biddle Correspondence). Library of Congress, Washington, D.C., State University of New York at Stony Brook. (microfilm)

Biddle, Nicholas. Papers. Library of Congress, Washington, D.C., State University of New York at Stony Brook. (microfilm)

Buchanan, James. Papers. The Historical Society of Pennsylvania, Philadelphia.

———. The Library of Congress, Washington, D.C.

Cass, Lewis. Papers. University of Michigan Library, Ann Arbor.

Dallas, George M. Papers. The Historical Society of Pennsylvania, Philadelphia.

———. Diary, 1848–49. The Historical Society of Pennsylvania, Philadelphia.

———. Papers (Library Company Collection). The Historical Society of Pennsylvania, Philadelphia.

———. Huntington Library, San Marino, California.

———. Letters. Rosenbach Museum, Philadelphia.

———. Letters. University of Michigan Library, Michigan Historical Collections, Ann Arbor.

———. Letters. Temple University, Philadelphia.

———. Letters. The Library of Congress, Washington, D.C.

The Historical Society of Pennsylvania Collections, Philadelphia.

    Conarroe Papers

    Coryell, Lewis S. Papers

    Dreer Collection (in boxes)

    Dreer Collection (Presidents)

    Etting Papers (Bank of the United States)

    Gardiner, Edward C. Collection (Henry C. Carey Papers)

    Gilpin, Henry. Papers

    Gratz Collection

    Ingersoll, Charles J. Papers

    Nixon, John and Henry. Papers

    Society Autograph Collection

    Society Miscellaneous Collection

    Townsend-LeMaistre Collection (Isaac D. Barnard Correspondence)

    Vaux, Robert. Papers

    Wolf, George. Papers

Marcy, William L. Papers. Library of Congress, Washington, D.C.
Miscellaneous Papers. Princeton University, Princeton, New Jersey.
Monroe, James. Papers. University of Virginia, Charlottesville.
Pierce, Franklin. Papers. Library of Congress, Washington, D.C.; University of Nebraska, Lincoln. (microfilm)
Polk, James Knox. Papers. Library of Congress, Washington, D.C.
Rives, William C. Papers. Library of Congress, Washington, D.C.
Rush Family Papers. Princeton University, Princeton, New Jersey.
Van Buren, Martin. Papers. Library of Congress, Washington, D.C.; University of Nebraska, Lincoln. (microfilm)
Walker, Robert J. Papers. Library of Congress, Washington, D.C.

Published Collections

Correspondence

"Some Unpublished Correspondence of John Adams and Richard Rush, 1811–1822." *Pennsylvania Magazine of History and Biography* 61 (April 1937): 137–64.
Adams, Henry, ed. *The Writings of Albert Gallatin.* 3 vols. Philadelphia: Lippincott, 1879.
Bassett, John Spencer, ed. *The Correspondence of Andrew Jackson.* 6 vols. Washington, D.C.: Carnegie Institution of Washington, 1926–33.
Dallas, Lt. Col. Alexander J. *A History of the Family Dallas from 1262 to 1894.* Philadelphia, 1895.
Dallas, Julia, ed. *George M. Dallas: Letters from London, 1856–1860.* Philadelphia: Lippincott, 1869.
Donnan, Elizabeth, ed. *The Papers of James Bayard, 1796–1815* (American Historical Association Annual Report for 1913, II). Washington, D.C.: Government Printing Office, 1915.
Hay, T. R., ed. "John C. Calhoun and the Presidential Campaign of 1824 (some unpublished Calhoun letters, II)." *American Historical Review* 40 (January 1935): 287–300.
Jameson, J. Franklin, ed. *Correspondence of John C. Calhoun* (American Historical Association Annual Report for 1899, II). Washington, D.C.: Government Printing Office, 1900.
Manning, William, ed. *Diplomatic Correspondence of the United States: InterAmerican Affairs, 1831–1860.* 12 vols. Washington, D.C.: Carnegie Endowment for International Peace, 1932–39.
Moore, John Bassett, ed. *The Works of James Buchanan.* 12 vols. Philadelphia: Lippincott, 1908–11.
Nichols, Roy F., ed. "The Library: The Mystery of the Dallas Papers (Part I)." *Pennsylvania Magazine of History and Biography* 73 (July 1949): 349–92.
Phillips, U. B., ed. *The Correspondence of Robert Toombs, Alexander H. Stephens and Howell Cobb* (American Historical Association Annual Report for 1911, II). Washington, D.C.: Government Printing Office, 1913.

McGrane, Reginald C., ed. *The Correspondence of Nicholas Biddle.* Boston: Houghton
Mifflin, 1919.

Staples, Arthur G., ed. *The Letters of John Fairfield.* Lewiston, Me.: Lewiston Journal
Co., 1922.

"Walker-Heiss Papers." *Tennessee Historical Magazine,* December 1915, pp. 331–45.

Diaries

Adams, Charles F., ed. *The Memoirs of John Quincy Adams.* 12 vols. Philadelphia:
Lippincott, 1877.

Dallas, Susan, ed. *George M. Dallas Diary (While He was United States Minister to
Russia, 1837–1839, and to England, 1856–1861).* Philadelphia: Lippincott, 1892.

Fitzpatrick, John D., ed. *The Autobiography of Martin Van Buren* (American Historical Association Annual Report for 1918, II). Washington, D.C.: Government
Printing Office, 1920.

Forney, John W. *Anecdotes of Public Men.* 2 vols. New York: Harper and Brothers,
1873–81.

Nevins, Allan, ed. *The Diary of Philip Hone, 1828–1851.* 2 vols. New York: Dodd,
Mead, 1927.

Nichols, Roy F., ed. "The Library: The Mystery of the Dallas Papers (Part II)."
Pennsylvania Magazine of History and Biography 73 (October 1949): 475–517.

———. "The Missing Diaries of George M. Dallas." *Pennsylvania Magazine of History and Biography* 75 (July 1951): 295–338.

Quaife, Milo M., ed. *The Diary of James K. Polk (1845–1849).* 4 vols. Chicago: A. C.
McClurg, 1910.

"Memoirs of a Senator from Pennsylvania, Jonathan Roberts, 1771–1854." *Pennsylvania Magazine of History and Biography* 62 (July 1938): 361–409.

Wainwright, Nicholas B., ed. *A Philadelphia Perspective: The Diary of Sidney George
Fisher Covering the Years, 1834–1871.* Philadelphia: The Historical Society of
Pennsylvania, 1967.

Wallace, Sarah A. and Gillespie, Francis E., eds. *The Journal of Benjamin Moran,
1857–1865.* 2 vols. Chicago: University of Chicago Press, 1948.

Public Documents

U.S. *Register of Debates in Congress, 1825–1837.* Washington, D.C., 1825–37, 29 vols.
22d Congress, 1st and 2d Sessions.

U.S., *Congressional Globe, Containing the Debates and Proceedings, 1833–1873.* Washington, D.C., 109 vols. 25th Congress–36th Congress.

U.S., 25th Congress, 2d Session, 1837–38, *Senate Document No. 1.*

U.S., 34th Congress, 3d Session, 1856–57, *Senate Executive Journal,* Volume X.

U.S., 35th Congress, 1st Session, 1857–58, *Senate Executive Document No. 61.*

U.S., 36th Congress, 2d Session, 1859–60, *House Executive Documents No. 2 and No.
7.*

U.S., Department of State, *Diplomatic Instructions of the Department of State* (Great Britain, 30 July 1849–12 August 1861).
U.S., Department of State, *Despatches from United States Ministers to Great Britain* (14 March 1856–20 May 1859).

Newspapers and Periodicals

Harrisburg Chronicle, 1813–40.
Harrisburg Democratic Union, 1843–49.
Harrisburg Pennsylvania Intelligencer, 1831–33.
Harrisburg Pennsylvania Reporter, 1831–33.
Harrisburg Pennsylvania Telegraph, 1831–33, 1844–49.
Hartford Courant, 1858–65.
London Times, 1846–60
National Intelligencer, 1831–48.
New York Times, 1851–65.
New York Tribune, 1844–65.
Niles' Weekly Register, 1831–48.
Pennsylvania Freeman (Philadelphia), 1844–48.
Philadelphia National Gazette, 1828.
Philadelphia North American, 1844–49, 1856–57.
Philadelphia Public Ledger, 1844–49.
Pittsburgh Daily Morning Post, 1844–49.
Pittsburgh Daily Gazette, 1844–65.
Washington Globe, 1831–45.
Washington Union, 1845–49.

Secondary Sources

Books

Adams, Henry. *The Life of Albert Gallatin*. Philadelphia: Lippincott, 1880.
Beale, Marie. *Decatur House and Its Inhabitants*. Washington, D.C.: National Trust for Historic Preservation, 1954.
Bemis, Samuel R., ed. *American Secretaries of State and Their Diplomacy*. 10 vols. New York: Knopf, 1927–29.
Coleman, John F. *The Disruption of the Pennsylvania Democracy, 1848–1860*. Harrisburg: The Pennsylvania Historical and Museum Commission, 1975.
Crippen, Lee F. *Simon Cameron: Ante-Bellum Years*. Oxford, O.: The Mississippi Valley Press, 1942.

Dusinberre, William. *Civil War Issues in Philadelphia, 1856–1865.* Philadelphia: University of Pennsylvania Press, 1965.

Eiselen, Malcolm. *The Rise of Pennsylvania Protectionism.* Philadelphia: University of Pennsylvania Press, 1932.

Fuller, J. D. P. *The Movement for the Acquisition of All Mexico, 1846–1848.* Baltimore: The Johns Hopkins Press, 1936.

Govan, Thomas P. *Nicholas Biddle.* Chicago: University of Chicago Press, 1959.

Graebner, Norman A. *Empire on the Pacific, A Study in American Continental Expansion.* New York: Ronald Press, 1955.

Holt, W. Stull. *Treaties Defeated by the Senate.* Baltimore: The Johns Hopkins Press, 1933.

Kehl, James A. *Ill Feeling in the Era of Good Feelings; Western Pennsylvania Political Battles, 1815–1825.* Pittsburgh: University of Pittsburgh Press, 1956.

Klein, Philip S. *Pennsylvania Politics (1817–1832): A Game Without Rules.* Philadelphia: Historical Society of Pennsylvania, 1940.

———. *President James Buchanan.* University Park: Pennsylvania State University Press, 1962.

Konkle, Burton A. *The Life of Chief Justice Ellis Lewis, 1798–1871.* Philadelphia: Campion, 1907.

Lambert, Oscar D. *Presidential Politics in the United States, 1841–1844.* Durham, N. C.: Duke University Press, 1936.

McCarthy, Charles. *The Antimason Party: A Study of Political Antimasonry in the United States, 1827–1840* (American Historical Association Annual Report for 1902, I). Washington, D.C.: Government Printing Office, 1903.

McClure, Alexander K. *Old Time Notes of Pennsylvania.* Philadelphia: John C. Winston, 1905.

McCoy, Charles A. *Polk and the Presidency.* Austin: University of Texas Press, 1960.

Meigs, William M. *The Life of John Caldwell Calhoun.* New York: Neale, 1917.

Merk, Frederick. *Manifest Destiny and Mission in American History.* New York: Knopf, 1963.

Morrison, Chaplain W. *Democratic Politics and Sectionalism.* Chapel Hill: University of North Carolina Press, 1967.

Nagel, Paul C. *One Nation Indivisible: The Union in American Thought, 1776–1861.* New York: Oxford University Press, 1964.

Nichols, Roy F. *The Democratic Machine, 1850–1854.* New York: Columbia University Press, 1923.

———. *Franklin Pierce: Young Hickory of the Granite Hills.* Philadelphia: University of Pennsylvania Press, 1931.

Remini, Robert. *The Election of Andrew Jackson.* Philadelphia: Lippincott, 1963.

Russell, Robert R. *Improvement of Communications with the Pacific Coast as an Issue in American Politics, 1783–1864.* Cedar Rapids, Iowa: Torch Press, 1948.

Scharf, J. T. and Westcott, T. *A History of Philadelphia.* 3 vols. Philadelphia: L. H. Everts, 1884.

Schroeder, John H. *Mr. Polk's War: American Opposition and Dissent, 1846–1848.* Madison: University of Wisconsin Press, 1973.

Scroggs, William O. *Filibusters and Financiers: The Story of William Walker and His Associates.* New York: Macmillan, 1916.

Sellers, Charles. *James K. Polk: Continentalist (1843–1846).* Princeton, N.J.: Princeton University Press, 1966.

Shenton, James P. *Robert John Walker.* New York: Columbia University Press, 1961.

Smith, E. B. *The Magnificent Missourian: The Life of Thomas Hart Benton.* Philadelphia: Lippincott, 1958.

Snyder, Charles M. *The Jacksonian Heritage: Pennsylvania Politics, 1833–1848.* Harrisburg: Pennsylvania Historical and Museum Commission, 1958.

Soulsby, Hugh G. *The Right of Search and the Slave Trade in Anglo-American Relations, 1814–1862.* Baltimore: The Johns Hopkins Press, 1933.

Spencer, Ivor D. *The Victor and the Spoils: A Life of William L. Marcy.* Providence, R. I.: Brown University Press, 1959.

Stanwood, Edward. *American Tariff Controversies in the Nineteenth Century.* 2 vols. Boston: Houghton Mifflin, 1903.

Taussig, F. W. *The Tariff History of the United States.* New York: G. P. Putnam's Sons, 1893.

Thomas, Benjamin P. *Russo-American Relations 1815–1867.* Baltimore: The Johns Hopkins Press, 1930.

Walters, Raymond. *Alexander James Dallas.* Philadelphia: University of Pennsylvania Press, 1943.

Warner, Sam B. *The Private City: Philadelphia in Three Periods of Its Growth.* Philadelphia: University of Pennsylvania Press, 1968.

Weinberg, Albert K. *Manifest Destiny.* Baltimore: The Johns Hopkins Press, 1935.

Wilburn, Jean Alexander. *Biddle's Bank: The Crucial Years.* New York: Columbia University Press, 1967.

Williams, Mary W. *Anglo-American Isthmian Diplomacy, 1815–1915.* New York: Russell and Russell, 1965. First published in 1914.

Willson, Beckles. *America's Ambassadors to England, 1785–1929.* New York: Frederick A. Stokes, 1929.

Wiltse, Charles M. *John C. Calhoun, Nationalist, 1782–1828.* New York: Bobbs-Merrill, 1944.

Articles

Ambacher, Bruce. "The Pennsylvania Origins of Popular Sovereignty." *Pennsylvania Magazine of History and Biography* 98 (July 1974): 339–52.

————. "Dallas, Cuba and the Election of 1856," *Pennsylvania Magazine of History and Biography* 97 (July 1973): 318–32.

Brebner, J. H. Bartlet. "Joseph Howe and the Crimean War Enlistment Controversy Between Great Britain and the United States." *Canadian Historical Review* 11 (December 1930): 300–27.

Curti, Merle. "Young America." *American Historical Review* 32 (October 1926): 34–55.

Donovan, Sister Therese A. "Difficulties of a Diplomat: George Mifflin Dallas in London." *Pennsylvania Magazine of History and Biography* 92 (October 1968): 421–40.

————. "President Pierce's Ministers at the Court of St. James." *Pennsylvania Magazine of History and Biography* 91 (October 1967): 457–70.

Fuller, J. D. P. "The Slavery Question and the Movement to Acquire Mexico, 1846–1848." *Mississippi Valley Historical Review* 21 (June 1934): 31–48.

Graebner, Norman A. "James K. Polk: A Study in Federal Patronage." *Mississippi Valley Historical Review* 38 (March 1952): 613–32.

Merk, Frederick. "Presidential Fevers." *Mississippi Valley Historical Review* 47 (June 1960): 3–33.

Phillips, Kim T. "Democrats of the Old School in the Era of Good Feelings." *Pennsylvania Magazine of History and Biography* 95 (1971): 363–82.

Post, Albert. "Early Efforts to Abolish Capital Punishment." *Pennsylvania Magazine of History and Biography* 68 (January 1944): 38–53.

Rippy, Fred J. "Diplomacy of the United States Regarding the Isthmus of Tehuantepec, 1848–1860." *Mississippi Valley Historical Review* 6 (March 1920): 503–31.

Van Alstyne, Richard. "John F. Crampton, Conspirator or Dupe?" *American Historical Review* 41 (April 1936): 492–502.

———. "British Diplomacy and the Clayton-Bulwer Treaty, 1850–1860." *Journal of Modern History* 11 (June 1939): 149–83.

———. "Anglo-American Relations, 1853–1857." *American Historical Review* 42 (April 1937): 491–500.

———. "The British Right of Search and the African Slave Trade." *Journal of Modern History* 2 (March 1930): 37–47.

Wainwright, Nicholas B. "Butler vs. Butler: A Divorce Case Incident." *Pennsylvania Magazine of History and Biography* 79 (January 1955): 101–7.

Theses and Dissertations

Ambacher, Bruce. "George M. Dallas and the Family Party." Ph.D. dissertation, Temple University, 1970.

Bartlett, Marguerite G. "Chief Phases of Pennsylvania Politics in the Jacksonian Era." Ph.D. dissertation, University of Pennsylvania, 1919.

Beck, Virginia. "The Political Career of George M. Dallas." Master's thesis, University of Pittsburgh, 1932.

Felton, Paul E. "The History of the Atlantic and Great Western Railroad." Ph.D. dissertation, University of Pittsburgh, 1943.

Harris, Thomas L. "America and England in 1861." Ph.D. dissertation, University of Indiana (Bloomington), 1928.

Harshbarger, Emmett L. "The African Slave Trade in Anglo-American Diplomacy." Ph.D. dissertation, Ohio State University, 1933.

Lambert, Oscar D. "The Presidential Election of 1844." Ph.D. dissertation, Johns Hopkins University, 1929.

Levett, Ella P. "Negotiations for Release from the Inter-Oceanic Obligations of the Clayton-Bulwer Treaty." Ph.D. dissertation, University of Chicago, 1941.

Long, John W. "The San Juan Island Boundary Controversy." Ph.D. dissertation, Duke University, 1949.

Scribner, Robert L. "The Diplomacy of William L. Marcy: Secretary of State, 1853–1857." Ph.D. dissertation, University of Virginia, 1949.

Slick, S. E. "The Life of William Wilkins." Master's thesis, University of Pittsburgh, 1926.

Van Alstyne, Richard. "British-American Diplomatic Relations, 1850–1860." Ph.D. dissertation, Stanford University, 1928.

Index

Taylor, Zachary, 126; and 1848 election, 131; Dallas views him, 132
Tehuantepec, Isthmus of, 152
Texas issue in 1844, 84–85, 98
Toombs, Robert, 179
Trist, Nicholas, 125
Tucker, David H., 143, 191n9
Tucker, Elizabeth Dallas (daughter of George M.), 191n9
Tyler, John, 49, 55, 82, 83, 168

Upshur, Abel P., 61

Van Buren, John, 130
Van Buren, Martin: challenges Calhoun, 30, 31, 36, 40; as vice presidential choice, 50–51, 60, 61; and election of 1836, 62; offers Dallas Russian mission, 63; and patronage, 80–82, 94, 103; defeated in 1840, 82; and 1844 presidential race, 83–86 *passim;* views 1844 ticket, 88; and Free Soil Party, 131, 208n13
Vaux, Robert, 106
Victoria (Queen of England), 148, 175
Vigil, Augustin, 150

Walker, Robert John: description and background, 84; and Dallas's nomination, 86–87; and 1844 campaign, 92; appointed Secretary of the Treasury, 101–2, 109; and Tariff of 1846, 111, 134; and Charles Sibbald legal case, 135, 178
Walker, William, 148, 150, 159, 211n9. *See also* Central America, Costa Rica, Nicaragua
War of 1812, 12
Washington, George, 160
Webster, Daniel, 39, 46, 53, 109, 135, 138
Webster-Ashburton Treaty, 87, 168–73 *passim*
Welsh, Henry, 105
Westcott, James, 108
Whig Party, 55, 56, 58–59; and 1836 election, 62; and 1844 election, 88, 95, 97–98. *See also* Anti-Masonic Party
Wilkins, Matilda Dallas (sister of George M.), 64, 191n2
Wilkins, William, 3; joins Family Party, 18, 28; elected to the Senate, 32; on Bank recharter, 38, 41–42; on tariff and internal improvements, 44–45, 197n24; on nullification, 48–49; as vice presidential choice, 50–51; relations with Jackson, 52; Minister to Russia, 55, 64, 66, 69; and Texas clique, 91, 191n2, 191n12, 195n3
Willis, John, 95
Wilmot, David, 107, 111, 127
Wilmot Proviso, 126–28, 130, 131–32
Wolf, George: elected governor, 29; reelected, 51–52; alliance with Buchanan, 54–55, 56; problems as governor, 57–58
Wood, Samuel, 57
Woodbury, Levi, 86, 130
Woodward, George, 104, 110, 177
Wright, Hendrick, 105
Wright, Silas, 86, 87, 94, 103, 125
Wyke, Charles, 163

Yancey, William, 130, 179, 180
"Young America," 141–42